The Making of the 20th Century

*This series of specially commissioned titles focuses atten-
tion on significant and often controversial events and
themes of world history in the present century. Each
book provides sufficient narrative and explanation for
the newcomer to the subject while offering, for more
advanced study, detailed source-references and biblio-
graphies, together with interpretation and reassessment
in the light of recent scholarship.*

*In the choice of subjects there is a balance between
breadth in some spheres and detail in others; between the
essentially political and matters economic or social. The
series cannot be a comprehensive account of everything
that has happened in the twentieth century, but it provides a guide to recent research and explains something
of the times of extraordinary change and complexity in
which we live. It is directed in the main to students of
contemporary history and international relations, but
includes titles which are of direct relevance to courses in
economics, sociology, politics and geography.*

The Making of the 20th Century

Series Editor: GEOFFREY WARNER

Weimar and the Rise of Hitler

Fourth edition

First published 2000 by
MACMILLAN PRESS LTD
Houndmills, Basingstoke, Hampshire RG21 6XS
and London
Companies and representatives
throughout the world

ISBN 0–333–73472–6 hardcover
ISBN 0–333–73473–4 paperback

A catalogue record for this book is available
from the British Library.

This book is printed on paper suitable for recycling and
made from fully managed and sustained forest sources.

10   9   8   7   6   5   4   3   2   1
09 08 07 06 05 04 03 02 01 00

Printed in Hong Kong

Published in the United States of America by
ST. MARTIN'S PRESS, INC.,
Scholarly and Reference Division,
175 Fifth Avenue, New York, N.Y. 10010

ISBN 0–312–23350–7 (cloth)
ISBN 0–312–23351–5 (paper)

To my parents

Contents

Abbreviations

BVP	*Bayerische Volkspartei* (Bavarian People's Party)
DAP	*Deutsche Arbeiterpartei* (German Workers' Party)
DDP	*Deutsche Demokratische Partei* (German Democratic Party)
DNVP	*Deutschnationale Volkspartei* (German National People's Party – German Nationalists)
DVP	*Deutsche Volkspartei* (German People's Party)
KPD	*Kommunistische Partei Deutschlands* (German Communist Party)
NSDAP	*Nationalsozialistische Deutsche Arbeiterpartei* (National Socialist German Workers' Party – Nazis)
SPD	*Sozialdemokratische Partei Deutschlands* (German Social Democratic Party – Majority Social Democrats)
USPD	*Unabhängige Sozialdemokratische Partei Deutschlands* (German Independent Social Democratic Party)
ZAG	*Zentralarbeitsgemeinschaft* (Central Working Association of Employers and Trade Unions)

Preface to the First Edition

In this book I have attempted to provide an introduction to the political history of the Weimar Republic. The failure of German democracy in the years after the First World War was of crucial importance, not only for Germany but for the world as a whole. It is necessary to understand the causes of this failure, and to avoid a natural tendency to over-simplify them. Very often they have been sought in the national character and historical development of the Germans, in the nature of Western capitalism, in the weaknesses of the Republican constitution or in the hypnotic power of Adolf Hitler. Some of these explanations are more respectable than others; none alone can begin to satisfy any serious enquiry.

One unforeseen by-product of Hitler's catastrophic war was the opening of German official records to historians. During the last two decades a great many valuable monographs have been published which throw light on the problems besetting the Weimar Republic. I have attempted to incorporate some of their findings into this book, but the need for compression precludes a detailed or definitive treatment. If I am able to stimulate the reader to delve more deeply into this fascinating and complicated subject I shall feel that my work has been justified.

My thanks are first of all due to my College for providing me with the facilities without which this book could not have been written. I should also like to acknowledge with gratitude the help I have received from Christopher Thorne and Miss Elizabeth Wiskemann. I am especially indebted to Sir John Wheeler-Bennett for his kindness in reading my manuscript and for his invaluable comments. I have benefited greatly from discussions with my Oxford colleagues, especially Tim Mason, Jonathan Wright and Modris Eksteins. Needless to say, I am entirely responsible for the opinions expressed in the book and for any errors which it may contain.

I wish to acknowledge the care and accuracy of my typists, Miss D. Twamley and Miss. E. Harrison, and finally I should like to thank my wife for her constant encouragement.

A. J. N.
St Antony's College, Oxford
March 1968

Introduction to the Fourth Edition

It is a great pleasure for me to be able to introduce a fourth edition of this book, the first edition having been published over thirty years ago. The third edition, which appeared in 1991, was already considerably expanded in terms of length. Thanks to the generosity of my publishers, I have also been able to incorporate a considerable amount of new material in this edition.

As I pointed out in my preface to the third edition, this book does not pretend to be a definitive or exhaustive history of the Weimar Republic. For that I should need to explore economic and social issues in more depth than is possible in an introductory account, and political events would need to be treated in much more detail. I make no apology for adopting a different approach. It seems to me that, before readers can begin to appreciate the rich variety of specialist material which exists on this period of German history, they require an overview of the general contours of the subject. It is that which this book seeks to provide.

When I revised the book in the early 1990s, I was concerned to address controversies about the nature of the German revolution, 1918/19, and the relationship between political upheavals in Germany and economic crises – especially the hyperinflation of 1923 and the catastrophic depression which began in the autumn of 1929. These issues still loom large in the ongoing discussions about Weimar, and I have endeavoured to incorporate new insights where appropriate. In particular I am happy to pay tribute to two books which deal with inflation, Niall Ferguson's *Paper and Iron*, which describes the impact of inflation on the economy of Hamburg, and Gerald D. Feldman's magisterial history of the German inflation, *The Great Disorder*. Both these studies reinforce my view, expressed in earlier editions, that the inflation had a catastrophic effect, not only on the economic stability but also on the political atmosphere of the Weimar Republic. Even if inflation may have brought benefits to some individuals or enterprises, the overall perception was that it was ruining most people. The German middle class, in particular, felt that its social position had been undermined, and blamed the Republic for that.

I have always tended to believe, however, that politics rather than economics were the most important factor in wrecking Germany's first attempt at democracy. So far as inflation is concerned, German money was effectively wiped out once again in the currency reform of 1948. Nevertheless, the Federal Republic, which was founded in the following year, established itself as a stable and prosperous democracy. Despite the social tensions caused by mass unemployment and bankruptcies during the great depression, it has to be remembered that other countries experienced the economic crisis of the early 1930s without jettisoning their democratic systems. It was the political legacy of the Wilhelmine Empire which was to prove so damaging to the Weimar Republic in the years 1918–33. This legacy took many forms, but perhaps the most pernicious was the widespread acceptance of a particularly intolerant type of ethnic nationalism, which assumed that the interests of the nation-state overrode considerations of individual rights, international trade or international harmony. This attitude had been widespread among German educated and propertied classes before 1914, but the experience of the World War intensified its appeal so that it reached well into the ranks of the labour movement. The amount of blood and treasure invested in the First World War made it difficult for Germans to contemplate a future in which the German Reich was not victorious. This was evident in July 1917, when the Reichstag passed a resolution in favour of a negotiated peace, a resolution which was not only ignored by the Imperial government, but which provoked furious opposition from those who saw it as tantamount to treason. The success of the Fatherland Party, a pro-war front organisation set up by the General Staff in September 1917, demonstrated the strength of feeling for a victorious peace. The circles which propagated this view were later responsible for disseminating the belief that Germany had not actually been defeated in the war at all, but had been 'stabbed in the back' by pacifists and left-wing subversives. The Versailles Peace Treaty – which still left the Germans considerably more territory than united Germany has today, and which was rapidly ameliorated by such schemes as the Dawes Plan – was totally rejected by the overwhelming majority of Germany's politicians, and that rejection clouded Germany's foreign policy throughout the Republican period.

Furthermore, the fundamental objectives of German political parties were far less conducive to pluralistic parliamentary democracy than was the case in West Germany after 1949. The labour movement was divided between a radical revolutionary Communist Party subservient to Moscow and a more moderate Social Democratic Party which, to please its left-wing members, still retained the class war rhetoric of the pre-war period. In any case, neither the Social Democrats nor the Roman Catholic Centre Party were believers in free-market capitalism, so that political emancipation did not march together with economic freedom as was the case after 1949. Even the liberal parties were too engrossed with Germany's national interests to support international free trade. Instead, various forms of collectivism and state intervention distorted the economy, while the emancipatory aspects of the Weimar Constitution were obscured by national resentments and post-war hardship.

In recent years historians have been discussing whether there really was an alternative to the Third Reich in January 1933.[1] Of course, Hitler's appointment by President Hindenburg was not necessary. But the alternatives are less clear. Apart from the Social Democrats, none of the Weimar parties was wholly committed to parliamentary democracy on the Western model. None was willing to make the concessions to Germany's former enemies – above all France – which would have encouraged that international co-operation which was the only means of overcoming the World depression. The contrast with the situation in the 1950s, when Adenauer initiated his successful policy of integrating Germany into a Western European Community in collaboration with the French, is striking.

Immediately after the Second World War the great German historian, Friedich Meinecke, attempted to explain the causes of what he called the German catastrophe. Since he could have access to only a limited range of sources, his interpretation was necessarily impressionistic, but it was based on a wealth of personal experience. Meinecke believed that individual values were the most important factor governing human behaviour, despite the need to take economic and social developments into account.

He regarded the intellectual and moral climate of nationalistic egoism which affected the German middle class during and after the First World War as the most fateful cause of Germany's disastrous lapse into barbarism under the leadership of Adolf Hitler.[2] For many years his views have been regarded as respectable but quaintly old-fashioned. As we look back over more than half a century their wisdom becomes more obvious.

The history of the Weimar Republic is a warning to all of us that xenophobia and self-indulgent nationalism can poison the political culture of a modern industrial society. This is a lesson the Germans have learned. We must hope that the rest of us in Europe can do likewise.

My thanks are once again due to my publishers, and in particular to Terka Bagley for encouraging me to revise this volume. As always, any errors of fact or interpretation are entirely my responsibility.

A. J. Nicholls
July 1999

Notes

1. See, for example, Rödder, 'Reflexionen über das Ende der Weimarer Republik. Die Präsidialkabinette 1930–1932/3.
2. See, for example, his remarks on the foundation of the *Vaterlandspartei* in the autumn of 1917. Meinecke, *Die Deutsche Katastrophe*, pp. 48–50.

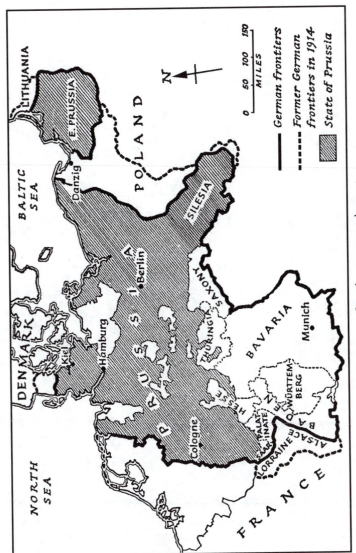

Germany after the peace settlement

1 The Lost War

On 29 September 1918 the German Army High Command advised its emperor, Kaiser Wilhelm II, that Germany must sue for peace. This marked a dramatic reversal of fortunes in the Great War. The previous spring had seen the launching of a massive German offensive on the Western Front. Its architect, General Ludendorff, had confidently predicted that it would bring the final triumph of German arms. Instead, by the autumn, German forces were in retreat and their allies defecting. Ludendorff and his titular superior, Field-Marshal Hindenburg, had to admit that military force alone could not save Germany.

Ludendorff recommended that the responsibility for negotiations should be laid on the shoulders of civilian politicians – who had had precious little influence on German policy since the summer of 1917. The government should also be given a wider and more popular character. It was hoped that this 'revolution from above' would appease public disaffection over a lost war.

Before the outbreak of hostilities in 1914 the German Empire had been a constitutional state with a democratically elected parliament (the Reichstag). Although the Kaiser's government was not appointed by the Reichstag and could not be held responsible to it in the manner of French or British governments, ministers needed the support of a parliamentary majority if they were to govern smoothly. Some of the parties on the left of the political spectrum – the Progressives and the large German Social Democratic Party – wanted an extension of parliamentary power. They hoped to see Germany's national government and local administration put under effective democratic control. In particular they wanted to reform the electoral system in Prussia, the largest state in the federal structure of the German Empire, where the right-wing parties were assured of predominant influence as the result of an unequal franchise. Generally speaking the same political elements were eager that Germany should pursue a foreign policy of international co-operation and peaceful development, although they were proud of their nation's achievements and were determined to further its interests.

On the other hand there were many powerful sectors of German society which felt that the Empire was not being assertive enough in the field of foreign affairs, that the liberal nature of Germany's political structure was a source of weakness, and that parliamentary government was a luxury which no nation as isolated and exposed as Germany could afford. These same critics of a liberal state also tended to be hostile to the growing urbanisation of their society, with the consequent expansion of a politically conscious working class. They disliked any form of cosmopolitan outlook.

Before 1914 the Imperial Government had usually looked for support in the Reichstag to one or other of the right-wing parties, the Conservatives or the National Liberals. The Centre Party, which represented the interests of the Roman Catholic minority in Germany, was at times persuaded to support the Government, but Roman Catholics were still regarded as outsiders by the Kaiser. As for the Social Democrats, the largest party in the Reichstag, they were politically detested as revolutionaries and socially unacceptable as members of an inferior class. It was true that the Social Democrats did have a revolutionary programme, but by 1914 their party had become far too accustomed to legality and peaceful agitation to desire a bloody confrontation with the ruling classes.

It was important that in German life political parties were regarded with distaste. Party intrigue was contrasted with the civil servant's sense of duty. Parliamentary squabbles were compared unfavourably with the loyalty and obedience of the Imperial Army. Many otherwise cultured and sophisticated Germans believed that there was something dirty about the business of politics. It was a belief by no means confined to Germany, but it was to have unfortunate consequences.

When the Great War broke out all the German parties rallied to their country's cause. Some of those on the left hoped that this would lead to political reforms. They were disappointed. Doubts also began to arise about the purely defensive nature of the war which Germany was waging, and there were fears that, if the Kaiser emerged victorious, his government would be encouraged to pursue a reactionary policy. This was particularly true after a political crisis in the summer of 1917, when the army leadership became the real voice of authority.[1]

Some Social Democrats had always regretted their party's support for the war effort, and others soon joined them. In April 1917 the party split over this issue, and a minority broke away to form the Independent Social Democratic Party (USPD), dedicated to a rapid peace and the transformation of German society. On the left of the USPD there stood an even more radical group known as Spartakists, who wished to see extreme action taken against the Imperial regime. Its two most important leaders, Rosa Luxemburg and Karl Liebknecht, spent the last years of the war in prison.

On a less radical plane the Reichstag parties critical of the Imperial Government's conduct of the war began to consider how they could best improve the situation. In July 1917 an inter-party committee was set up to discuss means of pressing the Kaiser's ministers to adopt a more realistic view of Germany's military prospects. Two of the four parties represented on the committee, the SPD and the Progressives,* were also eager to build up a parliamentary majority to achieve political reforms.

The committee continued to meet from time to time for the rest of the war, although the National Liberals left it towards the end of 1917. The zeal with which the parties pursued their aims of political reform and a negotiated peace waxed and waned according to the state of hostilities. But the habit of consultation between the leaders of the Social Democrats, Progressives and Centre seemed to foreshadow a political constellation which might become powerful if the Kaiser's military authorities lost their position of autocratic power. Outside parliament the mood of the nation was gradually changing. The miseries and bereavements of the war affected the mass of the civilian population. A shortage of labour, horses and fertilisers was damaging the productivity of German farmers, while the temptations of the black market were more attractive than rigorously controlled sales supervised by the authorities. Prices, which had been stable before the war, rose sharply despite government controls. Ignoring the black market, food prices more than doubled

---

* The others were the predominantly Roman Catholic Centre Party and the National Liberals. The Independent Social Democrats were not in the committee.[2]

between January 1914 and January 1917. By the end of 1918 the German mark had lost about three-quarters of its pre-war value.[3] Urban workers were especially badly affected by food shortages, and their discontent manifested itself in occasional riots.

Although real wages in industry fell during the war, middle-class Germans felt that they were losing financially *vis-à-vis* wealthy capitalists and supposedly overpaid munitions workers. Frictions between farmers and urban dwellers grew as food shortages worsened. Regional resentments manifested themselves as arguments broke out over which parts of Germany were bearing the heaviest burdens. In particular, anti-Semitism was fanned by the scurrilous claim that the small Jewish population of Germany was evading military service. There was no truth in this, but it was given official status by a so-called 'Jew count' (*Judenzählung*) in 1916 implemented by the military authorities. Certainly the war gave anti-Semitism, which had previously been less noticeable in Germany than in either Austria-Hungary or Russia, a powerful stimulus, providing as it did a simplistic explanation of Germany's misfortunes.[4]

The army was also affected by misery at home and prospects of an inglorious death at the front. Even before the spring offensive of 1918 there had been signs of deteriorating morale among the troops. This was especially true of those on the Eastern front, who felt they had won their war by defeating the Russians and had no desire to seek glory with Ludendorff in the West. There were numerous complaints about malingering among soldiers being transferred from the East. The defeats in the summer of 1918 made matters worse, and by the autumn the situation had deteriorated to such an extent that the army could no longer be counted on as an effective guarantor of the Imperial regime. In the battle area discipline still held, but camps and barracks inside Germany housed many soldiers who were substandard from the military viewpoint. Wounded, sick, temperamentally unsuited for front-line duty, or simply politically unreliable, these men acted as a disturbing leaven among the raw recruits training for their spell in the front line. State authorities were not well placed to combat serious internal unrest. Police forces were depleted owing to the war. The best officers and NCOs were at the front. Nor was co-operation between the civilian and military authorities always as good as it might have been.

The domestic background was not, therefore, very reassuring when Hindenburg and Ludendorff decided that Germany must seek an armistice. It was, indeed, to be an armistice of a very one-sided character, since it would enable their armies to withdraw unscathed to the German frontier and stay there in a defensive posture.

Ludendorff knew very well that the Allies would be unlikely to accept his conditions. When one of his staff officers asked him if he would agree to a truce if he were Marshal Foch* he replied, 'Of course not, I should press on hard. But perhaps this offer will not be unwelcome to him. In war one can never be sure.'[5] Ludendorff himself admitted he was grasping at a straw. As for the reorganisation of the Government, his motives were a mixture of calculation and spite. On the one hand he was genuinely concerned with the problem of maintaining order at home so that the army could be held together. On the other he loathed reformist politicians and wanted to saddle them with the responsibility for defeat. On 1 October he told his commanders that those people should be brought into the Government 'whom we have to thank for bringing us to this pass. We shall therefore see these gentlemen come into the Ministry. They must make the peace that has now to be concluded. They must now eat the dish which they have prepared for us.' It was small wonder that the colonel who recorded these words was reminded of Siegfried, mortally wounded by Hagen's spear plunged in his back.[6] It is in the nature of men to blame others for their own mistakes and Ludendorff was no exception. For him the German collapse had been caused by weakness and conspiracy at home. The army was blameless. It was the beginning of a legend which was to haunt Germany until 1945, when the Red Army stood triumphant in the ruins of Berlin.

Ludendorff's sudden urge to create a parliamentary regime ran parallel with the efforts which some members of the Reichstag majority – especially the Progressives and Social Democrats – had been making to build up resistance against the Imperial authorities' handling of the situation and at last impose parliamentary government on the Empire. The Inter-Fractional Committee of the Reichstag had been keeping itself informed as far as was

* The Allied commander-in-chief.

possible about the war situation, and the leaders of the Social
Democratic, Progressive and Centre Parties were aware that
the position was grave. They thought, however, that enough
time would be granted to Germany to negotiate an acceptable
peace if a government which enjoyed their confidence could
be created. Their efforts were forestalled by Ludendorff's volte-
face. Instead of Germany receiving a parliamentary regime as
the result of Reichstag pressure, she apparently obtained it by
the grace of the High Command.

The man selected to be Chancellor in the new government was
Prince Max of Baden. He was the protégé of the Progressive Party
leader Haussmann, who thought that he combined sound ideas
with the social prestige necessary to withstand pressure from the
army.[7] Prince Max had no desire to be responsible for a sudden
armistice offer, since this would damage public morale and might
lead to the accusation that politicians were betraying the army. He
knew that, unless he was cautious, he might find himself the
object of a favourite German saying, 'The pen has thrown away
what the sword has won.'[8] He therefore urged that a more general offer of peace be made before a specific appeal for an armistice, and refused to transmit such an appeal until a ministry had
been formed. His new government was to be of a much more
democratic character than previous Imperial administrations.
The decision to widen the basis of the ministry meant that leaders
of the parliamentary parties had to be told of the military crisis.
Many of them were shocked and astonished.

This shock had its effect on the so-called 'parliamentarisation'
which was supposed to accompany Prince Max's elevation to the
Chancellorship. It was quite clear that this was a deathbed con-
version so far as the Kaiser and the High Command were concerned. The parties which had been most eager for constitutional
changes – the Social Democrats, the Progressives and the Centre
Party – had not won them by asserting their own parliamentary
influence. They owed them to Germany's foes. An invitation to
enter the Government at that stage was an invitation to share in
the greatest humiliation ever inflicted on Germany. Many Social
Democrats would have preferred to decline it. The fact that the
new Reich Chancellor was a prince and a major-general hardly
made the government more attractive from their viewpoint. But
their leader, Friedrich Ebert, was convinced that his party should

not refuse to serve. It ought not to be said of the Social Democrats that they left their country in the lurch in its darkest hour. Ebert was a sincere patriot, as were most of his colleagues. He had not wanted to betray his country in 1914, and he would not weaken now.

By participating in the Government the Majority Social Democrats lost the chance of steering the growing anti-war movement for their own purposes. The Independent Social Democrats were quick to accuse them of bolstering up a rotten regime which ought to be allowed to collapse.

As the month of October wore on and peace was not concluded, popular hostility to the nation's leadership grew more intense. On 24 October the representative of the Saxon government in Berlin reported:

> Two moods are predominant among the masses. The first is a yearning for peace which has now grown to an extreme pitch. The second is an unmistakable bitterness over the fact that previous governments did not recognize the limits of German strength but went on nourishing the belief in Germany's invincibility so effectively that broad circles of the population were lulled into a sense of false security...[9]

With victory clearly impossible, public opinion swung behind those demanding immediate peace. If the institutions of the Empire were obstacles to that demand they would have to be eliminated.

The internal crisis had been directly affected by the course of the armistice negotiations. Prince Max was finally prevailed upon to issue an appeal to President Wilson, and from the answers received it became clear not only that the Western Allies would insist on the elimination of Germany's capacity to continue the war, but also that the Kaiser himself was a major obstacle to peace.

An American Note of 14 October spoke of the need to destroy those forces in Germany which threatened the peace of the world. Nine days later the message was made more explicit.

By 31 October external pressure for abdication had become so intense that the cabinet was forced to discuss the matter very seriously. The Social Democratic spokesman at the meeting,

Philipp Scheidemann, urged that the Kaiser should be asked to abdicate. This was a wise proposal, but no decision was taken. Meanwhile, on 29 October, Wilhelm II had left Berlin for the military headquarters at Spa in occupied Belgium. It seemed likely that he might try to use loyal front soldiers to crush subversion behind the lines. Some officers, including Heinrich Brüning, who was to become Reich Chancellor in 1930, would have supported him.[10]

It was at this juncture that discipline in the armed services began to break down. The trouble started among naval units in Kiel and Wilhelmshaven. Since the battle of Jutland in 1916 the German High Seas Fleet had been virtually confined to the North Sea ports as a defensive screen for U-boat warfare. On 28 October it was ordered to sea for a major operation in the English Channel.

The German naval staff were determined that hostilities should not be allowed to end without an impressive action by their fleet. They wanted to be sure that the German navy would outlive the war. The Kaiser had approved the operation, but Prince Max's government was not properly informed, even though the naval attack might well have prejudiced the armistice negotiations then in progress.[11] As it happened, the naval chiefs were thwarted by opposition from their own ranks.

The sailors, among whom resentment at harsh discipline and enforced idleness had already found expression in mutinous outbreaks, refused to obey orders. Attempts to punish them led to demonstrations. Troops were called out to restore the situation, but proved unreliable. After some bloodshed the authorities wavered. Their position was usurped by a committee of rebellious soldiers and sailors. Red flags were hoisted. The German revolution had begun.

Notes

Full details of the titles and articles cited in the references can be found in the Bibliography.

1. For a discussion of the nature of the power of the High Command see Kitchen, *The Silent Dictatorship: The Politics of the German High Command*

under Hitler and Ludendorff. A somewhat different view is taken by Gerald Feldman, *Army, Industry and Labour in Germany, 1914–1918*, and this book is also invaluable for its description of the impact of the war on labour relations.

2. See Matthias, *Der Interfraktionelle Ausschuss*, vol. I, pp. xxxiii–iv.
3. Bessel, *Germany after the First World War*, p. 31.
4. Kershaw, *Hitler, 1889–1936*, p. 100; Kauders, *German Politics and the Jews, Düsseldorf and Nuremberg 1910–1933*, pp. 56–8; Feldman, *The Great Disorder*, pp. 61–2.
5. Michaelis, Schraepler and Scheel (eds.), *Ursachen und Folgen. Vom deutschen Zusammenbruch 1918 und 1945 bis zur staatlichen Neuordnung Deutschlands in der Gegenwart*, vol. II, p. 324. Hereafter cited as *Ursachen und Folgen*.
6. Ibid., pp. 322–4.
7. Matthias and Morsey, *Die Regierung des Prinzen Max von Baden*, pp. xxii–ix. Also Robson, 'Left-Wing Liberalism in Germany, 1900–1919', D.Phil. thesis, University of Oxford, 1966, p. 350.
8. *Ursachen und Folgen*, vol. II, p. 327.
9. Cited in Kolb, *Arbiterräte*, pp. 18–19.
10. Burdick and Lutz, *Political Institutions*, p. 27. See also Patch, *Brüning*, pp. 22–3.
11. For a discussion of the German navy's attitude towards the operations at the end of October see Deist, 'Seekriegsleitung und Flottenrebellion 1918', pp. 341 ff.; see also Winkler, *Weimar, 1918–1933*, p. 25.

2 The German Revolution

The Kiel mutiny was the first of a chain of revolts which spread across Germany in the next few days and which finally disrupted the German Empire. It is common to stress their unpolitical nature. More than one German historian has pointed out that dissidents in the armed forces hoisted the Red Flag because it was the only banner under which they could be sure of evading punishment for their action. Strikers or demonstrators could hope for reform; mutineers had to opt for revolution.[1]

Certainly the left-wing political parties were ill-prepared when revolution came. The SPD, although it had put peace and democratic reform in the forefront of its programme, wanted no violent upheaval, and would have been happy to accept a constitutional monarchy. The Independent Socialists were more willing to exploit mass unrest in their campaign for an immediate end to the war. Some of them worked together with radical elements among the factory workers in Berlin and other large cities to further revolutionary agitation. But they did not really imagine that the powerful machinery of the German State would be vulnerable to working-class assault for many months. The same view was held by the leaders of the truly revolutionary pressure group on the left of the USPD, the Gruppe Internationale or Spartakists. Most of the Spartakist militants were, in any case, under some sort of official restraint in October 1918. It was the sudden demoralisation created within Germany by the news of impending defeat which paralysed the repressive forces of the old order and conditioned the masses to accept a major political change.

Nevertheless the revolution did not take place by accident. Despite a great deal of repression the Independents had been agitating in Germany for an end to hostilities, the freeing of political prisoners, an end to restrictions on public expression, better food and working conditions and really democratic government. In the context of Germany in 1918 this was a revolutionary programme, and many members of the more

10

militant element in the USPD were willing to recognise it as such. There was, indeed, confusion in the party's rank and file about how far revolution should be designed to end the war and how far agitation to end the war should be exploited to create a revolution. Most of the more prominent members of the USPD – for example, Hugo Haase and Karl Kautsky – were more interested in peace than revolution. But in Berlin groups of radical factory shop stewards and militant members of the Independent Socialist Youth group were less moderately inclined.

Many of the unknown and obscure men who took the lead at crucial moments in the German revolution had been exposed to Independent Social Democratic propaganda or had themselves actually been involved in subversive political activity. At Kiel, for example, the sailors could remember the harsh sentences meted out to leaders of an earlier – and very restrained – political manifestation, in which some of the accused had admitted links with the Independent Social Democratic Party.[2]

The soldiers in rear areas played a key role in overthrowing the German Empire. They alone could have suppressed the revolutionary movement. In fact they were more affected by anti-war feeling than almost any other section of the population. There were, of course, many troops who had no political views and no inclination to revolt, but they saw little sense in shooting their countrymen just to continue a war that had already been lost. The rank and file of obedient soldiers upon whom authority depended had only one overwhelming desire: to go home.

A broad pattern of revolution began to make itself apparent. Mass meetings in favour of peace and political reform would be held, followed by marches and demonstrations. Soldiers and sailors usually made up the most radical element in these activities, and were in the vanguard of any riotous outbreaks which developed from them. The police and military would try to ban such manifestations, but would find they had no power to enforce restrictions. Official retreats encouraged more daring action by the demonstrators. Majority Socialist leaders usually tried to gain control of the crowds and prevent them from transgressing the bounds of peaceful demonstration, and sometimes they were successful. But in other cases more zealous agitators – sometimes members of the USPD – would lead the crowds to barracks, prisons or government offices. Soldiers would be disarmed and persuaded to join the revolution. Political prisoners were released. Municipal and, in some cases, governmental authority was taken over by the rebels. Revolutionary power would be exercised by so-called 'Workers' and Soldiers' Councils' or 'Soviets'.

These bodies undoubtedly owed their conception to the Russian revolution, but there was great vagueness about their precise form and function. Few Germans had a very clear idea of what was happening in Russia. In any case, the behaviour of the Bolsheviks had aroused strong criticism throughout the German Labour movement, and not least in the USPD. So far as the purpose of the Workers' and Soldiers' Councils was concerned, confusion reigned within both the socialist parties, but it was most marked among the Independents. For the most part the Majority Socialists tended to see the councils simply as devices to maintain law and order in a turbulent situation. They hoped that they would quickly disappear. Many of the Independents had more ambitious plans, wanting to use the councils as organs of working-class self-expression which could draw the masses into political activity in a manner impossible with a more conventional parliamentary constitution. They could also be used to create genuinely democratic institutions in Germany before any more formal decisions were taken by an elected parliament. Such a development could be carried into the social field, and many Independents thought that initial steps towards the socialisation of Germany's economy should be taken by the councils without waiting for any parliamentary sanction. Lastly, there were those who felt that the councils should be instruments of proletarian dictatorship which would replace bourgeois parliaments altogether. In November 1918 their numbers were quite insignificant.[3]

During the first few days after the Kiel disturbances power had changed hands in only a few north-western cities and only on a local level. But on 7 November a more serious event took place. In Munich, the capital of Bavaria, a by-election campaign had been transformed into a determined agitation for a German Republic. Faced with a complete breakdown of police and military authority, the last of the Wittelsbach kings, the aged Ludwig III, left his palace in the middle of the night and never returned to it. On the following day it was announced that Bavaria was a Republic. Its new premier was an Independent Social Democrat, Kurt Eisner, who had only recently been released from prison.[4]

With this blow at the monarchical system the fate of the German Empire was really sealed. The Majority Socialists could not afford to let the Independents take the lead in winning power. They had to act quickly if their party was to control events in the future.

The situation in Berlin had been deteriorating, although it was not yet so desperate as in cities to the west and south. A group of factory shop stewards in the capital's heavy industrial plants were preparing for a revolution to take place on 11 November.[5] Workers' and Soldiers' Councils were being set up, despite the express prohibition of the Army High Command. The Majority Social Democrats had managed to prevent any serious outburst among Berlin's factory workers, but by 7 November the party felt it could wait no longer. An ultimatum was presented to the cabinet; if the Kaiser and the Crown Prince did not abdicate within two days the SPD would leave the coalition.

The Imperial military authorities were trying to resist subversion in the capital. They put particular trust in the crack troops of the Naumburger *Jäger* who had only recently been brought into Berlin. It was hoped that they would be able to crush an attempt at rebellion. However, early in the morning of 9 November soldiers in *Jäger* barracks asked the Majority Social Democrats to send them a speaker to explain the political situation. Otto Wels, an experienced SPD functionary, persuaded them to help put an end to the war by supporting the people against the Kaiser, whose obstinacy was prolonging the bloodshed. The *Jäger* then mounted guard over the offices of the SPD newspaper, *Vorwärts*, securing it from radical left-wing threats.[6] The position of the SPD was strengthened, and the possibility of resistance to the revolution itself had effectively disappeared. Later the same morning Prince Max announced the Kaiser's abdication and handed over his post as Reich Chancellor to Friedrich Ebert. At the same time Ebert offered equal participation in his new government to the Independent Social Democrats.

It was too late to save the monarchy. As the day wore on large crowds of soldiers and workers marched on the government buildings in the centre of the city. It became known that Karl Liebknecht was about to proclaim a German Republic. Once again the danger loomed that the SPD would lose command of events to a really radical group. Faced with this situation

Scheidemann went to a window of the Reichstag building and announced to the cheering spectators below that Germany had become a Republic. The Wilhelmine Empire was at an end.[7]

That same day the Kaiser, having refused to abdicate while there was still time to save his dynasty, followed the advice of his Army Chief of Staff, General Groener, and fled from Spa to take refuge in the neutral Netherlands. He had had no choice in the matter. It had become obvious that Germany's soldiers would not fight their comrades to save the Hohenzollerns.

Many Majority Social Democrats were not enthusiastic about a Republic. Ebert would have preferred a democratic system within a constitutional monarchy, and feared that discontented royalists might weaken a new Republican state. Most of the gains that his party hoped for could have been settled within a constitutional monarchy. Even the new National Assembly, which was to replace the old Reichstag, had been suggested by Prince Max before the Kaiser abdicated. But it was clear by 9 November that popular hostility to Prussian militarism associated with the Kaiser and his family had become so intense that a Republic was inevitable. The Kaiser's flight from Berlin to Spa had reinforced public distrust.[8] Ebert and his colleagues were mainly concerned about the effect which chaos in Germany might have on the conduct of the peace negotiations, and wanted to create a stable government as quickly as possible.

On the morning of 10 November the Imperial cabinet met for the last time. Ebert took the chair as Chancellor. A German armistice commission under Erzberger had already gone to negotiate with the Western Allies, and had relayed the conditions to be imposed upon the German armed forces back to Berlin. Ebert told his colleagues:

> There is no alternative to accepting the armistice terms. It is however, already apparent that these conditions will not produce a just peace. The sacrifices imposed on us are tremendous, they must lead to our people's doom.[9]

Germany's representatives signed the armistice on the following day, and hostilities ceased. But Ebert was haunted by the fear that a collapse of military discipline or public order in Germany might bring Entente troops across the Rhine. Reports from

German embassies in neutral countries suggested that if any sign of Bolshevism appeared in Germany an invasion might follow.[10]

It was not a situation in which to embark on political experiments. However, now that the Republic had come, Ebert and his colleagues had to make the best of it. They set about their task with a determination not equalled among their Independent Socialist rivals.

Real power in Berlin rested at that moment with the Workers' and Soldiers' Councils. The Majority Social Democrats conducted vigorous propaganda to ensure that delegates sympathetic to them were elected to these. Otto Wels himself was a very effective propagandist for the SPD and his efforts were particularly successful among the soldiers.[11] He and other SPD functionaries were more experienced than their rivals and were often better known. Most of those voting for the councils did not think that there ought to be a split in the socialist ranks at that moment.

An Executive Committee of the Workers' and Soldiers' Councils in Berlin was also set up, but its functions were left vague and an attempt to prevent the Majority Social Democrats receiving representation on it was thwarted. Otto Wels became 'commandant' of Berlin, thereby taking responsibility for the military there. The Berlin police chief ceded his power to a radical independent social democrat, Emil Eichhorn.

Ebert also persuaded the leadership of the Independent Social Democratic Party – which was very confused about its aims now that the revolution had actually broken out – to co-operate with him in forming a government. When a meeting of Berlin Workers' and Soldiers' Councils was held on 10 November it sanctioned a ruling cabinet of six – three Majority Social Democrats and three Independents. Ebert was chairman. It was true that the new government was called a 'Council of People's Representatives', but the name was not of great importance. To all intents and purposes, Ebert remained Reich Chancellor.

The new revolutionary government was an uneasy but not impossible coalition. Its three Social Democratic members, Ebert, Scheidemann and Landsberg, were eager to re-establish order in Germany and to organise the election of a National Assembly to draw up a new constitution. Once these objectives were gained it would be possible to negotiate a Peace Treaty with the Entente and set about the reconstruction of Germany's economic life. They assumed that democratic elections would produce a very powerful socialist group in the new National Assembly. They had no reason to believe that the sort of Germany they wanted could not be created with the aid of existing bureaucratic institutions, especially since they had themselves been drawn into the Imperial Government before the revolution had broken out.

Their leader, Friedrich Ebert, was forty-nine years old, the son of a master tailor in Heidelberg. A fine organiser, he had made his career in the administrative machine of the Social Democratic Party. It had been thanks to men of his stamp that the party had been able to build up its membership and electoral support so successfully before 1914. He was skilled in the arts of negotiation and conciliation, but could on occasion give way to outbursts of temperament.[12] Ebert was at any rate a man of strong and determined will. In him the SPD possessed a clear-headed leader, but one whose mental horizons were narrow.

The Independents were not such a closely-knit group as their SPD colleagues. By far the most radical was Emil Barth, who had been collecting arms for a revolution since the beginning of 1918.[13] The others, Hugo Haase and Wilhelm Dittmann, were of a different stamp. Both had been Reichstag deputies in 1914 and were therefore old colleagues of the Majority Social Democrats. On the face of it there was no clear reason why the two sections of the socialist cabinet should not work together. Now that the war was over the main objective of the USPD had apparently been achieved. Certainly there was no thought of a Red dictatorship on the Russian model.

It soon turned out, however, that the difficulties in the way of socialist co-operation were very formidable. The personal rancour created by the split in the German Labour movement during the war was not easily forgotten. The SPD leaders had been associated with the war effort, and had finally been taken into the government. The Independents had been ostracised as subversives or even traitors. Some of them had suffered imprisonment; many had committed illegal acts. They, in turn, regarded the collaborationist attitude of the SPD as a betrayal of socialist principles.

Then there were differences about the way in which the revolution ought to be exploited. Mindful of his country's military situation. Ebert wanted to end disorders in Germany as soon as possible and call elections to a National Assembly. The Independents saw the events of 9 November as a victory, and the end of the war as a heroic achievement. They did not want a Soviet dictatorship, but they did believe German society ought to be fundamentally altered. Before a National Assembly was elected they thought that the country should be given time to adjust itself to the revolution. In particular, the working classes should be mobilised for political action through the agency of the Workers' and Soldiers' Councils.

The Independents also wanted immediate steps taken towards socialising large-scale industry, whereas Ebert and his colleagues wanted such decisions left to the National Assembly. The German trade union organisation had negotiated an industrial bargaining agreement with employers and did not wish to see this undermined by 'excesses' on the part of the Workers' Councils. The Independents argued that, unless radical change was carried through as part of the revolution, it might never come at all. Time was to prove them right. However, it must also be noted that the sort of changes they suggested were hardly appropriate to an advanced industrial society which had just suffered grievous economic damage as the result of a debilitating war. The caution of their SPD colleagues was not without justification, although it may have been excessive. One distinguished German historian claims that Ebert's majority Social Democrats saw themselves less as the founding fathers of a new democracy and more as receivers administering a bankrupt Wilhelmine Empire.[14]

If personal experience and policies divided the SPD from their coalition partners, their relations with the officials of the old Empire deepened the cleavage between them. The bureaucrats in the Reich Ministries behaved as though Ebert – officially only the chairman of a governing committee – were an old-style Reich Chancellor. His instructions were treated as binding orders, whereas Independent Socialist members of the committee found their directives being referred to him for ratification. The agenda of cabinet meetings was drawn up by Ebert and he led the discussions. The division of labour on the committee also meant that the SPD members had the most important tasks allotted to them.[15]

The immediate problems which faced the People's Commissioners were the re-establishment of government authority throughout Germany and the evacuation of German troops from all areas west of the Rhine. The latter was a condition of the armistice and had to be fulfilled if Germany was to avoid invasion. Both issues involved delicate relationships with the Workers' and Soldiers' Councils, and in particular with the executive committee established in Berlin.

This committee claimed that Ebert and the other People's Representatives were only functioning with its consent, and implied that if they did not rule according to its wishes they could be replaced. In order to ensure that revolutionary influence prevailed in Berlin it tried to set up a 'Red Guard'. It also encouraged Workers' and Soldiers' Councils to try and exercise control over civil servants and municipal officials. In both these enterprises it failed miserably. The Soldiers' Councils themselves opposed any force in Berlin which might rival their own.[16] The authority of German officialdom proved too great for the Workers' Councils. Generally speaking, they were unable to exercise any real control over internal administration.

When the committee convened a National Congress of German Workers' and Soldiers' Councils in Berlin on 16 December the result was a triumph for Ebert. The Congress voted in favour of rapid elections for a national constituent assembly. A Central Committee was set up dominated by Majority Social Democrats. Attempts by the Congress to press socialisation and army reform on the Government were evaded by procrastination and technical objections.

Despite the failures of the executive committee, Ebert's government was still faced with the problem of organising an effective armed force to protect itself. The Soldiers' Councils had real power among the troops in Berlin. Yet these could not be used as the foundation for a Republican army. They were far too concerned with undermining the authority of their superiors. In any case, many units were beginning to break up. By the middle of December the army was in dissolution. Those who remained in the barracks did so as much to obtain food and shelter as to act as defenders of the new regime. Some of them, like Adolf Hitler in Munich, were disgusted with the collapse of their old, proud regiments and blamed the revolution for their humiliation.

Indeed, a myth rapidly grew up that the returning heroes of the German army had been jeered at and even spat upon by mobs of pacifist revolutionaries when they arrived home in November and December 1918. This was actually far from the truth. Although there was friction between some front soldiers and those in the home barracks, the dissolution of the old army proceeded remarkably smoothly. Most repatriated soldiers were given civic receptions and other expressions of their country's gratitude, some of which encouraged the misleading impression that the army had not been defeated at all. Demobilised soldiers usually received clothes and a small gratuity, and demobilisation committees helped them recover their former occupations, often at the expense of women workers or foreign labour. The problem was rather that some soldiers found it difficult to adjust to the realities of civilian life in war-weary Germany, with food supplies inferior to those they were used to in the army, and living conditions generally worse than they had been before the war. It should not be thought, however, that most of the troops who returned to Germany and quickly demobilised disapproved of the revolution. After all, it had possibly saved their lives by ending the war. The largest voluntary ex-servicemen's association, the Reich Association of War Wounded, War Participants and War Bereaved (Reichsbund der Kriegsbeschädigten, Kriegsteilnehmer und Kriegshinterbliebenen) was anti-militarist in its attitudes.[17] Many of those who joined the Freikorps or nationalist paramilitary formations later on were too young to have fought in the war themselves, although their officers and NCOs were usually experienced fighters.

For Ebert the problem of maintaining order and discipline in the army seemed far more serious than the need to build up new contingents loyal to socialism or the Republic. His views on the military situation were, therefore, very similar to those held by the old Imperial High Command. General Groener, who had tackled the unenviable task of advising the Kaiser to leave Germany, was the most intelligent and effective leader of the old officer corps. Groener had got in touch with Ebert soon after the Republic had been proclaimed. A private wire linked the High Command to the Reich Chancellery and consultations between the two men could be conducted without difficulty. Ebert did not publicise his contacts with Groener, but he saw nothing wrong in them. The High Command offered to co-operate with the Republican government if it in turn was prepared to maintain discipline in the armed forces. This was entirely consistent with Ebert's programme. Groener seemed at that time to be in a weak position *vis-à-vis* the socialist politicians, since he needed their help to maintain his position.

For the time being Groener and his nominal superior, Field-Marshal Hindenburg, wanted above all to prevent revolutionary disaffection spreading to the soldiers on the front in the west. They calculated, quite correctly, that these forces would be willing to be led home by their officers without mutinous disturbance. Soldiers' Councils among the field army units were later established under the supervision of officers and were usually loyal to them. Once in Germany, it was hoped, the Front Army would provide both the officer corps and the Government with a reliable force with which to stabilise an apparently insecure situation. This proposition was just as attractive to Ebert as it was to the officer corps.[18] The executive committee of the Berlin Workers' and Soldiers' Councils did not know of these arrangements between Groener and Ebert, but they suspected quite rightly that the SPD leaders had a very different view of the army's future from their own.

There is no doubt that more could have been done to create an armed force that was emotionally loyal to the Republic. In December 1918 the old army was in ruins and Groener was unable to offer the Government effective protection. The administration of military affairs was under the control of the Prussian War Ministry, and the Independent Social Democrats in the Government urged that an officer known to approve of the revolution be appointed as its head. Ebert passed over their suggestion. He preferred Colonel Reinhardt, who described himself as a 'convinced monarchist, but one who would never use the troops entrusted to him to attack the government'.[19]

It was small wonder that many of the Independent Social Democrats and their supporters in the Workers' and Soldiers' Councils took the view that Ebert was giving way to counter-revolutionary pressure. Their fears were increased by a virulent press campaign against the more radical revolutionaries and the 'excesses' of the councils.

Shortly before Christmas 1918 a conflict erupted in Berlin between the city commandant, Otto Wels, and the so-called People's Naval Division, a group of sailors occupying part of the *Marstall*, formerly the stables of the royal palace in the centre of the capital. Wels had been trying to persuade the sailors to evacuate the building, but they wanted a substantial payment before doing so, and tried to negotiate this through Emil Barth, the most radical of the Independent Social Democratic People's Commissioners. During the dispute two sailors were killed by government soldiers and Wels was then taken prisoner by the naval division. Ebert and the Majority Social Democrats called on the old army leadership for help, and Groener was quite happy to send troops into action against radical revolutionaries. The *Marstall* was bombarded by a unit loyal to the old High Command. When it seemed that the defenders were on the point of surrender they received reinforcements sent by Eichhorn, the Independent Social Democrat who had taken over as police president in Berlin. The army had to admit defeat and the Majority Social Democrats were forced to negotiate a humiliating settlement with the sailors. Wels was released but had to resign as city commandant.[20]

The whole affair was damaging to German social democracy because it deepened the split in the Berlin working-class movement and strengthened the enemies of moderation on both the right and the left. Efforts to create a loyal, democratic army were blighted, while the radicals on the left of the USPD were encouraged to believe they could seize power by force. An ill-tempered post-mortem within the provisional government led to accusations of bad faith by the Independents against Ebert and his colleagues. In the early hours of 29 December the USPD People's Commissioners resigned their posts. The revolutionary socialist coalition was at an end. Ebert and his Majority Socialist colleagues carried on alone.

They faced a tense situation made worse by Germany's economic difficulties. War production naturally fell away with the end of hostilities. At the same time men returning from the front demanded jobs. Industry was very short of raw materials, and the fact that the Allies maintained their blockade of Germany even after the armistice had been signed did not facilitate a resumption of peacetime production. Germany was, in any case, cut off from most of her pre-war export markets. Unemployment, especially in big towns like Berlin and Munich, began to become a serious problem. The Spartakists and radical Independents did their best to mobilise support among unemployed workers.

The radical shop stewards and the left wing of the Independent Social Democrats were now totally opposed to Ebert's government and determined to resist it through the medium of the Workers' and Soldiers' Councils. Their influence in the USPD was growing and divisions between them and more moderate elements were becoming very serious. The most consistent radical voices on the left belonged to the Spartakist Union whose leaders, Rosa Luxemburg and Karl Liebknecht, argued that the November revolution was a sham and that the proletariat must be mobilised to take over power itself. On 31 December the Spartakists held a Congress at which it was decided to break away from the Independents and form a separate German Communist Party. The radical shop stewards in Berlin considered joining the new party, but no satisfactory terms could be worked out for them. Under the leadership of Rosa Luxemburg the party seemed likely to follow an independent course, even though Karl Radek, a Bolshevik agent of Lenin, had been present at the foundation Congress.[21]

The language of the German Communists, as expressed at meetings and in their paper *Die Rote Fahne* (The Red Flag), was very violent and seemed to be encouraging immediate insurrection. Actually Rosa Luxemburg saw it as the party's task to educate the German masses by demonstrating the conservative nature of the Ebert government. Only then, in her view, would they be roused to demand revolutionary action. Until that mass support was available she and Karl Liebknecht had no desire to initiate a coup. But many of their supporters were less sophisticated. They were eager to risk a conflict while Berlin was still in an atmosphere of turmoil.

Its occasion was the dismissal from office of Emil Eichhorn, the left-wing Independent Social Democrat who held the post of Police President in Berlin. He refused to make way, and large-scale demonstrations took place in his favour. The Independent Social Democrats, radical shop stewards and Communists who provoked these demonstrations were carried away with enthusiasm at their success. They established a revolutionary committee and declared Ebert's government deposed. Fighting broke out. The German revolution seemed about to enter a new and more extreme phase.

In fact the 'Spartakist rising', as it later became known, was virtually unplanned and chaotic in execution. Although Rosa Luxemburg's Communist (Spartakist) Party was identified with the rising in government propaganda, Rosa Luxemburg herself had not thought that the time was ripe for such a move. Once fighting had started, however, she believed that the workers' leaders ought not to desert them or encourage them to surrender.[22] Her party reaped the benefits of repression, notoriety and martyrdom. For the German Labour movement as a whole the fighting brought nothing but tragedy.

Most of the rank and file in both Social Democratic Parties in Berlin wanted to avoid fraternal conflict. It is possible that a determined effort by Ebert and his colleagues to negotiate with the Independents and the radical shop stewards might have led to a compromise.[23] But this would have implied that the Government could not assert its authority in Berlin. Negotiations with the USPD would also have involved taking steps to create a more genuinely revolutionary administration, particularly in the fields of military organisation and police. Ebert was not the man to risk the chaos which such doubtful experiments might bring with them. In view of Germany's desperate situation and the complete confusion of the German radical left, it is hard to condemn him. Nevertheless, the effects of his actions were unhappy for the future of the Republic.

The rebels were crushed after some bitter fighting. The new Defence Minister in Ebert's government, Gustav Noske, made use of volunteer units raised by the old Army Command and paid by the Prussian War Ministry. These *Freikorps* formations were led by Imperial officers, most of whom were violently opposed to the revolution. On 19 January Rosa Luxemburg and Karl Liebknecht were murdered by officers and men in one of these units. Their killing was a brutal and unnecessary crime carried out by politically ignorant men. Noske became regarded on the left as the butcher of his class.

This was not the only atrocity to besmirch Republican arms in 1919, and most victims of such violence were men of the left.

Noske's forces freed Berlin from the fear of a Communist insurrection, but at the expense of working-class unity. The damage
done to the German Labour movement by its early experiences
in the revolution was never repaired. Proletarian solidarity
remained an empty slogan until Hitler subjected all German
workers to the control of the Nazi Labour Front.

On 19 January the Social Democrats lost their monopoly of
German political life. In the elections for the National Assembly
both socialist parties put together were in a minority. The tide
of the German revolution had turned. Its ebb was to be a rapid
one.

The revolution has often been described as a failure. In the
sense that it did not bring socialism to Germany this is true. Yet it
may be doubted whether the German people were prepared to
accept large-scale social experiments in 1918. Certainly those who
urged radical measures were very confused in both their aims and
methods. The organs of working-class self-expression, the Workers' and Soldiers' Councils, could not assert themselves against
experienced labour leaders and civil servants. The councils' influence on the economy was anything but positive. To take one
example, in the coal mines of the Ruhr area the councils urged
socialisation of the pits, by which they evidently meant a form of
workers' control. This demand upset the miners' trade union and
was not even supported by the socialist parties. But in January
1919 the miners backed it up with a wave of strikes.[24] The
Republican authorities could not give in to the miners demands.
Workers' control would have meant higher costs and lower production at a time when every ton of coal was vital for the entire
economy. The result was working-class disillusionment damaging
to both trade unions and the Majority Socialist Party.

To have attempted to 'socialise' the German economy in the
winter of 1918/19 would have been a formula for disaster. The
economy was already choked with restrictions established during
the war. The result of this controlled economy (*Zwangswirtschaft*)
was increasing distortion of market forces and resentment
amongst both consumers and producers. Farmers were angry
that they could not charge market prices for their produce;
city dwellers accused the farmers of profiteering on the black
market. Shopkeepers and small businessmen also found life
difficult under the *Zwangswirtschaft;* they blamed trade unions

and big business. Rent controls did ameliorate living costs for poorer tenants, but also helped to exacerbate the housing shortage.[25]

Politically the nationalisation of a major industry, like coal, might have weakened those powerful German entrepreneurs who were most hostile to the labour movement and most disdainful of democracy. A quarter of the country's coalfields were already owned by the Prussian state, and the administration of such an industry would not have presented insuperable problems. German railways were publicly owned, and functioned well in the Republican period. Yet the mere creation of a state-owned industry would not have satisfied socialist radicals, and it would have generated immense opposition from industrial vested interests at a time when Germany needed economic recuperation. The Majority Social Democrats' slogan was 'Reconstruction first; then socialisation.'[26] It was not heroic, but it showed common sense.

It also fitted in with the policy of the trade unions, whose major interest lay in establishing themselves as recognised negotiating partners within major industrial enterprises, and in obtaining state protection for labour contracts. Even before the November revolution broke out, the head of the German trade union movement, Carl Legien, had negotiated a compromise with the leading Ruhr industrialist, Hugo Stinnes, according to which the private entrepreneurs would keep and manage their own enterprises, but would recognise trade unions and accept the eight-hour day, a long-standing demand of German industrial labour. Plans for socialisation adumbrated by the provisional government early in 1919 were soon dropped. A Central Working Association (*Zentralarbeitsgemeinschaft*, or *ZAG*) of industrialists, trade union leaders and government officials was established to try to steer the economy, and various schemes of a *dirigist* character were produced in the new Reich ministry of economics. None of these had any positive results. Insofar as they increased an existing tendency for German industry to look to the state for assistance, and to undermine competition by price-fixing activities, they were probably harmful. Certainly they reinforced middle-class suspicions that an unholy alliance between union bosses and big business was ruining the small man in Germany. In actual fact, the representatives of heavy industry chafed under their commitments to the trade unions and did all they could to put the clock back to the pre-war period. In 1924 the ZAG collapsed. There was plenty of combustible material in German society if circumstances proved right for a conflagration.

On the other hand, the revolution had provided Germany with an armistice and a Republic. It was clear that her new political institutions would be genuinely democratic in a sense they had never been before. Pressure from outside parliament had achieved a greater degree of parliamentarisation than had been possible under the Empire. The reform movement within the former Reichstag had never looked strong enough to assert itself against the Imperial regime – the revolution had toppled that regime altogether. Germany had not been transformed. Yet the new Republic promised to be a freer and more egalitarian State than its Imperial predecessor.

Notes

1. For instance, Rosenberg, *The Birth of the German Republic*, pp. 13–14. Also Heiber, *Republik von Weimar*, p. 14. The following accounts of the revolution are well worth consulting: Carsten, *Revolution in Central Europe, 1918–1919*; Matthias, *Zwischen Räten und Geheimräten: Die Deutsche Revolutionsregierung, 1918–1919*; E. Matthias, 'German Social Democracy in the Weimar Republic', in Nicholls and Matthias (eds.), *German Democracy and the Triumph of Hitler*; and Ryder, *The German Revolution of 1918: A Study of German Socialism in War and Revolt*. Wolfgang Mommsen, 'The German Revolution 1918–1920: Political Revolution and Social Protest Movement', in Bessel and Feuchtwanger, *Social Change and Political Development in Weimar Germany*; Kluge, *Soldatenräte und Revolution, Studien zur Militärpolitik in Deutschland, 1918/19*; Ritter and Miller (eds.), *Die Deutsche Revolution, 1918–19 Dokumente*; Tampke, *The Ruhr and Revolution*.

   A stimulating, if controversial, assessment of the German revolution is given by Rürup in his article 'Problems of the German Revolution, 1918–19'. Two important monographs on the USPD should also be consulted: Morgan, *The Socialist Left and the German Revolution: A History of the German Independent Social Democratic Party, 1917–1922*, and Wheeler, *USPD und Internationale. Sozialistisches Internationalismus in der Zeit der Revolution*.

2. See, for example, the statements made in Wilhelmshaven by the sailors Reichpeitsch and Kolbis in August 1917. *Ursachen und Folgen*, vol. I, p. 228.

3. For a discussion of German attitudes towards the Workers' and Soldiers' Councils, see Tormin, *Zwischen Rätediktatur und Soziale Demokratie*, pp. 26–52.

4. The best account of these events in English is in Mitchell's *Revolution in Bavaria, 1918–1919*.

5. Kolb, *Arbeiterräte*, pp. 42, 62, citing Müller, *Vom Kaiserreich zur Republik*, vol. I, p. 139. See also Barth, *Aus der Werkstatt der Deutschen Revolution*, pp. 49–51.

6. Winkler, *Von der Revolution zur Stabilisierung, Arbeiter and Arbeiterbewegung in der Weimarer Republik, 1918 bis 1924*, p. 45.

7. Scheidemann, *The Making of the New Germany*, vol. II, pp. 261–4.

8. Winkler, *Weimar, 1918–1933*, p. 33; Eyck, *History of the Weimar Republic*, vol. I, p. 45.

9. Burdick and Lutz, *Political Institutions*, p. 39.

10. Ibid., p. 70.

11. Winkler, *Revolution*, p. 55.

12. Kotowski, *Friedrich Ebert*, pp. 154–6.

13. Barth, *Werkstatt*, pp. 24 ff.

14. Winkler, *Weimar, 1918–1933*, p. 39.

15. Kolb, *Arbeiterräte*, p. 123.

16. Burdick and Lutz, *Political Institutions*, p. 48; also *Ursachen und Folgen*, vol. III, p. 13.

17. Bessel, *Germany after the First World War*, pp. 84–90, 258.

18. For a discussion of the hopes the High Command placed in the front army and its attitude to Soldiers' Councils see Carsten, *Reichswehr*, pp. 7–12. Also Gordon, *The Reichswehr*, p. 9.

19. Burdick and Lutz, *Political Institutions*, p. 166.

20. Winkler, *Revolution*, pp. 109–11.

21. For details of this congress see Waldman, *Spartakist Uprising*, pp. 149–58. Also Flechtheim, *Kommunistische Partei*, pp. 45–7; Angress, *Stillborn Revolution*, pp. 23–7; Nettl, *Rosa Luxemburg*, vol. II, pp. 753–61.

22. For a fuller discussion of the complex motives and often contradictory behaviour within the Communist Party at this time see Nettl, *Rosa Luxemburg*, pp. 761–8.

23. See, for example, Kolb, *Arbeiterräte*, p. 239.

24. W. Mommsen, 'German Revolution', pp. 31–6.

25. Bessel, *Germany after the First World War*, pp. 174–94.

26. Winkler, *Revolution*, pp. 191–8.

3 The Foundations of the New Republic

To most Germans the defeat of the Spartakist rising seemed to be a victory for moderation and legality. Ebert, who personified both these qualities, achieved another important objective on 19 January, when Germany went to the polls to elect a Constituent National Assembly. The elections were held in an atmosphere of crisis. Their smooth completion was a triumph for the Republican government. For the first time all adult Germans of both sexes were voting for a truly powerful representative body.

The return to constitutional forms gave Germany's non-socialist parties a chance to assert themselves for the first time since the revolution. From Ebert's point of view, this was quite a healthy development. He had asked Haussmann, the Progressive Party leader, to stay in his government in November 1918. Although this had proved impossible, the collaboration between Majority Social Democrats and the other parties of the old Reichstag majority – Centre and Progressives – might well be revived in the new Republic.

Changes which had taken place in the old Reichstag parties since the revolution had apparently made such collaboration more likely. The Progressives – who had always been in favour of genuine parliamentary government – swung sharply to the left and merged into a new party, the Democrats. This had been founded by a group of intellectuals, journalists and businessmen who felt that the old liberalism had not been decisive or bold enough to make an impression on German society. The majority of the Progressive Party was persuaded to join it, giving the Democrats a political machine with which to fight the elections. Very soon Progressives began to dominate the party.[1] At the same time negotiations were going on between the Progressives and the more right-wing National Liberals, whose members had been badly shaken by the collapse of the Empire.

For a moment it looked as though the forces of German liberalism – which had been split since the time of Bismarck – would unite on a platform of Republican democracy. That this did not happen was due initially to the over-confidence of the new Democratic leaders who refused to give the old National Liberals adequate status in the new organisation. Although some of the National Liberals swallowed unfavourable terms and joined the new party, others remained outside.

They were rallied by Gustav Stresemann, the most energetic National Liberal leader, whose Pan-German record in the war had made him unpalatable to the Democrats. On 15 December 1918, at a meeting of the National Liberal executive attended by only a fraction of those eligible, Stresemann's supporters were able to gain a slender majority for the merger of the party into an organisation under his leadership called the German People's Party (DVP).[2] Later on a good deal of attention was paid to this failure to achieve liberal unity, and Stresemann's part in it received particular scrutiny. At the time he did not seem nearly so important, especially to the triumphant Democrats.[3] In any case it is very doubtful if a real chance of lasting union was cast aside in December 1918. The revolution had frightened many of the old guard into accepting a programme of complete democracy and social reform, but once normality returned their natural aversion to radical egalitarianism would reassert itself.

For the time being Stresemann's People's Party remained weak in numbers and organisation. Its programme was vague and ambivalent, since its candidates sometimes adopted a moderately Republican pose and sometimes revealed themselves as monarchists. In fact, Stresemann and his followers were still attached to the monarchy, and wished to combat the threat of socialist legislation against the propertied classes.[4]

The Democrats, on the other hand, enthusiastically committed themselves to the Republic, and to a programme of democratic reform. For many of them, however, the revolution in November had been a bitter pill to swallow. The Progressives had seen in Prince Max's government the achievement of their political goal; the peaceful and orderly democratisation of Germany. The revolution had upset this development and threatened the country with anarchy. It had also forced the Social Democrats to adopt a more radical posture just at the moment when they seemed ready to co-operate most effectively with the middle-class parties.[5] Despite the dynamism of democratic intellectuals and the support of various white-collar pressure groups such as the German Farmers' League and the German Officials' League, the DDP was ideologically and socially divided. Its main aim in the January elections was to prevent a socialist majority appearing in the National Assembly.[6]

The Roman Catholic Centre Party had not welcomed the revolution. Even before it had broken out the Centre had been divided in its attitude towards Prince Max's government. The collapse of the Empire took the Centre completely by surprise. Its leaders reacted with astonishment and dismay. Trimborn, president of the party's Rhineland section, voiced a general feeling when he described the revolution as a 'national disaster'. There was great confusion about the way in which the party should react to the new situation. Most of its functionaries were loyal to the Empire, but the trade union wing of the party – important in the western provinces of Germany – wanted to exploit the revolution to gain social reforms. There was a real danger that the Centre would disintegrate. Salvation came from an unlikely quarter. The new socialist government in Prussia included Adolf Hoffmann, an Independent Social Democrat, as Education Minister. Hoffmann was eager to free education from clerical influence. So great was the furore aroused by his plans to secularise schools that the Centre in Prussia rallied its forces to oppose him. Defence of Roman Catholic rights once more became a political issue, and it restored the wavering unity of the socially heterogeneous Centre Party.[7]

The last important non-socialist group to contest the election stood uncompromisingly, if somewhat nervously, on the right. This was the German National People's Party, or DNVP. The DNVP was a coalition of conservative and right-radical groups represented in the old Reichstag. The major conservative party, the DKP, which had drawn a good deal of its strength from the landed interests in Germany's eastern provinces, put its electoral machine at the disposal of the DNVP. Nevertheless many old conservative leaders were forced to play a relatively inconspicuous role in the new organisation because it was feared that the electorate would reject such obviously backward-looking social elements.[8] Although more than a quarter of the DNVP's elected representatives in the National Assembly were returned in the provinces of East and West Prussia, Posen and Pomerania,[9] the party was not just a mouthpiece of the Junkers, but had attracted to itself other powerful vested interests alarmed by social disturbance. The party regarded itself with justice as the most uncompromising opponent of the November revolution.

The election results have usually been represented as a victory for the Republic. The Majority Social Democrats, the Centre Party and the Democrats between them obtained a solid majority. On the left, the Spartakists boycotted the election and the Independent Social Democrats only returned 22 deputies out of 423. The DNVP and Stresemann's DVP combined could only muster 14.7 per cent of the vote, which gave a total of 63 seats to the anti-Republican right. Hence monarchism on the one hand and radical socialism on the other seemed to have been defeated. Nevertheless, this impression of the election, which was strengthened by the rapid entry of Democrats and Centre Party members into a coalition government with the SPD, is slightly misleading.

The election campaign was fought by the moderate parties as much to protect Germany from socialist dictatorship as to preserve the Republic against reaction. Ever since the outbreak of the revolution their main objective had been to return as quickly as possible to normal forms of parliamentary government. As soon as they had recovered from the first shock of seeing the Empire collapse they, and the majority of the press, began to attack symptoms of anarchy in Germany and to demand law, order and a National Assembly. Many newspapers were almost hysterical in their assaults on the Spartakists, while the Workers' and Soldiers' Councils were seen as rivals to properly elected democratic institutions.

The other major domestic topic to concern the electorate was social policy. The parties recognised that a strong distaste for an unrestricted form of capitalism, with its apparent encouragement of class conflict, existed in Germany at the end of the war. It was almost as though the Germans had come to desire social change as a consolation prize for their military defeat. Both groups of socialists promised socialisation; the Independents with great fervour. Such a policy did not recommend itself to the other parties. They all produced schemes of social reform, diminishing in effectiveness from left to right, but at the same time they stressed their wish to protect private property.

The Democrats presented themselves as being above the class struggle, and ready to defend individual rights.* The Centre Party rejected any attacks on private property. Its speakers were egged on by episcopal pronouncements to the effect that between Christianity and Socialism there could be no compromise – 'only either – or'.[11] The general impression given was that religion and property were threatened, and that the Centre was a safe refuge from atheist revolution. The two right-wing parties, the DVP and the DNVP, were naturally just as critical of social democracy.

To sum up, the election result of January 1919 was a vote for democracy but against social revolution. It sealed the fate of the workers' councils and made the implementation of socialisation plans unlikely. The reformist alliance of moderate Social Democrats, progressive Liberals and Roman Catholic Centre which had been eclipsed in November 1918 now took over power. Unfortunately there were no strong grounds for confidence in its ability to function effectively. The events of the revolution had deepened the cleavage between the working-class supporters of the SPD and the nervous liberals or Roman Catholics who had voted for their coalition partners. It was not a good beginning for a government facing immensely difficult tasks.

The National Assembly met in Weimar on 6 February 1919. Weimar lies about 150 miles south-west of Berlin, and was chosen as the home of the National Assembly because the capital was not considered safe.

The Assembly's main task was to agree on the form of the new German State and draw up a constitution. Negotiations over this were inevitably long and complicated. Apart from obvious problems which beset all constitution makers – the type of political representation to be chosen, the division of powers within the State, and the nature of the executive – the Germans had to tackle a difficulty which had troubled the founders of their previous Empire: the existence of the German Federal States.

---

* The banker Hjalmar Schacht, for example, writing in 1926 when revolution was not regarded with favour, claimed that the prime object of those who founded the Democratic Party was to establish internal order in Germany and save the country from Bolshevism.[10]

These states, or *Länder* as they are more properly called, pre-dated the Empire. Many of them, like Saxony, Bavaria and Würt-temberg, had long histories and a strong sense of local patriotism. They were, however, very uneven in size, and their geographical position was not designed to facilitate a federal type of government. By far the largest was the kingdom of Prussia, which had dominated Germany before the revolution. It contained 57 per cent of Germany's population and extended from the Rhine to the Russian frontier. Under the Imperial constitution the Länder had been allowed to keep their own governments and their own parliamentary institutions. Most of the domestic administration in Germany was carried out by officials in the employ of Land governments. Prussia, whose electoral system had been weighted in favour of the propertied classes, was naturally very important in this administrative scheme, and its government had always been a bulwark of Imperial authority. It was not surprising that reformers in the Empire had wanted to see Prussia's dominating position abolished. Social Democrats and left-wing liberals were in favour of rationalising Germany's administrative structure so as to create a stronger central government in Berlin and smaller, more uniform administrative units for local affairs.[12] It was, of course, also assumed that both national and local authorities would be strictly democratic in their election and methods.

The Minister of the Interior in the new coalition government was a Democrat, Hugo Preuss, who taught Constitutional Law at the Commercial University in Berlin.[13] As early as 14 November 1918 he had been empowered by Ebert to draw up plans for a constitution. A firm believer in drastic reform, he particularly admired the British system of local government, although his ideas about it were rather utopian. His ideal conception of a new Germany would have involved not only a radical reconstruc-tion of the Länder so as to create units of roughly equal size, but also a great diminution in their status. They would have become little more than the provincial element in a pyramid of democrat-ically elected local authorities.[14] Such changes were clearly too sweeping to gain acceptance. Preuss therefore watered down his proposals to a certain extent, and when he published his draft constitution on 20 January 1919 the Reich was seen to preserve its federal character. But it was clear that some smaller Länder were likely to be eliminated, Prussia would be broken up and the powers of all the Länder reduced *vis-à-vis* the central government in Berlin.[15]

Preuss's plans had much to commend them in theory, but they soon ran into practical difficulties. At the root of these lay the interest which many party politicians felt in maintaining the old administrative structure. The events of the revolution in various Länder had strengthened particularist feelings there. Whatever theorists might say, the regional organisations of all parties – including the Socialists and the Democrats – had never been wildly keen to see their Länder emasculated. The events of the revolution had strengthened these particularist feelings, because the old opposition parties had been able to take over the reins of government in the Länder capitals as well as in Berlin. In particular, Prussia, once the bastion of Hohenzollern power, now became a stronghold of the Social Democrats, who – usually in alliance with the Centre – maintained almost uninterrupted leadership of the Prussian Land Government.

It was also unfortunate for Preuss that his draft should be published at a time when the Reich government itself looked very insecure. Many provincial politicians were afraid that Berlin might fall prey to Bolshevism. There was a widely-voiced fear that the dissolution of Prussia would encourage the French and the Poles to covet parts of her old territory. Hence Preuss's scheme ran into great opposition from the Länder, and Ebert's government felt in no position to ride roughshod over such objections. In any case some of Ebert's own colleagues felt alarm at the thought of Prussia being weakened.[16]

After a great deal of wrangling a compromise was arrived at whereby the Länder kept their historic form and their administrative institutions. Certain privileges in taxation, rail and postal services and military affairs which had been enjoyed by some of the southern states were abolished. Although some of the powers previously enjoyed by Land governments were now transferred to that of the Reich, the execution of Germany's laws was still mainly in the hands of officials controlled by the Länder. Police, judges and schoolteachers were employed by Land governments rather than by the authorities in Berlin. The major exception to this state of affairs lay in the field of taxation, where Erzberger – who became Germany's Finance Minister in June 1919 – insisted on establishing tax-gathering agencies under the direct control of the central government.[17] Procedure was established for the future modification of Land boundaries, but no major changes were ever made.* The Prussian state remained intact. In the long run, the Federal structure of the Republic was bound to cause problems because of the unbalanced nature of the Länder. Many of the smaller Länder – and even some of the larger ones like Bavaria – were financially insecure. Their situation was made more difficult because, as time went on, Reich legislation imposed more financially burdensome duties on the Länder without adding to their sources of income. They had to depend on payments from the Reich. When the economic situation grew worse towards the end of the 1920s, tension amongst the Länder – and between them and Reich governments – increased over this issue. Reform proposals were complicated by the disproportionate size of Prussia. The Prussian government wanted to maintain its powers, but hoped to centralise Germany by absorbing neighbouring Länder.[19] Conservative reformers disliked Prussia because it was dominated by the social democrats. Some wanted to give more power to the Reich government, but this did not please anti-socialists in non-Prussian Länder, especially those in Bavaria. The possibility of creating a reasonably well-balanced federal state, like the one which appeared in West Germany in 1949, did not really exist. This was a fundamental source of weakness in Republican politics. Given the difficult situation faced by the Republic in the early months of 1919 such a compromise arrangement was not surprising, but it could hardly be described as a happy solution. On the one hand the constitution was not decentralised enough for those who thought that the Länder should have as much autonomy as was compatible with the needs of German unity. On the other it did not establish a single, unrivalled source of power in the Reich.

The fact that Reich laws took priority over Land laws did not prevent Land governments ignoring orders from Berlin, or trying to obstruct them. On several occasions in the career of the Republic the conflict between Land and Reich authorities was to

---

* Thuringia was united as a Land in 1920, and in the same year Coburg was joined to Bavaria. Pyrmont joined Prussia in 1922. In 1928 there was an exchange of territory between Saxony and Prussia, and Waldeck joined Prussia. None of these changes was of a radical character.[18]

threaten the stability of the whole State. It certainly made effective policy-making in Berlin very difficult. At the same time party
politics remained organised on a Land basis so that regional
struggles for power could, and did, have an effect on relations
between the parties in Berlin. In addition the Länder governments themselves had a voice in the Reich legislature, the second
chamber of which, the Reichsrat, was made up of their representatives. Although the major initiative for legislation came from
the Reichstag, the Reichsrat could exercise considerable influence
over it.[20]

If the relationship between the Reich and the Länder was
never satisfactorily resolved, the constitution-makers also faced a
serious problem over the head of state. How would the Republic's
President be appointed? Should he be indirectly elected, like the
President of France, who was perceived in Germany to be a
weak figurehead, completely subordinate to parliament? Or
should he be a democratically elected commander of the
executive, as in the USA? A compromise was chosen. The President was to be elected by popular vote, but the Reich Chancellor
(Prime Minister), whom he nominated, was responsible to the
German parliament, the Reichstag. The President also enjoyed
the effectively unfettered right to dissolve the Reichstag, though it
was to be expected that he would do so on the advice of the
Reich Chancellor. All Weimar Reichstags were ended by presidential dissolution and not by the expiry of the legislative
period.[21]

The decision to provide a counterweight to the Reichstag in the
shape of an elected presidency was largely the work of the liberal
parties, who feared the 'absolutism of parliament' and the 'tyranny of the majority'. This reflected a traditional distrust of mass
democracy amongst the adherents of German liberalism. It created an awkward ambivalence in the constitution, since the President could claim a popular mandate which was as powerful, and
arguably more convincing, than that enjoyed by the Reichstag.
The latter was bound to be divided into several political camps.
German political culture in the Wilhelmine era had been traditionally contemptuous of political parties, which were regarded as
representing divisive sectional concerns rather than the national
interest. Under Article 48 of the constitution, the President was
given the right to govern by decree in the event of a national

emergency, so long as his measures were not rejected by a vote in the Reichstag.[22]

This meant that political parties were able to feel that, in difficult times, the presidency would be able to carry on the government, thus making it unnecessary for the parties themselves to shoulder responsibility for unpopular measures, or compromise their principles to maintain effective government.

The fact that between 1930 and 1933 German governments had to rely on the authority of President Hindenburg was a grave admission of weakness, but nevertheless it has not been satisfactorily explained what the alternative to presidential rule would have been, given the ideological cleavages between the parties in the Reichstag. Certainly the President's powers came in very useful for the defenders of the Republic during other turbulent times; notably the crisis year of 1923. Despite having the authority of popular election,* no president attempted a *coup d'état* along the lines of Louis Napoleon. Hitler established his dictatorship while he was Reich Chancellor.

At the heart of the constitution lay the Reichstag, the national parliament, which was to be elected by universal suffrage under a system of proportional representation. Unlike its Imperial predecessor, the Reichstag could make or break governments, which were responsible to it. Since such elections would normally only take place every four years, an element of direct democracy – the plebiscite – was introduced. These reforms enabled the Social Democratic Minister of the Interior, Eduard David, to boast that the German Republic was 'the most democratic democracy in the World'.[23] If anything, however, the plebiscite weakened democracy rather than strengthened it. Theoretically it was possible for disputes between the two houses of the legislature, the Reichstag and the Reichsrat, to be resolved by this means, but in practice this never happened. In addition, if 10 per cent of of the electorate petitioned for a particular piece of legislation and the Reichstag refused to carry it into law, the matter could be put before the whole nation for a plebiscitary decision. These provisions had little practical value. The plebiscite did not recommend itself to administrators as a means of overcoming constitutional difficulties because it might lead to popular unrest. They preferred

*Ebert was never popularly elected, so this only applies to Hindenburg.

negotiations behind the scenes. A number of attempts were made by political parties to organise plebiscites in favour of controversial measures, but none of these proposals ever succeeded.[24] The plebiscitary campaigns helped to poison the political atmosphere in Germany – a Communist-inspired attempt to confiscate the property the former royal houses in 1926 and a Nationalist assault on the Young Plan in 1929 were examples of such divisiveness. But otherwise the plebiscites did not play a vital part in the Republic's development.[25]

After the collapse of Hitler's Third Reich in 1945, the founding fathers of the Federal Republic of Germany drew clear lessons from the weakness of the parliamentary system of the Weimar Republic. The presidency was indirectly elected, and could never be regarded as an alternative source of power to the Federal Chancellor, and the plebiscitary element in the constitution was eradicated altogether.

One other feature of the Weimar political system has come in for particular criticism. This was the method of proportional representation under which members of the Reichstag were to be elected. Proportional representation had long been a political objective of the Social Democrats because, under the old Imperial method of Constituency elections, urban voters usually elected fewer members than country voters. Hence the vote of a Bavarian peasant counted for more than that of a factory hand in Berlin. The National Assembly had therefore been elected according to a method invented by a Belgian, de Hondte. The country was divided into thirty-eight large electoral districts, and parties put up lists of candidates in each of these.* The number of votes cast for a party in any electoral district decided how many candidates from its list would be sent to the Assembly. This system was continued under the new constitution, but was modified so that for every 60 000 votes a party received it could count one Reichstag member, while its surplus votes in all districts should be pooled to elect extra members from a national party list. In this way virtually no vote was wasted.[26]

It has often been argued that proportional representation weakened Germany by fostering a multiplicity of small parties and

---

* Elections were actually held in only thirty-seven of the districts, because the French did not allow voting in Alsace-Lorraine.

thus preventing the emergence of large political forces concerned with national issues. Another unattractive feature of the electoral system was that voters could not select persons when voting, only lists. Hence the position of candidates on a list was all-important, and this was decided by their party organisation in the region concerned. This seemed to make party officials more important than the electorate in the career of German politicians.

Such criticisms have some weight, but are not convincing explanations of the Republic's political difficulties. So far as the relationship between parties and electorate is concerned, it would be naive to imagine that single-member constituencies produce a much closer association between members of parliament and their voters. In Britain, for example, it is clear that most electors vote for the party rather than the candidate. The party machine is as important in small constituencies as it is in large ones. Nor was the need to please local sentiment absent from the minds of German committee-men. Some members of the Reichstag enjoyed greater popularity with their electors than others, but this is a phenomenon common to all electoral systems.

As for the question of small parties, and the supposed fragmentation of Germany's political life, it should be remembered that all of the major parties in the German National Assembly were direct successors of those represented in the Imperial Reichstag. In one case – the DNVP – the new party was an amalgamation of several old ones and therefore represented consolidation rather than diversification of forces. Other small groups, like the Danes and the Poles, had vanished. Smaller parties did become more successful electorally towards the end of the 1920s – and the liberal middle class was particularly affected by this development – but all the small groups put together never attracted more than 15 per cent of the total vote in German elections. It is also doubtful how far the proportional system helped those parties dedicated to the destruction of the Republic. The Nazis and the Communists were parties whose main strength initially lay outside parliament, and it is unlikely that any other electoral method would have held them back.

So far as Hitler's party was concerned, it may have benefited somewhat from proportional representation (PR) in the election of 1930, when it first became a serious parliamentary threat to the established parties. But by 1932 it had increased its support so much that under an electoral system such as that used in Britain it would have won considerably more seats than it gained from PR. Under the latter, Hitler did not even manage to win a majority for his party in the highly pressurised election of March 1933, when intimidation was rife. It could thus never be claimed that he had achieved absolute power as the result of a democratic, popular decision.

To contrast PR with a 'first-past-the-post' system such as that used in Britain is in any case misleading so far as Germany is concerned. The old Imperial election system had involved run-off elections in constituencies where no candidate received an overall majority. This encouraged pacts between parties and thereby helped smaller ones to survive. The PR system marked a further stage of refinement; it would have been inconceivable to change over to first-past-the-post in 1919. PR was seen as the most modern electoral system by the Social Democrats and as a safe method of containing them by the weaker liberal parties.[27]

Whatever problems faced the Weimar Republic they were not attributable to the democratic nature of its constitution. Far more important was the legacy of the old Wilhelmine Empire, in which parliamentary parties had been given rights of self-expression without being required to shoulder the duties of government. Strident nationalism, for example, had been a hallmark of pre-war German liberal and conservative parties, whose spokesmen were secure in the knowledge that they would never be called upon to make hard diplomatic choices themselves. In the Weimar Republic the political parties retained the lack of responsibility which had characterised their behaviour in the old Reichstag. This did not mean that their leaders were unpatriotic or deliberately feckless. But by tradition politicians who participated in coalition governments remained bound by the decisions of their own party delegation, and the delegation in its turn was mightily influenced by pressures from party organisations outside parliament. The result was that fruitful collaboration between party leaders in cabinet might be torpedoed by a party committee fearful of associating itself with electorally unpopular measures or persons. For this, as for the structural inadequacies of the German State, the Republic was less to be blamed than its Imperial predecessor.

The Republican constitution was in many ways an admirable piece of humane and enlightened statecraft. Unlike its Imperial predecessor of 1871, it included a list of individual rights which could only be suspended under exceptional circumstances. Article 109 of the Constitution established that all Germans were equal before the law. Men and women had equal civic rights and duties. In 1919, therefore, adult German women were not only confirmed in their right to vote, but could claim equality of treatment in such areas as education or appointment to the public service. Needless to say, in practice emancipation proved a slow process, but German women had certainly stolen a march on their neighbours in Britain and France. Unfortunately, in this, as in so many other areas, the time needed to reap the benefits of such a change was not to be vouchsafed to the Weimar Republic. Nevertheless, its constitution was a brave statement of fundamental liberal and democratic principles, and for this it deserves to be honoured.

The Republic's first parliamentary cabinet took office in February 1919. It was a coalition of Majority Socialists, Democrats and Centre. An alliance of moderate working-class social democracy, middle-class liberalism and organised Roman Catholicism, it came to be known as the Weimar Coalition. Such a combination aroused fury in the breasts of many who had been associated with the old Reich, for it seemed that the least patriotic elements had seized the reins of power and were feathering their own nests at Germany's expense. It was especially galling for them to see the Catholics, whom they had unjustly supposed were more loyal to Rome than Berlin, working hand in glove with irreligious Social Democrats. These negative views were widespread among sections of German society whose power and influence had by no means disappeared. The army, and later on the powerful ex-servicemen's association, the *Stahlhelm*, were especially prone to resentments of this kind. They were also to be encountered in the universities and among civil servants.

As for the coalition itself, co-operation was genuine among the leaders of the government parties in the National Assembly, but their motives were mixed and the attitude of their supporters unenthusiastic. The Democrats and Centre joined the government primarily to prevent the Social Democrats exercising a monopoly of power. The Centre Party, in particular, had serious doubts about committing itself to the new administration. Many of its rank and file upbraided the leadership for betraying the anti-socialist pledges made at the elections.[28]

The coalition was soon faced with great internal stress as the result of the Allied peace terms to Germany, presented on 1 May. Reluctance to shoulder responsibility for accepting a harsh peace caused ministers to resign, and the Democrats withdrew from the coalition for several months. Internal strife also discredited the government.

As Germany's constitution-makers debated in the National Theatre at Weimar, rumblings of proletarian disturbance provided a sinister chorus in the wings. In the spring of 1919 the Russian Bolshevik goal of world revolution seemed nearer than at any other time. That January the Soviet government, whose communications with the West were uneven and eccentric, established a new international socialist organisation – the Comintern. In March a Communist coup took place in Hungary, where Bela Kun set up a dictatorship in Budapest. German Austria appeared to be on the brink of revolution. There were strikes in the Ruhr and disturbances in Berlin. Most spectacular of all were the events in Bavaria. In February Kurt Eisner, having been overwhelmingly defeated at elections for a new Bavarian parliament, was on his way to announce his resignation, when an unsophisticated young aristocrat shot him dead.

In the wave of popular indignation which followed, the Workers' and Soldiers' Councils became the real source of authority in Munich. On 7 April a group of radicals declared Bavaria to be a Soviet Republic. A week later leadership of the Soviet was taken over by the Communist Party, at whose head stood a fanatical young Russian revolutionary, Eugen Leviné. A Red Army was recruited. Lenin sent his blessing to the Bavarians. It was not until 1 May 1919 that Noske's troops from northern Germany and some Bavarian Freikorps fought their way into Munich. The Soviet was crushed with much brutality. Many revolutionaries were shot without trial, and others received terms of imprisonment. Leviné himself, having courageously defended his beliefs before a special court, was condemned to death and executed.

The Munich Soviet was by no means the only instance of revolutionary disturbance in 1919. The spectacle of Reichswehr units, often still in the form of Freikorps, marching into German cities to suppress working-class unrest, became almost common-place. Although the Communists afterwards claimed that they had borne the brunt of such fighting, their organisation was feeble and their numbers insignificant. The Independent Social Democratic Party was still the spokesman – albeit a confused and divided spokesman – of the radical proletariat.

Yet the USPD never really adjusted itself to the post-war situation. It wanted both social revolution and democracy, and however desirable these objectives may have been, they were not compatible in the Germany of 1919. Many of the more distinguished members of the party had always rejected the concept of a Soviet dictatorship. Although they were bitter about the way their former comrades in the SPD had treated them, they were basically men of peace and compromise. For them the road back into the old Social Democratic Party was easier to tread than that which led to Bolshevik revolution.

At first, no such choice had to be made. The USPD, whose leaders were not burdened with government responsibility and whose speakers defended rebellious elements in parliament and the law courts, reaped a handsome reward in working-class gratitude. At the Republic's first Reichstag elections of June 1920 the party quadrupled its representation and more than doubled its vote. It was a hollow victory. Virtually isolated on the left, the Independents could do little in parliament and were divided on the extent to which they should carry the battle out into the streets. An immediate cause of dissension faced the party in the autumn of 1920 when it was suggested that the Independents should submit themselves to the discipline of the Third (Communist) International, directed from Moscow. A majority of the delegates at a Party Congress in October accepted this move, but in practice only about a third of the party's membership actually left to join the Communists.[29] Nevertheless, this was the beginning of the end for the Independents, and in 1922 the rump of the party voted to rejoin the Majority Social Democrats.

Hence, for all its weakness, the Communist Party possessed certain long-term advantages in the battle for the allegiance of the left. Its revolutionary martyrs – Liebknecht, Rosa Luxemburg, and even Leviné – achieved wider notoriety than their equivalents in the USPD, largely because the most prominent people in that party did not figure in revolutionary upheavals.

The party also gained from the sinister prestige of its Bolshevik patrons in Soviet Russia. It was natural that the Government should place most of the blame for violence on the 'Reds' or Communists, thus adding to the impression that the KPD was the only effective champion of proletarian dictatorship in Germany.

Unrest on the left forced the Republican government to rely more heavily on the repressive authorities associated with the old empire. First among these was the army, now renamed the *Reichswehr* and under the direction of staff officers whose emotional loyalties were almost entirely directed towards the old Reich of Bismarck. By the summer of 1919 they were beginning to recover their confidence after the shocks of the revolutionary period.

The new Reichswehr was the first unified army Germany had possessed in peacetime. Its headquarters were those of the former Prussian War Ministry in Berlin's Bendlerstrasse. The army was built up out of the loyal remnants of old units and some of the new Freikorps, although staff officers were not too enthusiastic about the self-willed attitude apparent in these formations. The official aim was to develop a consolidated and highly disciplined force, completely dependent on the orders of its military superiors. The question of obedience was supremely important; the existence of Soldiers' Councils had apparently threatened the internal cohesion of the army and undermined the status of the officers.

In fact the officer corps was fighting a very successful battle not only to survive, but also to maintain its exclusive control over the armed services. Bloodshed and disorder in various parts of the country in the first half of 1919 made the new Reichswehr indispensable to the government. Gustav Noske, the minister responsible, brooked no interference with the troops on ideological grounds. He was confident that he could work with the generals of the old army and obtain their loyal co-operation.

In any case, there seemed no alternative. Few socialists and trade unionists felt much enthusiasm for the army. Noske's appeals for co-operation in recruiting fell on stony ground within his own party. There were many reasons for this. The socialists had always been hostile to the military even though many of them – including Noske – had admitted before 1914 that there was a need for national defence. The behaviour of the military towards proletarian insurgents disgusted many trade unionists and alienated the socialist press. Apart from these political problems there was an institutional difficulty which became important after the peace treaty was signed. The Allies insisted that the new German army should not be based on conscription, but should consist of long-service professional soldiers. Very few urban workers desired to sign on for twelve years in a force whose political and social characteristics they found unattractive. The officer corps was able to recruit men to its own taste – indeed it had little choice. Most Reichswehr recruits were from rural areas, and few had Social Democratic, or even specifically Republican, sympathies.

Hence the spirit of the old army survived. The Solders' Councils dwindled in importance until they were eliminated. Noske, energetic though he was, could not prevent the staff officers – of whom a disproportionately large number had been kept in service as the army was demobilised – from keeping the control of military affairs very much in their own hands. As the political position of the Republican coalition became weaker so the independence of the men in the Bendlerstrasse grew more marked.

In the civil service the story was often similar, although always more complicated. When the revolution broke out most of the former officials in Reich and Land administrations had been asked to stay at their posts. Even the Workers' and Soldiers' Councils had reluctantly realised that to dispense with them was impossible. They had attempted to place the bureaucracy under proletarian supervision, but such efforts were never successful.

Although the more ambitious plans of the Workers' and Soldiers' Councils to supplant or subordinate the bureaucracy came to nothing it was clear that the new Republican coalition would wish to exert an influence over the recruitment and personnel of the civil service. It was also hoped that the power of officialdom would be diminished and that parliament would exercise greater control over civil servants than had been possible under the old regime.

No such developments took place. The civil service remained a powerful force at all levels of society. Its numbers swelled after 1919. The revolution did not damage the authority and status of the official; on the contrary, his position was strengthened. His security and freedom from party political pressure were guaranteed in the new Constitution; yet he still had the right to participate in political life and to stand for parliament.* In 1930 civil servants were to be found representing all shades of opinion in the Reichstag, nine of them in the Nazi Party.[30]

By no means all officials were hostile to the Republic, but many of them had been shocked by the violence and confusion of the November revolution. They then found themselves working for political parties which had usually been regarded by the official classes under the Empire as subversive or disloyal. This was especially true of the Social Democrats and the Centre. Although officials who served Wilhelm II had liked to regard themselves as above politics, those connected with law enforcement and local government had been expected to exert their influence in favour of loyal parties at election time, and they had usually done so.[31]

There was also the question of professional competence. German administrative officials regarded themselves as models of incorruptible efficiency, and this assessment was not unduly flattering. It was certainly accepted by most of the German middle classes. The training for a senior civil servant was lengthy and nearly always involved legal studies. Hence senior officials were not simply products of a particular class – although most of them came from socially superior backgrounds and the nobility was strongly represented[32] – but regarded themselves as part of a specialised elite. If the Republican parties were going to promote their own candidates into politically sensitive posts they would command respect from existing officials only if they possessed the right qualifications.

For the Centre Party and the Democrats this did not present too serious a problem, since lawyers were prominent in their ranks.[33] But the SPD had fewer men with the required background. Its leaders had worked their way up through trade unions, their party's administration or the party press. When such men were appointed to administrative or diplomatic posts

---

* Officials had been able to stand for parliament before 1918, but their allegiance to their monarchs and their Emperor was insisted upon and readily given.

it could be suggested that the standards of the service were being lowered for the benefit of party hacks. In actual fact some of the new officials performed very creditably. In the diplomatic service, for example, several ambassadorships were given to men whose careers had been made in the Labour movement, and they performed their tasks with distinction.[34]

The most important administrative area in which considerable changes were made was the state of Prussia. There the Ministry of the Interior was almost continuously under the control of the Social Democrats. The other coalition parties were also in a good position to press for appointments, although political support alone was rarely enough to secure an official post. Between 1919 and 1929 there were personnel changes in those departments of the senior Prussian civil service dealing with law enforcement and provincial administration. However, in many areas of the bureaucracy, such as finance, it was not possible even in Prussia to make personnel changes on political grounds. Furthermore, the changes which were made brought with them accusations of jobbery. In fact, many of the new appointees from the Social Democratic side had trade union experience, and this often proved an asset in dealing with labour problems. Although party political patronage was regarded as corrupt by nationalist opponents of the regime, many of those who took up government posts in Prussia lost money by doing so.[35] This was especially true of the early 1920s when, owing to inflation, an official's salary was losing its value all the time.

Nevertheless, the charge that the Republic had brought corruption and chaos became commonplace among its monarchist and nationalist opponents, and many bureaucrats believed it to be true. It was significant that many of them interpreted their oath to obey the constitution as not implying a commitment to the Republican state form.[36] When Hitler campaigned to 'cleanse' the administration of corrupt Republican elements he was echoing views expressed widely in far more respectable conservative circles.

One particular section of the bureaucracy exercised a definitely negative effect on the Republic's fortunes from the outset. This was the judiciary. The first reason was personal; most of the judges had been appointed by Imperial authorities before the November revolution. The second was legal. Jurists, being concerned with the law, naturally regarded revolution and the arbitrary acts of revolutionary bodies with distaste. The moderate Republicans were, for their part, hampered by the belief that judges ought to be irremovable in order to safeguard fair implementation of the law. Despite various proposals put forward in the Workers' and Soldiers' Councils, there was no such thing as 'revolutionary justice' in Germany.

On the contrary, German jurists glossed over the revolution; they assumed that the Republican government had inherited state authority of the old Reich through a kind of apostolic succession passing from Prince Max of Baden to Friedrich Ebert. Cases of a political nature were judged according to standards which had changed little since the time of Bismarck. It was an unhappy chance that the first political cases to come before the courts in Republican Germany involved conflict between the Republican authorities and their enemies on the left.

It was natural for jurists brought up in an authoritarian tradition to take a harsh view of militant revolutionaries and to condone excesses against them by the forces of law and order. The State Prosecutor in Munich who later became Bavaria's Minister of Justice and a member of Hitler's cabinet told one young socialist lawyer that the fighting in Munich in May 1919 should be regarded in the same light as a storm or similar natural disaster; there was no need to pursue the question of Freikorps atrocities too zealously.[37]

This sophistry in the administration of political justice, coinciding as it did with the personal prejudices of many judges, was soon to have more sinister implications. When attacks on the Republic began to come from the right rather than the left the law courts ceased to act as an effective shield. Attempted counter-revolution, political murder and libellous publications were often connived at in the courts because the judges thought the perpetrators more 'patriotic' than the new regime they were attacking. Respect for the law amongst violent extremists was in any case further reduced by the tendency of successive Republican governments to grant amnesties to political malefactors. To some traditional jurists it seemed that the Republican system lacked the will to uphold the rule of law.

Many judges were willing to abide by the letter of the Constitution, but they thought that above the Republic – which was the child of party politics – there stood a greater interest, that of the nation. This view, which was also common among other officials and army officers, implied that if Republican politics and what the judiciary considered to be the national interest came into conflict, the former might be cast aside. Since right-wing organisations were usually regarded as 'nationally-minded', this distinction worked to their advantage.

The inability of the new Republic to win the hearts of its servants was symbolised by their reluctance to accept the outward trappings of the new regime. During the early 1920s many civil servants in Prussia happened to take their holidays on the anniversary of the Republican Constitution, a day on which they would otherwise have been expected to demonstrate their loyalty to the new state form. The Republican flag, with its black, red and gold colours, was often not flown over public buildings. The army always avoided flying it wherever possible and was allowed a special war flag in the old Imperial colours with those of the Republic tucked away ignominiously in one corner.

The outlook for the Republic might have been rosier if a favourable climate of opinion had existed outside official circles. The Third French Republic had survived despite a largely monarchist officer corps and a parliament in which a majority hoped for a monarchist restoration. But after the signature of the Versailles Peace Treaty hopes of progress within the Republic tended to evaporate. In the universities and grammar schools bourgeois youth regarded the new democracy with contempt. Sixth-formers at one school who used the Weimar Constitution for air-gun practice were not untypical of their class and generation. German universities, despite grandiose projects for reform aired during the revolutionary period, remained predominantly a middle-class preserve, where the shame of Versailles was felt especially deeply. As was perhaps not unnatural, Western political ideas became unfashionable among intellectual youth and the search for a German solution to social and political problems led many to embrace authoritarian nationalism, some to admire Russian Communism, and a few even to advocate a mixture of both. This is not to suggest the there were no young people of liberal or social-democratic persuasion at universities. But the atmosphere in these institutions was not conducive to the development of a stable democracy.[38]

The churches, too, looked back to the old order with nostalgia. In practice they were treated very generously by the Republic. Despite socialist demands for a division of Church and State, neither the religious nor the financial status of the churches was damaged. But the Protestant Church resented losing the national status it had enjoyed under the Empire.[39] Most of its clergy remained openly monarchist. The Roman Catholic Church, for its part, was not so much impressed by the success of the Centre Party as by the threat to property and religion posed by an atheistical revolutionary movement.

It was therefore quite clear that the Republican parties faced an uphill task in associating the German people with their new State. The picture was not entirely black. The trade unions, for example, were committed to the Republic. Between 1914 and 1919 the socialist trade unions increased in membership from 2 to 5.5 million. By 1920 this figure rose to nearly 8 million, although it dropped away from the peak in the years that followed. The trade unions provided the backbone of the SPD's support electorally, they were a powerful source of financial aid and their newspapers had a readership of some 6 million.[40]

Yet the unions had their disadvantages as allies. They were mainly concerned with an economic struggle against capitalism and although their leaders were usually moderate men they spoke the language of the class war. This was in any case a characteristic of the whole working-class movement and helped to alienate the Social Democrats' colleagues in the Weimar coalition. The economic power of the unions was a possible weapon in the socialist armoury, though labour leaders had always been chary of using it. Its one apparent success came in the Kapp Putsch, but the value of a political strike was soon demonstrated to be very doubtful to a government dependent on middle-class votes.* Social Democracy could not hope to wield effective power while the working-class movement remained divided. The other organs of proletarian self-expression which might have aided their cause, the Workers' Councils, had been rapidly emasculated.[41]

Founded on a discredited revolution and burdened with a detested peace treaty, the Republic faced a grim future.

* For the Kapp Putsch see below, pp. 69–71.

Notes

1. Robson, 'Left-Wing Liberalism in Germany, 1900–1919', D. Phil. thesis, University of Oxford, 1966, pp. 424–6.
2. For details of this conflict between Stresemann and those eager to amalgamate the National Liberals with the DDP, see Jones, *German Liberalism*, p. 21 and Turner, *Stresemann*, pp. 13–25.
3. Robson, 'Left-Wing Liberalism', pp. 401, 407. For an interesting account of the early history of the DDP, see L. Albertin, 'German Liberalism and the Foundation of the Weimar Republic: A Missed Opportunity?', in Nicholls and Matthias, *German Democracy and the Triumph of Hitler*, pp. 29–46.
4. Turner, *Stresemann*, pp. 30, 35.
5. Robson, 'Left-Wing Liberalism', pp. 372–3, citing Matthias and Morsey, *Die Regierung des Prinzen Max von Baden*, pp. 631–3.
6. Jones, *German Liberalism*, p. 22.
7. See Morsey, *Zentrumspartei*, pp. 79, 95, 110–17.
8. For details of the founding of the DNVP see Hertzmann, *DNVP*, pp. 32 ff.
9. Hölfron (ed.), *Deutsche Nationalversammlung*, vol. I, p. 185. In 1912 the Old Conservatives had been the strongest right-wing party in Posen, Pomerania and East Prussia. The Free Conservatives were stronger in West Prussia.
10. Schacht, *Stabilization of the Mark*, pp. 36–7. He adheres to the same view in *My First Seventy-Six Years*, pp. 148–52.
11. Morsey, *Zentrumspartei*, p. 134.
12. On the attitudes of SPD and Democrats to the Constitution see Schulz, *Demokratie und Diktatur*, vol. I, pp. 30–1, 101 ff.
13. Eyck, *History of the Weimar Republic*, vol. I, p. 54.
14. Cf. Schulz, *Demokratie und Diktatur*, pp. 127–30.
15. For a discussion of the draft see Apelt, *Weimarer Verfassung*, pp. 56–64.
16. Schulz, *Demokratie und Diktatur*, pp. 136–8.
17. For Erzberger's part in framing the new taxation system see Epstein, *Matthias Erzberger*, pp. 334–8.
18. Apelt, *Weimarer Verfassung*, pp. 137–8.
19. Schulze, *Otto Braun*, pp. 584–601.
20. It could, for example, block legislation which did not command a two-thirds majority in the Reichstag. Apelt, *Weimarer Verfassung*, p. 245.
21. Gusy, *Die Weimarer Reichsverfassung*, p. 104.
22. For a discussion of the president's emergency powers see Boldt, 'Article 48 of the Weimar Constitution: its Historical and Political

Implications', in Nicholls and Matthias, *German Democracy and the Triumph of Hitler*, pp. 79–97. For social democratic and liberal attitudes to the presidency see Winkler, *Revolution*, pp. 231–2.

23. Winkler, *Weimar, 1918–1913*, p. 105.

24. One reason was that such a plebiscite needed the participation of a majority of the electorate if a positive result was to be valid. Hence if all those opposing the proposal abstained their votes would be added to those of the genuine abstainers, and only if there was a positive majority of all electors for the measure would it succeed in becoming law. Apelt, *Weimarer Verfassung*, pp. 249–50.

25. Gusy, *Die Weimarer Reichsverfassung*, pp. 97–8. Plebiscites could also be demanded at Land level, but only one of them ever succeeded. This was a joint Communist/Nazi campaign to dissolve the Oldenburg Landtag in April 1932. The result was that the Nazis ruled the Land thereafter.

26. Apelt, *Weimarer Verfassung*, pp. 179–80. This is a somewhat simplified account of the actual procedure.

27. Kolb, *Die Weimarer Republik*, p. 165.

28. Morsey, *Zentrumspartei*, pp. 169, 172.

29. Prager, *Geschichte der USPD*, pp. 222–9. Also Angress, *Stillborn Revolution*, pp. 71–2. See also Wheeler, *USPD*, pp. 246–61.

30. Bracher, *Auflösung*, p. 178.

31. Runge, *Politik und Beamtentum*, p. 21.

32. Ibid., pp. 169–71. A. J. Nicholls, 'Die höhere Beamtenschaft in der Weimarer Zeit – Betrachtungen zu Problemen ihrer Haltung and ihrer Fortbildung', in Albertin and Link (eds.), *Politische Parteien auf dem Wege zur parlamentarischen Demokratie in Deutschland, Entwicklungslinien bis zur Gegenwart*, pp. 195–207. For the whole question of the status and ethos of officials in Weimar see also Caplan, *Government without Administration, State and Civil Service in Weimar and Nazi Germany*, chs. 1–4.

33. Runge, *Politik und Beamtentum*, pp. 45–7. Also Morsey, *Zentrumspartei*, pp. 50–2, 155–6.

34. H. Holborn, in Craig and Gilbert (eds.), *The Diplomats*, p. 152.

35. Runge, *Politik und Beamtentum*, pp. 52–7.

36. Ibid., pp. 42, 230–1.

37. Hoegner, *Aussenseiter*, p. 15.

38. For a description of the cultural cleavages between various sections of Weimar Germany's society see Lacqueur, *Weimar: A Cultural History*, esp. pp. 41–3. The intellectual crisis in academic circles at this time is described in Ringer, *The Decline of the German Mandarins*, esp. ch. 7.

39. For a good description of the difficulties faced by Protestant Church leaders in the early years of the Republic see Wright, *'Above Parties'*.

40. Hunt, *German Social Democracy*, p. 168.
41. By 1920 there remained only the factory councils, and under a law passed in January of that year their powers were virtually restricted to the representation of employees' interests within a particular works or factory. See Oertzen, *Betriebsräte*, pp. 155–69.

4 The Republic Makes Peace

If Germany's domestic situation was bad, her international prospects were catastrophic. The revolution had broken out because the German people wanted peace. However well the new government carried out its tasks at home, the failure of peace negotiations would signal its collapse.

The November revolution did not bring about any fundamental changes in German foreign policy. Although Haase, the leader of the Independent Social Democrats, was responsible for foreign affairs, the personnel and attitudes of the German Foreign Ministry remained much as they had been under the Empire. Critical voices were to be heard demanding truly revolutionary developments in German diplomacy, but they were not heeded.

Some left-wing Independents and Spartakists wanted Germany to forge an alliance with the Bolshevik government in Russia. Proletarian solidarity should be the basis of German security. Such a policy was never taken seriously by the Republican leaders. It would have been anathema to Ebert, and Haase himself warned the cabinet that German overtures towards the Bolsheviks might provoke Allied invasion.[1] The Republic did not establish diplomatic relations with Russia. Another radical demand was that Germany should disassociate herself completely from the discredited policies of the Imperial Government. To do this Haase should purge the administration and diplomatic corps of all those compromised by annexationist tendencies during the war. He should admit that Wilhelm II's ministers had been guilty of aggression in 1914. Kurt Eisner, the Independent Social Democratic Premier in Bavaria, was the most forceful advocate of this course. He believed that by demonstrating her reformed character Germany would win the respect of the Western Powers. He went so far as to publish documents from the Bavarian archives demonstrating German complicity in Austrian aggression against Serbia at the outbreak of war. This gesture did nothing to alter the attitude of Germany's enemies, but it aroused predictable fury in Berlin, where Eisner was regarded as a traitor.

Nevertheless, the desire to win approval from the victors influenced the behaviour of Ebert's government. Peace negotiations begun by Prince Max of Baden in October 1918 had referred to President Wilson's famous Fourteen Points. These envisaged a peace of understanding based on national self-determination and international co-operation. Although no mention of the Fourteen Points was made in the armistice signed on 11 November, the Germans always claimed that any peace settlement ought to comply with them.

Since it was clear that Germany, defeated and helpless as she was, could hardly expect benevolence from the French or the British, her new leaders pinned what hopes they had on the Americans. Ebert and the Foreign Ministry wanted to present President Wilson with a picture of Germany as a stable, democratic country, eager to play her part in the World community. In December a new Foreign Minister was appointed. This was the former ambassador to Copenhagen, Count Brockdorff-Rantzau. He was at pains to stress German enthusiasm for the idea of the League of Nations, and declared that Germany would work for the victory of democracy throughout the world. He called for an end to secret diplomatic intrigues, such as those which had encompassed the Great War.

Although the Count had himself been critical of the Imperial government's policies during the war, much of his enthusiasm for a new international order was assumed for the benefit of the victor powers. The Army, the Foreign Office and the Government all thought that the democratic card was the one to play. It was not very effective. On 4 February 1919, for example, an American officer on a fact-finding mission to Berlin wrote a report which included the words:

> Of Brockdorff-Rantzau and the Foreign Office, I was impressed that no change had occurred and that no democratic spirit exists except as circumstances dictate for the moment. No realisation as to the changed conditions in the World and Germany's position in it are in evidence.[2]

The last sentence certainly applied to the average citizen. The German public was in no way prepared for a harsh peace. The Germans had always been told that the Reich was waging a defensive war, and did not therefore regard themselves as responsible for the disaster which had befallen Europe. In any case, the Imperial government and the Kaiser were gone, and so most people felt free from all liability for Imperial policies. As Ebert himself put it in his speech at the opening of the new German National Assembly in Weimar on 1 February 1919:

> Wherefore, by their own testimony, have our enemies fought? To destroy Kaiserism. That has now passed forever; the very fact of this assembly is proof of that. They fought to destroy 'Militarism'; it has been overthrown and lies in pieces never to rise again. According to their solemn proclamations our enemies have been fighting for justice, freedom and a lasting peace.[3]

Ebert himself was well aware that the Allies were unlikely to offer Germany a peace which would please his fellow-countrymen. The Germans had their own conception of what a just settlement should be. They expected to have to surrender Alsace-Lorraine to France and some limited amount of territory to the Poles. But in return they demanded that the German-speaking parts of the old Habsburg Empire should be allowed to join the Reich. On 12 November the Austrian parliament declared German Austria to be part of the German Republic. Ebert later assured the German National Assembly that negotiations would soon begin with Vienna to make Germany 'a nation of brothers'. Gustav Stresemann, formerly one of the most distinguished leaders of the National Liberal Party in the Reichstag, was prepared to give up his opposition to the Republic if union with Austria could be achieved.[4]

The Germans expected to be made full members of Wilson's League of Nations and to be given equality with other powers in the post-war world. They denied that the Allies had any right to impose an indemnity on Germany, although it was clear to them from the Fourteen Points that payment would had to be made for the restoration of devastated areas in Allied countries. On the whole the Germans' vision of the peace would have left their country rather more powerful *vis-à-vis* its European neighbours than when it entered the war.

It was not likely that the Allies would tolerate such a development. Their peacemakers were, indeed, faced with unique problems and it took them many months to hammer out their
proposals. The previous balance of power in Europe had been
totally destroyed. Russia was in a state of civil war and her government seemed quite unfitted to form part of a European concert.
The Habsburg Empire was in dissolution and the Ottoman
Empire had ceased to exist. France and Belgium suffered directly
as the result of war and occupation. Britain had sustained severe
financial and human losses. Italy ended the war in a state of
collapse. The United States had supported the Western war effort
with loans even before it became involved in the fighting. Despite
a genuine belief in the need for a new approach to international
affairs, the Allies could not be expected to sacrifice their own
interests in Germany's favour.

In particular the victors had to find some means of giving
permanent security to France. As Lord Balfour had somewhat
unkindly put it: 'The Franco-German problem appears insoluble,
for it is really a problem of making one Frenchman go as far as
two Germans.'[5]

Although the British and the Americans offered guarantees
to the French, many of them, including Marshal Foch, the commander-in-chief, would have preferred more tangible forms of
security. They thought in terms of establishing France's frontier
on the Rhine and dismembering the German Reich by giving
independence to some German areas in the south and west.
Such hopes were not realised in the peace settlement but they
did not die for several years.

On the question of indemnity the Allied Powers could point to
the fact that German industry had been undamaged by occupation in the war. If treated as an equal with the victors Germany's
powerful economy might soon dominate Europe.

The Allies presented their peace terms to the Germans on 1
May 1919. They were far more severe than anything the German
public had been led to expect. From that time on Germany's
foreign policy was systematically directed towards their revision.
All parties denounced the Allied proposals and the government
averred that it would never accept them.

Summed up very briefly the German case was as follows. First
there had been no negotiated settlement, but a *Diktat* forced on

Germany by threat of occupation. The Germans had not been able to put their case as equal participants in a peace conference. Although they had presented detailed written objections to the Treaty they had only been able to obtain a few alterations, and there the bargaining virtually ceased. The Allies attached a time limit to their revised draft. Refusal to agree would mean military invasion.

Secondly, it was argued that the terms imposed on Germany were incompatible with the Wilsonian Fourteen Points, even as revised by Wilson in the light of British and French objections. Germany lost 13 per cent of her territory and about six million subjects. She received nothing in return; Austria was not allowed to join the German Reich. The Germans bitterly resented the territorial settlement on their eastern frontier, where German minorities would be ruled by Poles. It order to give Poland an outlet to the sea the province of East Prussia was cut off from the Reich by a strip of territory joining Poland to the Baltic. This was the famous Polish Corridor. The population of the corridor was, in fact, predominantly Polish, but the port which stood at its head, Danzig, was German. Originally the Allies had intended to give Danzig to the Poles, but on the insistence of Lloyd George it was established as a Free City with an independent administration watched over by a Commissioner for the League of Nations. Further to the east the German city of Memel was ceded to Lithuania. Another eastern area over which there was fierce argument was Upper Silesia, whose population was mixed, but with an overall majority of Germans. After German protests at the Allied proposal to hand this province over to Poland it was agreed that a plebiscite should be organised there. Otherwise the Germans lost Alsace-Lorraine to France, frontier districts to Belgium and Denmark, and the important coal-mining region of the Saar Basin, which was placed under virtual French control for a minimum of fifteen years. This last measure was completely without justification so far as national self-determination was concerned, but was designed to guarantee compensation to the French for the damage done to their industry during the war.

Germany also lost all her colonies, which were distributed to the victors under the overall authority of the League of Nations. The League's involvement seemed a mere fig-leaf to the Germans. For one thing, they themselves were refused entry into the League; for another they did not believe that their enemies would permit colonial policy to be affected by an international body. In this German suspicions were completely justified.

Internationally Germany was not given equality of status with the victor powers. Brockdorff-Rantzau had already warned the Allies against treating Germany like a ship kept in quarantine as a plague risk.[6] But that was exactly what happened. Germany would only be allowed membership of the League of Nations when she had proved her peaceable character. This strengthened the already widespread feeling in Germany that the League would just be an Association of Victors designed to maintain the supremacy of·the Entente Powers. Germany had to submit to disarmament without receiving guarantees that her enemies would disarm also. The German army was to be cut to 100 000 men, and deprived of offensive weapons. The air force was destroyed; the navy reduced to insignificance. In the economic sphere Germany had to accord most-favoured-nation treatment to her enemies but had no such rights herself. A further humiliation was the fact that Allied troops were to remain in occupation in parts of the Rhineland for at least fifteen years as a guarantee that the terms of the treaty would be honoured, and that even after their withdrawal Germany should refrain from fortifying the left bank of the Rhine.

So far as economic and financial issues were concerned, the Germans lost overseas investments confiscated by the Allies. They lost most of their mercantile marine. They had to agree to pay reparations for damage done to Allied civilians during the war, and it became clear that this was to be interpreted in a very generous way, even including pensions paid to wounded servicemen and their families. The British and Dominion governments were responsible for broadening the scope of German reparations payments in this way. They realised that, unless this were done, the British Empire would receive very little financial recompense from Germany with which to counterbalance the heavy burden of their own war debts to the USA. This wider interpretation of reparations was hardly compatible with the correspondence between Prince Max's government and President Wilson before the armistice. It ensured that the reparations demands on Germany were bound to be unrealistically high, and that squabbles between the victors over their share of reparations would make a sensible settlement impossible.[7]

The Allies established commissions to supervise reparations and the disarmament clauses, so that the Germans could feel that their country was being controlled and exploited by her enemies. It was common to claim that the Allies were determined to extort the last drop of sweat from German workers for the benefit of Western capitalists. There is no doubt that the reparations clauses in the treaty were among the least felicitous elements in the peace settlement. Whatever the justice of Allied claims, the manner in which they were presented was bound to cause trouble in the future. Nobody could expect the Germans to work as well for foreigners as they would for themselves. If the Allies were determined to extort large sums from Germany over a long period they should have been prepared to do so by force. Only the French and the Belgians were ready to face this consequence.

It is certainly true that German criticisms of the treaty were exaggerated. In many cases there were good reasons why conditions which the Germans described as unacceptable should have been imposed on them. Austria was the most obvious example. The Allies could hardly allow Germany to end the war more powerful than she began it, and this would have been the case if a Greater Germany had been created. So far as the Polish Corridor and Danzig were concerned, the Poles had been promised access to the sea in Wilson's Fourteen Points. The settlement of nationality problems involved less injustice than had the frontiers of 1914, when French, Danish and Polish minorities had been included in Germany. The erection of tariff barriers against German goods and the economic burdens on Germany had to be set against the destruction of industrial areas in northern France and Belgium and the losses sustained by Allied merchant fleets as the result of U-boat warfare.

But much more important than the fairness or unfairness of the treaty was its impact on the new German Republic. How far is it true that the Versailles Treaty wrecked German democracy? That Germany's economy was ruined by reparations and her security was undermined by the restrictions on her army? That her status as a European Power was incompatible with the conditions she had to accept? Economically and demographically speaking there was no foundation in these assertions. German industry, despite the losses incurred, soon began to recover its productive capacity. There was a setback in 1923 but by 1927 the Gross National Product of the Weimar Republic had exceeded that of the entire German Reich in 1913. Germany's population was still half as large again as that of France and continued to rise. If the aim of French statesmen had been, as one English critic averred, to 'set the clock back and to undo what, since 1870, the progress of Germany had accomplished',[8] it had not been successful.

Germany's currency certainly suffered a complete disaster in the years following the peace treaty, and many outside experts, as well as virtually all Germans, blamed this on the reparations burden.[9] But there were other factors involved. Germany's internal debt had been greatly increased during the war, and of course she received no reparations to meet that. The Republican governments of the period also seemed incapable of imposing stringent fiscal measures on taxpayers and banks. This was directly related to the peace settlement, since it was believed that more effective government control would simply mean that more of Germany's wealth would drain away to the Allies.

From the economic point of view the Versailles Treaty offered very little hope of settling Europe's problems. It was possible to imagine, however, that as time passed the international organisation which had been established as part of the peace settlement might create improvements. Positive collaboration between victors and vanquished would be needed if the economic difficulties created by the war were to be overcome.

Much more serious was the political demoralisation which the treaty caused within the Reich itself. This was not so important among those already inclined to attack the Republic as among the democratic parties which supported it. The Nationalists and the Communists had already made it clear before June 1919 that they would not be contented with the new state form. Hitler would have raved against Versailles whatever its terms had been. The real damage the treaty did to Germany was to disillusion more moderate men who might otherwise have supported their new Republic. The parties most seriously harmed as a result were those which formed the Republican coalition, the Social Democrats, the Democrats and the Centre Party. These groups were forced to turn to the German people after an apparently

successful revolution with nothing to offer them but failure. The
political gains of that revolution had actually been considerable,
but in the public mind they remained unimpressive. The Germans had a new constitution; to many of them the old one had
seemed good enough. They had more freedom politically but
most of them had thought of themselves as free before. They
had responsible government; this 'responsibility' seemed to
mean confusion and even bloodshed in home affairs. The one
thing that the new order had brought them – peace – had been
transformed by a settlement which their newspapers and political
leaders all agreed was a form of prolonged slavery for Germany.
It was not an encouraging start.

Two particular issues connected with the peace settlement continued to poison the political atmosphere in Germany for many
years. The first was the question of war guilt. It had seemed self-
evident to the victor powers that the Germans had committed
aggression in 1914. Article 231 of the peace treaty required them
to accept responsibility for the war as the legal basis for Allied
reparations claims against Germany. The Germans vigorously
rejected this and demanded an impartial enquiry into the origins
of the war. By treating the matter as one of central importance the
Germans provoked the Allied governments to reiterate their view
that Germany had been the aggressor. This made compromise
more difficult.[10] In fact the Republican government was aware
that the Kaiser's regime had been implicated in provoking the
war. Karl Kautsky, a leading Marxist intellectual in the USPD, was
commissioned by Ebert to undertake an investigation into this
question, using German Foreign Office records. In April 1919 he
produced a collection of documents proving the complicity of the
Imperial government in the ultimatum to Serbia which had trig-
gered off the conflict. The Republican cabinet refused to publish
this, even though it would have helped to undermine the nationalist myth that Germany had been guiltless for the outbreak of
hostilities, and might have improved relations with the Entente
powers, who were convinced of Germany's guilt anyway.[11]

Even after the treaty was signed the German Foreign Office did
not relax its efforts to prove to the world that the Germans did not
start the Great War. It set up a special subsection, the *Kriegsschul-
dreferat*, to inspire and subsidise a campaign proving the Germans
innocent of responsibility.[12] Historians were mobilised to sift

through Germany's diplomatic documents and demonstrate that Imperial policies – though sometimes misguided – were not basically warlike. Every opportunity was taken to publicise expert opinion which seemed to support Germany's case. Academics in foreign countries – especially among neutral states and in the USA – were canvassed for interpretations of war guilt favourable to Germany. In the two decades after the war a school of 'revisionist' historians appeared, conducting an academic argument which had direct political implications. This is not to suggest that the historians in Germany and elsewhere who supported this campaign did not sincerely believe that their case was just, and the world of scholarship doubtless benefited from the diplomatic documents which became available as a result of the controversy. But during the Weimar Republic the consequences were not happy for Germany. By attacking the whole foundation of the Allied peace plan the Germans aroused the suspicion that they did not really intend to abide by it. At home it was believed that Germany could never be prosperous or safe so long as she was still 'shackled' by an unjust peace settlement. Diplomatically speaking it was not until Hitler came to power that the effects of the German campaign against war guilt came to be felt. Then it was the Nazis who reaped the benefit of the industrious efforts by academics, journalists and diplomats to undermine the moral basis of the European peace settlement.

The second issue was that of the so-called 'stab in the back'. Attempts to deny war guilt had domestic implications. If Germany had not been responsible for the war – as even Republican ministers claimed – then the Imperial authorities could not be blamed for the catastrophe which had befallen their country. Indeed, from the moral viewpoint Germany in no way deserved to be defeated in the war. How could this military injustice have come about? Was it not true that Germany had been on the brink of victory in the early summer of 1918? How could she possibly have won so many battles, gained so much enemy territory and still have been defeated?

For those who had pressed for ambitious annexations and total victory the answer was obvious. It was the fault not of superior Allied force, still less of superior Allied strategy. The real culprits were to be found within the frontiers of Germany. They were the weaklings and backsliders (the *Flaumacher*), the pacifists, socialists and other revolutionaries who had undermined Germany's war effort.

The German army, unbeaten in the field, had been stabbed in the back. The blame for Germany's defeat rested on the politicians at home. This accusation against the founders of Germany's Republic was not the result of disappointed idealism caused by the Treaty of Versailles. It had been current even before the war ended and had grown in strength ever since. Despite attempts to increase its credibility by attributing it to a British general, the 'stab in the back' was a home-grown product.* It became, like the war-guilt theory, a subject of endless discussion and publicity. Newspaper campaigns, libel actions and even a parliamentary committee of enquiry fanned the flames of controversy and reinforced the public impression that some sinister secret underlay Germany's defeat in the war. Republican politicians were once again on the defensive, and their own ambivalence towards the November revolution made it difficult for them to counterattack.

The decision to accept the peace treaty was not taken without agonising deliberations. Brockdorff-Rantzau refused to sign it, and the Prime Minister, Scheidemann, resigned. In addition to opposition from the political parties and most of the press, powerful military pressure was exerted on the Government to refuse the Western peace terms. Reinhardt, the Prussian Minister of War and chief of the new German army, feared that signature of the treaty would provoke mutiny among his troops. The proposed restrictions on Germany's armed forces were a direct threat to the careers of all men in uniform. Plans were adumbrated for a last-ditch resistance in the eastern provinces of Germany, it being believed that the Poles could be successfully opposed if they intervened. There were important men in the officer corps urging a military coup against the government if it capitulated

---

* The aim was to cite foreign opinion in support of a German myth. Actually two British officers – Lieutenant-General Maurice and Major-General Malcolm – were credited with inventing the stab in the back. Maurice's published statements were exaggerated in the German press and Malcolm himself had simply paraphrased a long-winded diatribe by Ludendorff. The idea of the stab in the back pre-dated both British comments. This did not stop Hindenburg referring to 'an English General' as his authority when blaming German defeat on disintegration behind the lines.[13]

to the Allies. Hopes for such a stroke were pinned on Field-Marshal Hindenburg, but – not for the first time in his career – the old war hero evaded responsibility for a political decision. It was left to his more energetic colleague, General Groener, to persuade the senior officers who controlled the armed forces that resistance to the treaty would result in the dismemberment of Germany. It was better to keep the German people together under humiliating conditions than to risk their complete disintegration.[14]

The National Assembly was still reluctant to capitulate to the Allies. The energetic intervention of Ebert – now acting President of the Republic – was needed to obtain an affirmative vote to the peace proposals. So great was the feeling of national humiliation that the parties who agreed to accept the Allied terms demanded a statement from their opponents recognising that only patriotic motives had influenced their decision.

On 28 June 1919 the peace treaty was signed in the Hall of Mirrors at Versailles by Hermann Müller, the Social Democratic Foreign Minister, and Dr Hans Bell, a Centre Party member who was Minister of Transport. The war had thus been formally brought to an end nearly eight months after hostilities had originally been suspended.

Should the treaty have been resisted? Might it not have been healthier if the national revulsion at the treaty had found expression in a physical conflict which would at least have forced the Allies to make themselves directly responsible for the imposition of their own peace terms? Would not even an enemy occupation have been preferable to a peace which burdened Germany's already enfeebled government with accusations of cowardice and treason? The experience of events after the Second World War, when a totally defeated Germany was occupied and administered for several years before independent German institutions appeared again, might be cited as a ground for believing that Ebert and his colleagues were wrong to act so cautiously in 1919, and that complete disaster might have been preferable to prolonged agony at the hands of the peacemakers. Certainly no atmosphere of peace descended on Germany with the signing of the treaty; if anything, hostility to the victor powers became more marked, and was reinforced by hatred for those at home regarded as tools of the enemy.

Yet, even with the advantage of hindsight, the arguments in favour of last-ditch resistance do not stand up to very close scrutiny. In 1945 Germany was totally defeated. There could be no question of having been tricked or betrayed into peace. In the summer of 1919 a successful Allied invasion of the country would still have been blamed on the duplicity of Wilson, the treason of the revolutionaries and the weakness of the moderate political parties. Then again, there is no evidence that the Allies intended to take responsibility for the government of Germany as they were compelled to do after 1945. President Wilson and his colleagues in Paris wished simply to force the German government to sign the treaty. The methods they intended to adopt would almost certainly have been successful. Marshal Foch claimed that his armies could not march immediately to Berlin, but must first advance to the line of the Weser and occupy the Main valley. Separate treaties could then be made with the South German states leaving Berlin isolated.[15] This would have given the Allies control of Germany's most vital industrial region, and would have implied that the recurrent German nightmare of national dismemberment might become a reality. No German government could be expected to risk the unity of the Reich. Nor is there much reason to suppose that dismemberment would have produced a lasting peace. It should be remembered that, however unfavourable the treaty was for the future development of German democracy, there was no means of knowing that the new Republic would founder as a result of it. The Third French Republic had come into being under similar conditions of trial and had survived. Neither Ebert nor the Allied leaders could be expected to foresee that events in Germany would take such a different and catastrophic course.[16]

Notes

1. Burdick and Lutz, *Political Institutions*, p. 70.
2. *Foreign Relations of the United States. The Paris Peace Conference 1919*, vol. XII, pp. 3–4.
3. Hölfron (ed.), *Deutsche Nationalversammlung*, vol. I, pp. 4–5. Translation as given in papers relating to the *Foreign Relations of the United States. The Paris Peace Conference 1919*, vol. XII, p. 9.

4. Turner, *Stresemann*, p. 37.
5. Earl of Swinton, *Sixty Years of Power*, p. 29.
6. Brockdorff-Rantzau, *Versailles*, p. 47. Speech to the German National Assembly, 14 February 1919.
7. Kent, *The Spoils of War: The Politics, Economics and Diplomacy of Reparations, 1918–1932*, pp. 39, 70.
8. Keynes, *Economic Consequences*, p. 32.
9. See, for example, the statements by Lord Brand in 'How a Banker Watched History Happen'.
10. For a discussion of this subject see H. Holborn in Craig and Gilbert, *The Diplomats*, pp. 138–45, and Dickmann, 'Die Kriegsschuldfrage auf der Friedenskonferenz von Paris 1919'.
11. Winkler, *Weimar, 1918–1933*, pp. 87–8.
12. See Geiss, 'The Outbreak of the First World War and German War Aims'.
13. See Petzold, *Die Dolchstosslegende*, p. 27, and Wheeler-Bennett, *Hindenberg*, p. 238.
14. Carsten, *Reichswehr*, pp. 40–2.
15. Mantoux, *Les Délibérations du Conseil des Quatre*, vol. II, pp. 22–3, 69, 430 ff. Also Zimmermann, *Deutsche Aussenpolitik*, pp. 61–3.
16. For a discussion of the impact of the Versailles Treaty on German opinion see E. Matthias, 'The Influence of the Versailles Treaty on the Internal Development of the Weimar Republic', in Nicholls and Matthias, *German Democracy and the Triumph of Hitler*, pp. 13–28.

5   1919–1922: Years of Crisis and Uncertainty

On 21 August 1919 Ebert, who had been acting as provisional President since the previous February, took the oath to the Constitution as Germany's first Republican head of state. The fact that he did not present himself for popular election as envisaged in the constitution illustrated the weakness of the new regime. Public opinion had been so outraged by the Versailles Treaty that an anti-Republican candidate might have defeated Ebert. Similarly, the Constituent National Assembly did not dissolve itself, but continued to function as Germany's legislature. The Weimar Coalition parties did not wish to face a parliamentary election.[1]

Public enthusiasm for the government was not increased when Matthias Erzberger – now Reich Finance Minister – introduced a comprehensive programme of taxation to deal with Germany's pressing financial problems. These had been inherited from the Imperial government, which had borrowed heavily during the war, and had been aggravated by the disturbed conditions after the revolution and the losses caused by the peace treaty. Erzberger was an energetic minister, and he gave Germany a coherent taxation system which placed the burden of sacrifice firmly on the wealthy. He imposed taxes on war profits, capital gains, inherited wealth and excess consumption. Income tax was graded to fall more severely on the rich, and was supplemented by a capital levy.[2] These measures, which were very advanced for their era, naturally aroused the fury of the well-to-do. Erzberger was accused of being simply a financial agent of Germany's enemies, squeezing money from the Germans for the benefit of the victor powers. A vitriolic campaign of public denunciation was whipped up against him, spearheaded by Karl Helfferich, a former Vice-Chancellor and financial expert under Wilhelm II. Erzberger was so discredited as a result that he had to retire from politics in the spring of 1920.

At almost the same time the Republic was rocked by the first serious attempt at counter-revolution since November 1918. This was the Kapp Putsch. Its major cause was discontent in the army. The Versailles Treaty required heavy reductions in Germany's armed forces. Many of the Freikorps formations recruited in 1919 to uphold internal order or protect Germany's eastern frontiers could expect to be disbanded. Their members faced unemployment. The feeling among most of their officers was fiercely hostile to the Republican government.

The commander of the Reichswehr district which included Berlin was General von Lüttwitz. He began to conspire with a number of reactionary civilians, chief among whom was a former Prussian civil servant, Wolfgang Kapp, who had been associated with demands for an annexationist peace during the war. Kapp's participation was symptomatic of another malevolent force behind the attack on German democracy, the landowning elite east of the Elbe, the so-called Junkers. They were bitter at losing their pre-eminence in German society, and particularly resented social democratic efforts to improve the wretched pay and conditions of labourers on their estates. In Pomerania, especially, labourers were dismissed in the autumn of 1919 to be replaced by Freikorps veterans. Arms depots were set up on East Elbian farms. The struggle between Junkers and the Prussian government would soon spread to Berlin. The Republic's Defence Minister, Gustav Noske, was not informed about these intrigues by his military and bureacratic subordinates.[3]

Also involved in the conspiracy was General Ludendorff. He had fled the country in terror after the revolution, but in February 1919 had returned to Berlin and established an anti-Republican salon there, frequented by reactionaries of various types.[4]

Matters came to a head in March 1920, when Noske attempted to disband two naval brigades stationed near Berlin. On the night of 12/13 March these units marched into the capital unopposed. Noske and General Reinhardt wanted to offer resistance, but their military colleagues would not support them. General von Seeckt, the most influential staff officer in the Defence Ministry, spoke out firmly against the army involving itself in what he saw as a political battle. He put the interest of the army before his duty to defend the Government.[5]

President Ebert, Reich Chancellor Bauer and most of the cabinet fled the city and went to Stuttgart. The National Assembly joined them there. The Vice-Chancellor, Eugen Schiffer of the Democratic Party, was left behind to watch events in Berlin.

The Kapp–Lüttwitz regime, called to power by the mutinous marine Freikorps, was quite incapable of any constructive policy. Collaboration between the military and civilian elements in the coup was notable for its absence, and what plans there were proved impossible to realise.[6] More important were the reactions to it and the results of its failure. Organised labour gave the most unequivocal demonstration of hostility to the Putsch. The trade unions called a general strike, which was apparently proclaimed with the blessing of Ebert and the social democratic ministers in the government, although in fact only Noske seems to have actually approved it.[7] In Berlin Kapp and Lüttwitz found themselves controlling a dead city. The civil service and the army were also unhelpful, but their attitude was less clearcut. Ministerial officials did not work for the new regime. General von Seeckt, who had become the most important man in the army after Reinhardt's humiliation, left his office and donned civilian clothes. Nevertheless, a group of his staff officers adopted a resolution declaring that they 'stood aloof' from events in Berlin, that they understood negotiations were going on between Kapp and the old (sic) administration and that they were willing to preserve law and order until a government which had the confidence of the nation was established. This was no ringing declaration of loyalty to the Republican ministry. Kapp and Lüttwitz expressed their thanks when it was communicated to them.[8] Even more disturbing for Ebert and Bauer was the fact that in some provincial areas army commanders were clearly in favour of Kapp, as was virtually the whole of the navy.

The Putsch also attracted sympathy from the two right-wing parties. The German Nationalists avoided any formal commitment to Kapp, but they issued a statement condemning the legal government for not holding parliamentary elections. Stresemann and his colleagues in the German People's Party were quite favourably impressed with Kapp, and seemed ready to negotiate with him.[9] None of these overtures were of any help to the Putschists. As days went by it became clear that they could wield no effective authority. Kapp and Lüttwitz fled the country, leaving Bauer's government apparently triumphant.

The ignominious collapse of the Putsch ought to have been a victory for the Republic. The right-wing parties had been seriously compromised. Reactionary elements in the army and the civil service had revealed both their disloyalty and their impotence. Public opinion was overwhelmingly hostile to the Putsch. Yet most of the politicians and officials who might have feared reprisals managed to wriggle off the hook on which they had apparently impaled themselves. They owed their deliverance partly to confusion within Bauer's government and partly to a new fear of revolution from the left.

Bauer and his colleagues were prepared to take stern measures against Kapp's supporters, but were embarrassed to find that in Berlin Vice-Chancellor Schiffer and other coalition party members had apparently offered promises of leniency to the leaders of the Putsch.[10] Even more important were the attempts by militant elements in the labour movement to use resistance to Kapp as an excuse for revolutionary activity. The trade union leadership in Berlin tried to force Ebert to appoint a purely socialist government which would introduce immediate socialisation of industry and create a new Republican army. The President was able to resist these demands, but he could not save Reich Chancellor Bauer, who had to resign.

The new government was headed by Hermann Müller, another Social Democrat. Noske had been forced to give up the Defence Ministry. General Reinhardt had already resigned after his failure to protect the Government, and General von Seeckt became chief of the Reichswehr. Noske's successor was a right-wing Democrat called Otto Gessler. He had no particular desire to impose civilian authority on the army, and von Seeckt was able to keep the officer corps aloof from Republican politics. No serious consequences overtook the army as the result of the Kapp Putsch. Indeed, some soldiers who had been loyal to the Republic fared worse than their mutinous superiors.[11]

Von Seeckt's position was made easier by outbreaks of left-wing violence in the Ruhr. It was thought that a Communist coup was imminent. As usual, the Communists were credited with more than they deserved. They had originally opposed trade union strike action against Kapp, claiming that the workers ought not to become involved in a clash between counter-revolutionary elements. Only when it became clear that the resistance to Kapp had overwhelming working-class support did the Communists change their tactics. Then they did all they could to exploit the strike, hoping to extend it into a demand for proletarian dictatorship. Even in this they had been forestalled. A spontaneous revolt broke out in the Ruhr in which Independent Social Democrats, anarcho-syndicalists and some supporters of the Majority Social Democratic Party were as important as the Communists.[12] Arms were distributed and barricades erected. The Reichswehr marched in to crush the insurgents, which it did with brutal efficiency.

The fighting in the Ruhr did no good to the cause of the Majority Social Democratic Party. Once again it seemed to be encouraging counter-revolutionary officers to suppress the working classes. The Independent Social Democrats gained in popularity as a result.

On the other hand, the demands of the trade unions and the fighting in the Ruhr scandalised the non-socialist parties in the coalition. The Centre, in particular, regretted its association with the general strike, and wanted to distance itself at once from revolutionary elements. One result of this was that Chancellor Müller agreed to call elections for a new Reichstag.

The Kapp Putsch has been seen as the turning-point in Republican fortunes – the moment when democracy in Germany lost its way. It certainly demonstrated the Republic's weaknesses, but it may be doubted whether it was more than a symptom of diseases which already existed. Noske's fall diminished political control over the army, but this had never been very effective. In any case, von Seeckt, for all his desire to preserve the purity of his officer corps, was a cautious man, and his regime in the Bendlerstrasse did not encourage political adventures. So far as the German Nationalist Party was concerned, it was chastened rather than encouraged by the failure of the Putsch, and was eager to disown it. Among both the DNVP and Stresemann's People's Party the view gained ground that power exercised according to the constitution should be the aim of the German Right. Indeed, in many ways the worst result of the Putsch was the 1920 elections.

Held on 6 June 1920, they were a fresh disaster for the Republican parties. The SPD, Democrats and Centre between them lost eight of the nineteen million votes they had mustered at the National Assembly elections eighteen months earlier. They were now in a minority, although their opponents were completely split.

On the left, the Independent Social Democrats had begun to approach the SPD in size and electoral support. On the right, Stresemann's People's Party trebled its vote and returned sixty-five Reichstag deputies; the German Nationalists polled over a million more votes than in 1919 and returned seventy-five deputies.

Defeat at the polls caused Chancellor Müller to resign. The SPD, the party most committed to supporting the Republic, left the Government. An elderly but respected leader of the Centre Party, Fehrenbach, formed a new cabinet, which included representatives of Stresemann's People's Party. Stresemann himself became chairman of the Reichstag's Foreign Affairs Committee.

Fehrenbach's ministry was beset with diplomatic and economic problems. Germany's former enemies accused her of defaulting on her reparations obligations and of evading the disarmament clauses in the Versailles Treaty. There was truth in both claims; but the Government in Berlin could not always help itself.

So far as reparations were concerned, the Germans had been left in apprehensive uncertainty about the extent of their indebtedness. In 1919 the Allies could not agree on a total figure which would be large enough to appease their own public and small enough to give the Germans even a theoretical chance of paying it. The task of setting a final figure was given to an inter-Allied Reparations Commission, and in the meantime Germany had to make large deliveries of gold, convertible currency, goods and raw materials. It was realised in London and Paris that the Germans would have difficulty in meeting projected Allied reparations demands. France and Britain had themselves incurred heavy debts to the USA during the war, and the British, in particular, would have been willing to treat Germany more leniently if inter-Allied indebtedness were reduced. From the very first, however, the Americans refused to consider such a solution. The fact that America had avoided accepting any obligation to support a system of international security also helped to throw the French and the British back on a strict interpretation of the Peace Treaty as the best guarantee of their safety. High protective tariffs in the United States made European economic reconstruction even more difficult. A number of attempts were made to reach an agreement over reparations between Germany and the Allies, but they all failed.

On the question of disarmament the Germans had been slow to fulfil their obligations, and the Reichswehr leaders undoubtedly hoped to maintain larger forces than those envisaged in the Treaty. General Seeckt and his colleagues were to become practised in the arts of evasion. Most Reich governments closed their eyes to such activities, illegal though they were. Nevertheless, in some cases they simply lacked the power to meet Allied requirements, being unable, for instance, to dissolve large 'Home Guard' forces retained by the right-wing government in Bavaria.

The crisis over reparations and disarmament came to a head in the spring of 1921. On 27 April the Allied Reparations Commission finally set the total German reparations debt at 132 thousand million gold marks – a figure lower than some originally mentioned by the Allies, but considerably more than those offered by the Germans.

On 5 May 1921 the Allies delivered an ultimatum. Germany had to accept an Allied schedule of reparations payments and complete her disarmament. She should bring men designated as war criminals to trial. If these terms were not accepted the Allies would occupy the Ruhr – Germany's most important industrial complex. A number of west German cities had already been occupied in connection with an earlier ultimatum, and the Germans had no reason to hope that they were faced with an idle threat.

Fehrenbach had already resigned when the ultimatum was delivered. His successor was a man of much more forceful character. This was Josef Wirth, also of the Centre Party. In some ways he was the most attractive leader the Republic had produced since its foundation. He certainly earned the distinction of being Germany's youngest Chancellor since that office had been established in 1871. His appointment marked a shift away from the rightward trend in German politics, since Stresemann's People's Party left the Government, and the Social Democrats rejoined the coalition.

Coming from Baden, in the German south-west, Wirth represented the more democratic and socially reformist tendency within the Centre Party. As finance minister in Fehrenbach's cabinet he had aroused displeasure among right-wing parties for his stress on direct taxation. His grasp of financial technicalities was to stand him in good stead when grappling with reparations problems. Unlike many other Centre Party politicians he had no employment other than politics, to which he devoted himself with great energy. His attractive personality, parliamentary skill and direct but effective technique as a platform speaker had aided his meteoric rise from a schoolteaching post in Baden to the summit of German political life. In many ways he was an example of the best the Weimar Republic could provide; his career would have been impossible under the old Empire. By the same token, his bluff manner and convivial disposition aroused distaste among those who preferred the more colourless behaviour of Imperial officials.

Wirth's name is associated above all with the policy known as 'fulfilment'. He was loyal to the Republic and believed that with careful and clever diplomacy Germany could improve her position in the world. 'Patience, more patience and still more patience' was his recipe for success, and it was sensible advice at a time when Germany was isolated and defenceless.[13] This did not mean that he wanted to surrender to Germany's enemies. On the contrary, he hoped that by adopting a less obstructive attitude than earlier governments he could weaken the united Allied front against Germany and modify the conditions imposed upon her.

At home Wirth's aim was to inaugurate a policy of reconstruction and reconciliation, laying stress on loyalty to the Republican constitution. 'He who loves his country will follow the flag of the German Republic' was his slogan.[14] It was a view which had not previously been accepted by all his Centre Party colleagues and was even less attractive to many members of Stresemann's People's Party. Yet, as the political situation developed without either a socialist revolution or a monarchist restoration, more and more of the bourgeois politicians were coming to feel that their best policy would be to come to terms with the Republic and work within its constitution. Stresemann, in particular, was unhappy at being excluded from power, and hoped to bring his party back into the Government when a favourable opportunity presented itself. It was unfortunate that the progressive devaluation of the currency, which had taken a sudden turn for the worse with the Allied ultimatum, was intensifying feelings of desperation among the public at large at a time when political leaders were more ready for compromise. Extremism on both the left and the right became more attractive to average citizens as their economic condition worsened.

Violence in politics did not disappear with the end of the revolution. Nationalist fanatics were responsible for a number of outrages against prominent Republicans or persons whom they suspected of betraying secrets about clandestine military activity. In August 1921 a particularly shocking case occurred when Matthias Erzberger, the former Finance Minister, was assassinated in the Black Forest.

Initially, however, Wirth's fulfilment policy showed some good results. The Germans accepted the Allied ultimatum in an agreement signed in London on 11 May. The following month the Bavarians were forced to disband their Home Guard. A number of Germans were brought to trial on war crimes charges. As was to be expected, the judgements were anything but harsh. Wirth made determined efforts to meet the Allied reparations demands, but here the difficulties facing him were too great to be overcome. German currency was losing its value all the time. Despite more stringent taxation measures the budget could not be balanced. The Allied Powers demanded major reforms in German domestic policy to enable the currency to be stabilised. Reparations should then be paid for out of a budgetary surplus. It was the German case that no realistic reform could be carried out while the country was burdened with such heavy reparations debts. The need to make large transfers of gold and convertible currency from Germany to the creditor nations was a large strain on Germany's reserves and weakened the mark. This in turn meant that no credit was forthcoming from abroad because foreign bankers did not believe financial stability could be achieved while the country was having to face such a large reparations burden.

On the whole it seems clear that – whatever the theoretical merits of the Allied case – in practice the Germans were right. Soon even Wirth's efforts over reparations failed. Germany had to declare that she would be unable to make the payments due at the beginning of 1922. 'Fulfilment' seemed to be leading Germany into a blind alley.

Wirth had quickly begun to lose faith in the possibility of concessions from Britain and France, although he had not renounced fulfilment. Instead he switched his attention to the east, hoping to strengthen Germany's diplomatic position by drawing closer to Soviet Russia. Moves for a better relationship with Lenin's Bolshevik government had been going on for some time. As early as 6 May 1921 the Germans signed a commercial agreement with Russia. It was not very wide in scope, but it confirmed German *de jure* recognition of the Soviet regime and envisaged an increase in trade between the two countries.

This Eastern policy was not just commercial. The German army was also involved. General von Seeckt had already authorised contacts with the Russians with a view to possible collaboration. Russia was not a signatory of the Versailles peace settlement. Arrangements with her might enable the Reichswehr to evade some of the restrictions put upon it by the Western Powers. By using Russian help the German army hoped to be able to keep abreast of developments in air and tank warfare, despite the prohibitions on such activities imposed by Versailles. Military personnel could be trained and forbidden armaments produced under Soviet auspices. In return the Russians would benefit from German technical help and administrative expertise.

The practical collaboration which von Seeckt hoped to achieve by making arrangements with the Russians did not in his case imply the slightest fondness for Communism or willingness to compromise with it in Germany. But there were on both the extreme left and nationalist right in Germany men who believed that their country's future lay in an arrangement with the East. Hatred of Western democracy and plutocratic capitalism – the enemies which had apparently caused Germany's downfall – encouraged a feeling of solidarity between the outcasts of Europe: Germany and Russia.

In the German Foreign Ministry the most enthusiastic supporter of a pro-Russian policy was the head of the Eastern Division, Count Ago von Maltzan. In the summer of 1921 he and Wirth agreed that closer relations with the Soviet Union ought to be the primary aim of German diplomacy.[15] The Germans could thereby hope to gain more room for manoeuvre in foreign affairs. There was also a defensive aspect to Wirth's policy. The Soviet government was trying to normalise relations with the West. Germany would thus have competition from Britain and

France in the bid for Russian favours. Lloyd George, in particular, became very interested in the expansion of Anglo-Russian trade. The British Prime Minister had promised Britain's soldiers a 'world fit for heroes to live in' when they returned from the war. Instead they found a stagnating economy and large-scale unemployment. Favourable terms of trade with Russia would brighten the prospect. For their part the French were eager to obtain compensation from Russia for the Tsarist loans repudiated by the Bolshevik government. As a lever to obtain Soviet compliance on both trade and debt questions the Western Allies might hope to use Article 116 of the Versailles Treaty, which reserved to Russia the right to make reparations demands against Germany for damage done during the war.

Furthermore, from the German military viewpoint it was most unlikely that a consortium in which Britain and France exerted much influence would tolerate secret German arms projects. Although Wirth made it his business not to enquire too closely into von Seeckt's dealings with the Red Army, he certainly knew that contacts existed. It was through his intervention that secret funds were made available to the Reichswehr for arms projects in Russia.[16] Wirth and von Maltzan both felt that the Russian connection was too valuable to be allowed to go by default.

Matters came to a head when Lloyd George persuaded his allies to call a European Economic Conference at Genoa in April 1922. Russia and Germany were both invited; the first time that the two outsiders in European politics had sat together at an international conference. The Soviet government did not have high hopes of gaining commercial advantages from Britain and France at Genoa. It therefore sent representatives to Berlin in an attempt to reach a formal agreement with the German government before the conference began. The Russian Foreign Minister, Chicherin, personally stopped off in the German capital to ensure the success of this project. A protocol was drawn up by Chicherin and von Maltzan which was virtually a treaty of friendship between the two countries.[17]

No formal agreement was made owing to reservations about association with Soviet Russia among Wirth's political colleagues. President Ebert had always disliked the Bolsheviks and had no desire to forge links with them. He had not been fully informed of Germany's moves towards Russia. Rathenau, the Foreign

Minister, was also reluctant to announce a treaty with Russia before the Genoa Conference because this might damage Germany's relations with the Western Powers. Rathenau harboured a faint hope that the conference might eventually lead to Allied concessions over reparations. On the other hand, important industrial interests favoured an agreement with Russia.

Yet when the German delegation – headed by Wirth and Rathenau – went to Genoa they found that Lloyd George was more eager to talk to the Russians than to them. It seemed that a scheme might be being worked out which would be prejudicial to German interests, and the Soviet delegation did all it could to heighten this impression when talking to the Germans,[18] although the latter may not have been taken in by this ruse.

At 2 a.m. on 16 April von Maltzan suddenly appeared in Rathenau's hotel room and told him that Chicherin was inviting the German delegation to a meeting at Rapallo later in the day. Rathenau was not in any case fundamentally opposed to a Soviet Treaty. It would be useful as a gesture of independence against the Western powers. By that evening a Treaty of Friendship had been concluded between the German and Soviet delegations. It safeguarded the Germans from any future Russian claims under the Versailles Treaty and ensured that Germany would enjoy most-favoured-nation treatment in its trade relations with Russia. There was no secret military protocol attached to the Rapallo Treaty, but its conclusion meant that collaboration between the Red Army and the Reichswehr was likely to be intensified, and this was in fact the case.[19]

News of the agreement naturally caused a sensation at Genoa and it was blamed for the meagre results produced by the conference. The French eagerly denounced German duplicity and Lloyd George was also indignant. On the face of it, however, there was little reason to suppose that the Germans lost much by their action. Lloyd George did not use Rapallo as an excuse for breaking up the Genoa Conference. On the contrary, he treated the Germans with more consideration, hoping they might help him gain concessions from Russia. The conference had never offered much chance of solving Germany's financial problems. British and American financial experts present at Genoa made it clear that an international loan to stabilise Germany's currency could only be raised if there was some prospect of a reparations settlement. Yet the French would not allow reparations to be put on the agenda at Genoa.[20]

Rapallo was the first real attempt by the Germans to take the initiative in foreign affairs and overcome their isolation. In many ways it was successful; the Russo-German contacts forged by the treaty continued and were the basis for more important economic co-operation later on. The fact that Germany had a link with Moscow gave her diplomatic advantages three years afterwards when she came to bargain with the West in a more favourable atmosphere. The military collaboration between the Reichswehr and the Red Army brought technical benefits to the former which were of considerable value when the army was rapidly expanded by Hitler in the 1930s. On the other hand, the Russo-German alignment alone could never be enough to overcome Germany's weakness *vis-à-vis* her former enemies. It may have encouraged the Germans to think that they could exert more pressure on Poland – with whom they had very bad relations for most of the 1920s – than was in fact the case. The Reichswehr could never become powerful enough to challenge Germany's conquerors by secret rearmament alone. It was the transformed diplomatic climate of the post-depression period which enabled Hitler to exploit opportunities never given to Republican politicians. One negative result of the apparent success of Rapallo was that it encouraged German diplomats and politicians to think that they could benefit by playing off East against West when dealing with their former enemies. The prospects for a rapprochement with France, which was essential if a democratic Germany was to regain a respected place in Europe without the constant prospect of military confrontation, were adversely affected by Rapallo, a point noted by some Republican politicians at the time. The French government under Poincaré prepared itself for drastic action in the near future.[21]

In May 1922 Wirth, after his return from Genoa, had completed a year in office as Chancellor – the longest run any leader had achieved since the Republic was founded. His colleagues in the Centre Party could feel that their Chancellor had extricated Germany from the period of crisis in which he had assumed power. Even if the conferences at Genoa had not led to any result they did seem to show a willingness on the part of other powers to listen to Germany's point of view. As one Centre Party newspaper claimed: 'a year ago they dictated to us; now they negotiate'.[22]

Indeed the early summer months of 1922 seemed remarkably calm. Germany had a stable coalition which one of the opposition parties, Stresemann's DVP, was doing its best to enter. Territorial disputes had been settled with Poland and Denmark. The reparations issue was hanging fire. But it was a calm before the storm.

On 24 June Foreign Minister Rathenau was murdered by nationalist terrorists. This act was well summed up by Stresemann in the remark:

> Political work often seems to me to be a labour of Sisyphus. Whenever one has rolled the stone up far enough so that one can believe in a stabilization of the general situation, then some fanatic plunges us into a misfortune.[23]

Germany suffered a severe loss of international prestige with Rathenau's death. The mark fell on world exchanges. In Berlin, Wirth reacted fiercely to the outrage and presented the Reichstag with the Law to Defend the Republic, giving the Government wide powers against enemies of the constitution. The Socialist trade unions organised strikes and demonstrations.

These events did not strengthen the coalition. Wirth's colleagues in the Centre Party, although shocked at Rathenau's murder, did not wish to embark on a campaign of radicalism. They disliked the militancy of Socialist trade unions. Catholic unions did not participate in the strikes. The fact was that the SPD was losing the sympathy of its coalition partners. It was clear in the summer of 1922 that the Independent Socialists and the SPD were moving closer together. Those Independents who had not gone over to the Communists were preparing to rejoin the SPD. After Rathenau's murder the two parties made a parliamentary alliance in the Reichstag. Social Democracy began to take on a more militant appearance.

In the early 1920s the more moderate elements in the SPD had seemed to be gaining the upper hand. At the Görlitz party conference of 1921 a platform was promulgated which aimed at creating a people's party of the left; the class war was played down and a conscious effort was made to appeal to voters outside the ranks of the industrial working class. But the lure of 'proletarian unity' presented by the possibility of winning back the Independent Socialists proved too powerful. If socialists were to be reunited, pragmatic attempts to work with 'bourgeois' parties would become more difficult. The price which had to be paid for reunion was therefore a tragically high one. It has been estimated that about one third of the members of the reunited Social Democratic Party harboured a Marxist proletarian self-image which inclined them to put class war ahead of parliamentary democracy in their list of priorities. Many of these radicals came from the Independents.[24] Several important Independent Socialist leaders, such as Rudolf Breitscheid and Rudolf Hilferding, and even a former communist leader, Paul Levi, were vocal in social democratic counsels. The result was a growing reluctance to co-operate with the parties of the centre-right just at the moment when those parties were beginning to show signs of working together within the parliamentary system.

Stresemann's People's Party, for example, was making strenuous efforts to conciliate the Democrats and Centre. When Rathenau was murdered Stresemann took the opportunity to align the DVP more firmly behind the Republican constitution than ever before. Though not finally renouncing monarchism, it adopted a resolution declaring:

> The dispute over the form of government must be put aside during our Fatherland's time of distress. We are of the conviction that the reconstruction of Germany is only possible within the framework of the Republican constitution.[25]

Stresemann went further and persuaded a large section of his supporters to vote for the controversial Law to Defend the Republic. Immediately afterwards it was agreed in principle that the Centre, Democratic and People's Party delegations in the Reichstag should consult together on important issues. This combination was to be given the high-sounding title of an 'Alliance of the constitutionally loyal middle' (*Verfassungstreue Mitte*). In September the SPD and the Independents finally merged. The Social Democratic Party thus became stronger in the Reichstag, and less enthusiastic for working within the government. Wirth himself had always worked well with Social Democrats, but his party grew restive and pressed for concessions to Stresemann. In November it insisted that the People's Party be admitted to the cabinet. The Social Democrats refused to accept this and Wirth had to resign. 'Working-class unity' proved to be Republican weakness.

A much more conservative cabinet was formed by Dr Wilhelm Cuno. Cuno was a former official of Wilhelm II who had become head of the Hamburg–America shipping line. His appointment was a retrograde step; it lessened the responsibility of parliamentary parties for the actions of the executive. Cuno's choice of ministers reflected a predilection for non-party 'experts' as against men of distinction in the Reichstag. His cabinet included a general, an ambassador, and the mayor of Essen, Hans Luther, who later described himself in his memoirs as a 'politician without a party'.

Cuno was quickly faced with a major crisis. The French government, led by the particularly intransigent Raymond Poincaré, was not prepared to prevaricate further on the question of reparations. German industry seemed to be booming under inflationary conditions,[26] and the French saw no reason why Germany should not meet her obligations to the Allies. At the end of December the French complained that Germany was defaulting on deliveries of telegraph poles. The Reparations Commission upheld their claim. On 11 January the French and the Belgians informed Cuno's government that they were sending a technical control commission to the Ruhr to supervise reparations deliveries. The occupation of Germany's most important industrial complex had begun.

Notes

1. Turner, *Stresemann*, p. 47.
2. Epstein, *Matthias Erzberger*, pp. 338–48. See also Witt, 'Tax Policy, Tax Assessment and Inflation', in Witt (ed.), *Wealth and Taxation in Central Europe*, pp. 137–60.
3. Winkler, *Revolution*, p. 297. Carsten, *A History of the Prussian Junkers*, pp. 156–8. Winkler, *Weimar, 1918–1933*, p. 121.
4. Goodspeed, *Ludendorff*, pp. 220–5.
5. Carsten, *Reichswehr*, pp. 79, 92–3. Also Erger, *Kapp-Lüttwitz-Putsch*, p. 143.

6. Gordon, *The Reichswehr*, pp. 110–11.
7. Winkler, *Weimar, 1918–1933*, pp. 122–3.
8. Carsten, *Reichswehr*, p. 82.
9. Turner, *Stresemann*, p. 52.
10. Erger, *Kapp-Lüttwitz-Putsch*, p. 282.
11. Carsten, *Reichswehr*, pp. 95–6.
12. Angress, *Stillborn Revolution*, p. 45.
13. Brecht, *Aus Nächster Nähe*, p. 344.
14. Ibid., p. 345.
15. Helbig, *Rapallo-Politik*, p. 57. See also Laubach, *Die Politik der Kabinette Wirth, 1921–22*, pp. 111–14.
16. Freund, *Unholy Alliance*, p. 97; Helbig, *Rapallo-Politik*, pp. 57–8; Carsten, *Reichswehr*, pp. 138, 141–2.
17. Helbig, *Rapallo-Politik*, pp. 77–83.
18. Freund, *Unholy Alliance*, p. 116. Helbig, *Rapallo-Politik*, pp. 89–90 states that the French were in fact suggesting to the Russians an arrangement whereby Russian repayment of Tsarist debts should be covered by German reparations. The Russians seem to have been willing to consider repayment of the debts, but in return demanded Allied compensation for damage caused by their intervention against the Bolsheviks in the Russian civil war. The differences between the two sides proved impossible to overcome.
19. For descriptions of the events at Rapallo see H. Pogge von Strandmann, 'Rapallo-Strategy in Defensive Diplomacy: New Sources and New Interpretations', in Berghahn and Kitchen (eds.), *Germany in the Age of Total War*, pp. 123–45. Also Fink *et al.*, *Genoa, Rapallo and European Reconstruction in 1992*, ch. 3; Freund, *Unholy Alliance*, pp. 115–19; Helbig, *Rapallo-Politik*, pp. 88 ff., Kessler, *Walther Rathenau*, pp. 319–59.
20. Erdmann, 'Deutschland, Rapallo und der Westen', pp. 151–2.
21. Winkler, *Weimar, 1918–1933*, pp. 170–2.
22. Morsey, *Zentrumspartei*, p. 50.
23. Turner, *Stresemann*, pp. 97–8.
24. Winkler, *Revolution*, p. 698.
25. Turner, *Stresemann*, p. 99.
26. For a description of the German iron and steel industry's progress in the inflation see Feldman, *Iron and Steel in the German Inflation, 1916–1923*, esp. ch. 4 and pp. 454–5.

6 Hitler and Republican Instability

As Germany's reparations problems grew more critical her internal security was being threatened by developments in Bavaria. Ever since the Kapp Putsch in March 1920, when the government in Munich had been entrusted to a monarchist official, Gustav von Kahr, Bavaria had become a centre for anti-Republican extremists.

The November revolution and the Munich Soviet Republic in April 1919 had been a great psychological shock to the propertied classes in Bavaria. Before the war their country had enjoyed political stability. The largest political party had been the Bavarian section of the Roman Catholic Centre. This had given fairly loyal – if sometimes fractious – support to the ministers appointed by Bavaria's Wittelsbach monarchs. After the November revolution a new organisation calling itself the Bavarian People's Party was established. It hoped to unite all conservative, Christian elements in the state, but in practice it inherited the supporters and most of the leaders of the old Bavarian Centre. On a national level it worked together with the Centre Party, and one of its members became a minister in the Weimar Coalition government. However, such collaboration soon became difficult. The new era had ushered in all sorts of unpleasant surprises for the Bavarians, not the least of which was the Weimar Constitution itself. It robbed them of the special rights they had enjoyed under the old Empire. Although these were not of great practical importance, their loss was wounding to Bavarian pride. Politically more significant was the centralising activity of Matthias Erzberger, whose tax-gathering techniques and obvious distaste for local privileges aroused anger south of the Main. The fact that he was a leader of the Centre Party strained the BVP/Centre association to breaking point, and in January 1920 the Bavarian People's Party disassociated itself from its Catholic colleagues in the rest of Germany. Its minister in the Berlin government had to resign.[1]

A further bone of contention between Munich and Berlin was the hospitality shown by the Bavarian government to private paramilitary organisations known as Patriotic Leagues (*Vaterländische Verbände*). These were often the remnants of former Freikorps units which had not been incorporated in the Reichswehr. They were generally anti- Republican in character and indulged in counter-revolutionary plots. The Bavarian army and police authorities turned a blind eye to the Leagues' activities and sometimes actively supported them. Von Kahr's regime also shielded murder gangs which liquidated those suspected of revealing secret arms caches to officials in Berlin or representatives of the Western Allies.

Certainly the administration of police authority in Bavaria was very one-sided. Von Kahr's Police President in Munich was Ernst Pöhner, a man who sincerely believed that the moral fibre of Germany had been undermined by the November revolution. He did all he could to support those who would fight Marxism and democracy. His attitude to the Republic is well illustrated in a conversation with a senior Reich official sent to investigate the Bavarian situation in February 1921.

Pöhner began by sneering violently at the Berlin government, which, he claimed, was no government at all. In Munich everyone was ready to die for von Kahr; who would die for Ebert, or Fehrenbach (the Reich Chancellor), or Gessler? He went on to describe the way in which he thought left-wing opponents should be treated by strong governments. If a strike was called in Berlin the government there would negotiate to try and end it. That was useless. Pöhner explained how he would deal with such a situation:

> You call the strike leaders together for a meeting and demand that the work be resumed next day. If the first says no you shoot him and ask the second. If he says no you shoot him too. Then the third will say yes. Then you have a total of two dead; using your negotiation methods there would be weeks of fighting with thousands dead.[2]

One beneficiary of such official attitudes in Bavaria was Adolf Hitler. He made his start in politics under the auspices of the Bavarian army. Bavaria was the school in which he learned his trade as a demagogue and party leader. The organisation he forged in these years was to carry him to power in Germany as a whole.

Born in 1889 in Braunau, on the Austrian side of the frontier with Bavaria, Hitler came from an unspectacular but hardly proletarian home. His father was a customs official, whose mother had only married some time after he had been born. Later on a great deal was made of the mystery surrounding Hitler's paternal grandfather. The possibility existed that he might actually have been a Jew. It was also pointed out that Hitler's father's name ought to have been that of his mother – Schickelgrüber. Since 'Heil Schickelgrüber' would hardly have been a rousing political slogan this was used as a propaganda weapon against the Nazi leader. In fact Adolf Hitler himself was quite legitimate and his name beyond question. Doubts concerning his ancestry were embarrassing to a politician propagating theories about racial purity, but there was no concrete proof that he had Jewish forebears.[3]

The importance attached to this point was symptomatic of the anti-Semitic atmosphere which seems to surround Hitler from his earliest recorded youth. The period before the First World War had seen a resurgence of this ancient prejudice in many parts of Central and Eastern Europe. It was bound up with a wider reaction against economic and political liberalism with which the Jews, who had benefited from the trend towards legal equality, were sometimes associated.

Anti-Semitism had originally owed a great deal of its force to religious hostility felt by Christians for Jews. But in the nineteenth century new and apparently more 'scientific' theories began to appear, according to which Jews were regarded as racially distinct from other Europeans. In fact such arguments had no scientific basis. Many of their supporters specifically denied the value of reason, preferring more emotional guides to action. Nevertheless, the belief that peoples were organic growths and that alien races would weaken or destroy them seemed more 'modern' than an attack on Jews as the enemies of Christianity. It also possessed the advantage of condemning all people of Jewish racial origin, no matter what their religious beliefs.

Tales of a Jewish 'world conspiracy' were already a common ingredient of anti-Semitic literature before the First World War.

One notorious description of mysterious Jewish cabals and plots against Christian society came to be known as the *Protocols of the Elders of Zion*. Of uncertain origin, it was enthusiastically disseminated by Russian anti-Semites before the First World War, and after Tsarism collapsed in 1917 it was exported to the West by White Russian refugees.[4]

In pre-war Germany organised political anti-Semitism had not been successful as a separate political movement, but anti-Semitic attitudes had begun to permeate apparently respectable movements such as the Pan-German League and the German Farmers' Association.[5] Racialist – or *Völkisch** – beliefs were current among middle-class youth dissatisfied with the achievements of united Germany and seeking a purer form of state than that represented by the Wilhelmine Empire. Owing to pogroms in Russia against Jewish communities many Russian Jews fled to the West, and some of them settled in Germany. Their numbers were often exaggerated, but it was widely believed that such 'Eastern Jews' were a subversive influence, especially among university students.[6] In Austria-Hungary Jewish populations in Vienna and Budapest were easy targets for racialists' abuse.

It was to Vienna that Hitler had gone as a young man, after a period of schooling in Linz. He wanted to study art, but was unable to qualify for the drawing academy. Instead he spent several years drifting aimlessly in the Austrian capital, dabbling in art and discussing politics with his Bohemian acquaintances. Vienna was a breeding ground for virulent nationalist, racialist and sectarian prejudices. It cannot be proved that Hitler was a convinced anti-Semite during his stay there, but he was certainly exposed to anti-Semitic ideas.[7]

In 1913 he left Austria and went to Munich. When the war broke out in August 1914 he volunteered for the Bavarian army, having listened amid a jubilant crowd to King Ludwig III declaring war against France and Russia. He was a good soldier, even if he did not rise above the rank of corporal. Serving on the Western Front, he was awarded the Iron Cross, first and second class. It seems that Hitler was very much happier in the army than he had been as a civilian; the organised chaos of war – so horrifying to

---

* *Völkisch* implied racial membership of and identification with the *Volk* (folk) who constituted a nation.

most men – simply provided him with a sense of purpose he had previously lacked.[8]

Germany's defeat came to him as a moral and physical shock. When the war ended he was in a military hospital recovering from the effects of a gas attack.[9] On his recovery he found himself in barracks in Munich, where the atmosphere was very different from that at the front. Many soldiers were simply staying in uniform to keep a roof over their heads. Authority in the Bavarian army was now shared uneasily between officers and Soldiers' Councils. In Munich the latter had the upper hand. April 1919 saw the proclamation of a Soviet Republic, which caused more dissension among the soldiers. Hitler does not seem to have participated in the conflicts which occurred at that time, though he must have been only too aware of them. Like many of his colleagues he remained neutral, possibly donning a red armband when it seemed necessary, but refusing to join the Red Army.[10] Nevertheless, Hitler had evidently impressed some of his army comrades as an opponent of the extreme left, for when, at the beginning of May 1919, 'White' forces supporting the legal government occupied Munich, he was rapidly put on a small committee to investigate the extent to which his battalion had been implicated in the Soviet Republic. He was thus allowed to stay in the army at a time when most of his comrades were being demobilised.[11]

The old officers in the Bavarian army had been shocked and humiliated by the November revolution and its consequences. They owed their return to Munich to Noske's forces from north Germany, and this was a further affront to their military pride. In their view the German people as a whole was demoralised, and unless it could be made to pull itself together the country was bound to fall into the arms of Bolshevism.

They were determined to create an army loyal to its officers and free of 'subversive' elements. They wanted to restore discipline and morale. This had to be done by careful selection of personnel and by political indoctrination or 'enlightenment'. A section of the army staff in Munich was set up to organise lectures and courses of instruction to explain the causes of the revolution to politically uneducated soldiers. The officers who set up such courses were not themselves very sophisticated politically, and their attitude towards Germany's problems largely coincided

with those of the nationalist opponents of the Republic. In particular they were eager to deny the charge that Imperial Germany
was responsible for starting the Great War.

Hitler was selected for training as a political educator. He
aroused the interest of his instructors – among whom there was
at least one distinguished university professor – by his rhetorical
talent and his determined anti-Semitism. This latter characteristic
was by no means unattractive to his superiors. The Munich Soviet
Republic was widely believed to have been the work of Eastern
Jews, and several leading participants in it actually had been of
Jewish origin.* Hostility to Jews was therefore equated with loyalty to 'law and order' by the army leaders.

The head of the propaganda department of the Bavarian Army
Command, Captain Karl Mayr, was at that time an enthusiastic
counter-revolutionary. He received good reports of Hitler's propaganda activity among returning German prisoners of war and
in other units. So Hitler was entrusted with more sophisticated
tasks. Mayr's organisation kept watch on all political activities in
Munich, hoping thereby to influence civilian as well as military
opinion in a suitable direction. One of the political groups in
which Mayr became interested was an obscure body called the
German Workers' Party (DAP). In September 1919 Hitler was
sent to one of its meetings. His demeanour impressed the party's
leaders and he was asked to become a member. It was to be the
beginning of a new career.[12]

The German Workers' Party itself had made no impact on
Munich at all when Hitler joined it. Its founder was a railway
worker called Anton Drexler, a man unfit for military service who
had felt it his duty in the closing stages of the war to exhort his
working-class comrades to support the war effort and struggle on
for a victorious peace. The party's aim was to put German workers under German leadership and ensure them freedom from
exploitation without going so far as to socialise industry. Employers' property should be respected so long as they did not abuse it.
There should be a clear distinction between workers and 'proletariat'. The skilled and the diligent should be given the

---

* There were, of course, plenty of native Bavarians in the Soviets, and the local
Jewish community was overwhelmingly opposed to the revolution. But such facts
were ignored at the time.

opportunity to identify themselves with the middle class.[13] After the fall of the Soviet Republic in May 1919 the DAP also began to stress the anti-Semitic element in its appeal. Nevertheless, it was still an unsuccessful and insignificant party when Hitler visited it on 12 September 1919.

Hitler afterwards claimed that he was the party's seventh member, but this is certainly untrue.[14] It is much more likely that he referred to his membership of the party's executive committee, to which he was almost immediately elected. Hitler's main task in the party was that for which he had been trained in the army: propaganda. He rapidly revealed himself to be the most effective orator within the ranks of the DAP.[15] On 24 February 1920 the party organised its first really large meeting in the Munich Hofbräuhaus – which had been a communist stronghold in the days of the Soviet Republic. Hitler was chosen to read out the terms of a new twenty-five-point party programme. The DAP also changed its name and became known as the National Socialist German Workers' Party, a title probably chosen to express solidarity with similarly named organisations in Germany, Austria and the Sudetenland.[16] From this time onwards the party began to make some impact on Munich and its environs, although it remained virtually unknown to the world at large.[17]

The party's new programme was a mixture of pan-German nationalism, racial exclusiveness and a resentful hostility to big business. It demanded a Greater German Reich and more land upon which to settle the country's surplus population. Citizenship should be restricted to people of German racial origin; aliens could not enjoy such rights, and Jews could never be citizens. The immigration of aliens into Germany should be stopped and those who had come into the country since August 1914 should be required to leave. The party did not specifically demand the abolition of parliamentary rule, but the corruption of parliamentary parties was attacked, as was Roman Law, which was to be replaced by a German Common Law. The press was to be cleansed of alien elements. Education was to be organised to disseminate respect for the State and build up a healthy nation. Religion would be tolerated as long as it did not threaten to undermine the State or offend German racial morals. The country should have a strong central government.

None of these ideas was original. Some points in the programme even bore a resemblance to sections in the Weimar
Constitution, although it is hardly likely that this was inten-
tional.[18] The desire for equality with other powers was a commonplace in 1920 and would have been accepted by nearly
everyone. Greater Germany was a traditional nationalist design
with its roots in the period before Bismarck. More adventurous
was the claim that Germany should gain land upon which to settle
her excess population, but that had been part of the Pan-German
League's programme during the war.[19] Indeed, the Nazis were
vague about this aspect of their policy, since they evidently considered it to refer to overseas colonies. The eastern orientation of
Hitler's colonial policy set out in *Mein Kampf* was absent from the
earliest objectives of the Nazi Party.[20] Attacks on Roman Law as a
Jewish institution were also conventional in anti-Semitic circles.
Sections on religion and centralised government were at least
partly an expression of nationalist hostility to Catholic Bavarian
separatism, against which Hitler and his colleagues were vigorously polemicising.

On the social and economic plane the party's policy was considerably indebted to the work of its idiosyncratic economic the-
orist, Gottfried Feder. Feder was obsessed with the belief that
finance capital – money invested to produce profit through interest – lay at the root of all society's problems. He regarded banks as
the equivalent of robber barons in the Middle Ages, and thought
that their influence should be greatly restricted. This did not
mean, however, that he believed in the nationalisation of private
property. On the contrary, he was often at pains to stress his
respect for property and for the enterprise of the individual
businessman.[21] Feder reflected the hostility to large-scale capitalism felt by many Germans in what might be described as the old
middle class – officials, independent businessmen, shopkeepers,
craftsmen and farmers.

It was this utopian socialism of the small proprietor that underlay the social elements in the Nazi programme. Each citizen had a
duty to work creatively for the common good. The 'tyranny of
interest' had to be broken. War profiteers were to be treated as
criminals, industrial trusts should be nationalised and there
should be profit-sharing in industry. Chain department stores
were to be expropriated and leased to local shopkeepers. Despite

the apparently revolutionary aspects of this programme it implied no large-scale attack on property for the benefit of the working classes. Point sixteen of the policy statement demanded the creation of a healthy middle class, by which was clearly meant the skilled craftsman, the farmer, the shopkeeper, the small businessman and the salaried employee. It was precisely these groups which were thought to have suffered most severely during the war, and who were threatened most severely by the inflation which followed it.

Some space has been devoted to an account of this programme, because the description of Hitler's followers as members of a 'socialist' workers' party has caused some confusion. The Nazi Party did not appeal only – or indeed mainly – to workers, and its socialism was of a kind which involved state controls but no major redistribution of wealth. This is not to suggest that it was ever the tool of big business or that it appealed exclusively to an ill-defined group called the lower middle class. But Hitler never allowed it to come into serious conflict with powerful vested interests among Germany's propertied classes, unless the Jews could be counted as such. His party never had a markedly proletarian character and when, later in the 1920s, attempts were made to stress its socially revolutionary tendencies, he successfully prevented National Socialism from being marked out as a specifically anti-capitalist movement.

Hitler himself was almost certainly not the sole author of the party programme, and in the years which followed he did not always seem very concerned about its fulfilment. He is supposed to have told Hermann Rauschning that 'it is for the masses. It points the direction of some of our endeavours – neither more nor less – it is like the dogma of the Church.'[22] Since Hitler admired the Church chiefly for the techniques with which it influenced the masses, this last comment reinforces an impression of cynicism towards the declared aims of his party. Yet there is no reason to assume that the Nazi programme did not coincide with Hitler's own political views. Some parts of it he regarded with more enthusiasm than others; this was to be expected. It is also not surprising that the social aspects of the programme – most of which were completely unrelated to the realities of German economic life – proved largely unworkable in practice. This is a fate not unknown to befall political programmes elsewhere. Indeed, if a party leader were only to be judged by the extent to which he carried out his promises, Hitler would have to be put in the highest class.

Two fundamental attitudes dominated Hitler's political career. The first was his hatred of the Jews, which never wavered from his earliest recorded statements until the day of his death in 1945. On 16 September 1919 he wrote to a soldier in his regiment:

> Everything which makes men strive for higher things, whether it be religion, socialism, or democracy is for him (the Jew) merely a means to an end, to satisfy his lust for money and power. His influence will result in national race tuberculosis.[23]

By attributing to the Jews a lust for power Hitler was unconsciously revealing his own compulsive urges in the same direction, for the second and more important motivating force in his life was a desire to achieve and exercise power over others. He always firmly believed that it was necessary and morally justifiable for the strong to rule – and even to destroy – the weak. Although he was to owe his success to the way in which he aroused mass support, he spoke of the masses with open contempt; as 'feminine', fickle and incapable of decision or rational calculation. They had to be bullied, cajoled and deceived by strong-willed leaders if they were to be politically effective. For this reason the techniques of mass manipulation fascinated Hitler and he mastered them in a fashion unrivalled by any of his contemporaries.[24] In this process the individual points of the programme were not so important as the general climate of opinion to which he appealed.

As we have already seen, the lost war and the disappointing peace had left many Germans feeling frustrated and resentful. Inflation, which had begun during the war and became rapidly worse after the revolution, was devaluing the salaries and savings of many who normally regarded themselves as safe from the economic fluctuations which might threaten the working or entrepreneurial classes. In an atmosphere of suspicion, violence and insecurity Hitler's propaganda played on emotion rather than reason; it satisfied a popular desire for certainty as against the intellectual difficulties posed by argument. Audiences came to Hitler to hear in the most uncompromising terms what they already wanted to believe – that their frustration and economic distress was entirely due to the revolution, the Republic and the betrayal of Germany's armed forces. Thus prepared they were impressed by the unwavering ferocity of Nazi assaults on those who were supposed to have engineered Germany's downfall: the Marxists and the Jews.

When Hitler joined the DAP it had, like most other parties, a relatively democratic structure and was run by a committee. Most of the committee's members were old colleagues of Drexler, the Party Chairman. Hitler became dissatisfied with this leadership. His own army background and rhetorical gifts soon put him in a powerful position *vis-à-vis* his colleagues. He also disagreed with them on the issue of national organisation. They were interested in linking their movement with other racialist societies in Germany and Austria. Hitler rightly despised most of these groups as generals without armies, hoping to create an imposing façade behind which they had no substantial membership. He also realised that any amalgamation with another party would reduce his own status in Munich.

Matters came to a head in the summer of 1921. Hitler threatened to resign from the party unless it was reorganised to give him dictatorial powers. The old committee was forced to capitulate. Hitler's local prestige had become so great that they dared not lose him. A three-man policy committee headed by Hitler was appointed to lead the Party. He also controlled an 'investigation' sub-committee, which regulated membership. Shortly after this the Nazis acquired a new business manager, the tough and efficient Max Amann. A former sergeant-major in Hitler's old regiment, Amann was completely loyal to him. With the neutralisation of the former party leadership, Hitler could rely on a more dependable local base than any other Völkisch politician in Germany. According to one report, the Munich branch of the party alone could boast of 2500 paying registered members in the early months of 1921.[25]

Most of his progress can fairly be ascribed to Hitler, for it was his personality and contacts which drew into the party men who were prepared to devote time and sometimes money to the Nazi cause. Some of them were none too respectable in their private lives; many did not fit in socially with the high-minded artisans surrounding Drexler.

So far as funds were concerned, the party depended largely on the collections at meetings, individual gifts from wealthier sympathisers and membership dues. In all respects Hitler's contribution was vital. It was he who moved large audiences with his oratory, he who charmed bourgeois families like the Bechsteins, and he who attracted new membership in the provinces and in Munich itself. Even if others might wield more influence with potential donors, Hitler provided the fire in the movement which made it seem worth supporting. From 1921 to 1923 the party continued to make steady progress, recruiting members and opening new branches. Although it had organisations in northern Germany, its main support still came from Bavaria. By January 1922 there were six thousand registered party members, a very respectable figure for a Völkisch organisation.

In the summer of 1921 Hitler also organised his own strong-arm squads which, by 1923, had developed into a paramilitary force of some considerable size. This SA, as it was called, staged provocative demonstrations and was sometimes involved in street fights with opponents. Its chief function, however, was to prevent Nazi speakers being embarrassed by interruptions. Hitler never relished discussion; his forte was the monologue rather than the debate. In some ways this made his party more attractive to his audiences, for it stressed the contrast between Nazi ruthlessness and power and the apparent feebleness of their democratic opponents. Hitler himself grew in confidence. Whereas in the early years he saw himself mainly as a propagandist, paving the way for a new regime led by others, the example of Mussolini's March on Rome in October 1922 greatly impressed him. He began to be referred to as 'Germany's Mussolini' and he allowed his supporters to present him as the leader for which Germany was waiting. The cult of the leader had made its appearance.[26]

Although he owed his growing prestige to the loyalty of his Munich organisation, Hitler did not confine his activities to Bavaria. He travelled widely in Germany and other German-speaking regions to address meetings and contact sympathisers. He was by no means a provincially-minded politician when matters reached crisis point in 1923. The disaster which was to engulf Chancellor Cuno and destroy Germany's currency found Hitler prepared to exploit his first chance to make a bid for national power.

Notes

1. The minister concerned was the Reich Finance Minister Dr Mayer, who became Ambassador in Paris.
2. Brecht, *Aus Nächster Nähe*, pp. 331–2.
3. See Hitler's family tree in Bullock, *Hitler*, pp. 28–9. For an account of his possible Jewish connection, Maser, *NSDAP*, pp. 46–8. See also Kershaw, *Hitler, 1889–1936*, pp. 3–13.
4. See Cohn, *Warrant for Genocide*, pp. 108–17, 126 ff.
5. See, for example, Kruck, *Alldeutschen Verbandes*. Also Pulzer, *Political Anti-Semitism*, pp. 190–1.
6. Williams, 'Russians in Germany: 1900–1914', especially pp. 130–4.
7. Hamann, *Hitlers Wien*, chs. 7–10.
8. Bullock, *Hitler*, pp. 53–4; Maser, *NSDAP*, pp. 123–7.
9. Maser, *NSDAP*, pp. 127–8.
10. Ibid., pp. 45, 132. Also Maser, *Hitler*, p. 103.
11. Kershaw, *Hitler, 1889–1936*, p. 121.
12. Deuerlein, 'Hitlers Eintritt in die Politik und in die Reichswehr'. Mayr later became a Social Democrat and an opponent of Hitler. He died in Buchenwald concentration camp in 1945. Kershaw, *Hitler, 1889–1936*, pp. 122–8.
13. Maser, *NSDAP*, pp. 150–1.
14. Ibid., p. 167. Hitler's actual party number was 555. See Kershaw, *Hitler, 1889–1936*, p. 127.
15. See Phelps, 'Hitler als Parteiredner'.
16. Bullock, *Hitler*, p. 66.
17. Phelps, 'Hitler als Parteiredner', p. 287.
18. Maser, *NSDAP*, pp. 472–4. The Nazi programme can be read in English in Noakes and Pridham, *Nazism 1919–1945. A Documentary Reader, Vol. 1, The Rise to Power, 1919–1934* pp. 14–16. See also Kershaw, *Hitler, 1889–1936*, pp. 144–5.
19. *Handbuch des Alldeutschen Verbandes*, 1917.
20. Phelps, 'Hitler als Parteiredner', p. 288.
21. See, for example, Feder, *Der Deutsche Staat*. On page 23 he writes: 'We National Socialists reject all forms of socialization or nationalization in the Marxist sense. Our economic ideal demands the greatest possible number of free enterprises, especially medium-size and small undertakings.'
22. Rauschning, *Hitler Speaks*, p. 188.
23. As given in Nolte, *Three Faces of Fascism*, p. 316. For the text of the letter in German see Deuerlein, 'Hitlers Eintritt in die Politik und in die Reichswehr', p. 205.

24. For a discussion of Hitler's power as a demagogue and its vital importance to the Nazi movement see Bullock, *Hitler*, pp. 68–73.

25. Franz-Willing, *Hitlerbewegung*, p. 103. Also Maser, *NSDAP*, p. 264, and Kershaw, *Hitler, 1889–1936*, pp. 163–5. For a discussion of Hitler's success in gaining control of the Nazi Party and the character of its organisation see Orlow, 'The Organisational History and Structure of the NSDAP, 1919–1923'.

26. Kershaw, *Hitler, 1889–1936*, pp. 182–5. For differing views about Hitler's self-perception see Tyrell, *Vom Trommler zum Führer*, and Horn, *Führerideologie und Parteiorganisation in der NSDAP, 1919–1923*.

7 Ruhr Occupation and Inflation

Cuno's government was in no position to fight the French, but it refused to surrender to Poincaré's strong-arm tactics. Cuno inaugurated a policy of passive resistance in the Ruhr. Businessmen, officials and workers were not to co-operate with the occupying powers. The Reich government met the financial losses involved in this resistance. Acts of sabotage were also organised by clandestine paramilitary groups under the authority of the Reichswehr.[1] One result of these measures was that the Franco-Belgian invasion became a much larger operation than had been at first envisaged. Repressive measures were taken against recalcitrant German mine-owners, miners and civil servants. They included jail after courts martial, and banishment from the occupied zone. Miners were shot down in clashes with French troops. A customs barrier was erected between the Ruhr area and the rest of the Reich.

This naturally represented an enormous financial and economic burden on the central government in Berlin. It was a burden that Cuno's regime was ill-fitted to bear. Germany's currency was in a desperate condition when Cuno assumed power. His defiance of the French only served to bury its slender chances of recovery. It should be emphasised that the inflation which had such a catastrophic and lasting effect on German society in the 1920s cannot simply be blamed on the French occupation of the Ruhr.[2] By the time Poincaré moved his troops across the Rhine the mark had already reached a stage of devaluation which had seriously undermined the value of many Germans' savings. At the beginning of 1920 the mark had fallen to one-tenth its pre-war value. In the summer of 1922 it was worth only one-hundredth of the old mark, and by January 1923 one pre-war gold mark would have had the purchasing power of over 1500 paper marks. This was, as one of Adolf Hitler's most distinguished biographers pointed out, a truly revolutionary development.[3] The socialist

99

phrases used by Germany's first Republican administration had scarcely touched large sections of the population. The inflation, on the other hand, was like a plague, affecting all classes whatever their political persuasion or social status. Some of those who were in a position to speculate were able to make great financial gains. But hundreds of thousands more saw their security destroyed and living standards jeopardised. Whatever compensations inflation may actually have had for individuals in the shape of reduced debts or a relatively easy job market, the vast majority of Germans believed that their prospects were being undermined as the result of an inflation which was systematically destroying their previously stable currency.

It is important to remember that the roots of inflation lay in the Kaiser's war, and that the Republic was faced with an inherently unhealthy financial situation when it took over what Ebert rightly described as a bankrupt concern. This situation had been camouflaged during the war by the government and the Reichsbank. The former placed military expenditure in an emergency budget which would supposedly be met by enemy indemnities when the war was won. In 1917 this budget showed a deficit of 13.7 billion* marks. From January 1916 the government imposed foreign exchange controls which artificially hindered a downward trend of the German mark on the foreign exchanges. For its part, the Reichsbank suspended gold payments and increased the money supply, using loan certificates from newly-created loan bureaux as security for the printing of banknotes.[4] Although in theory one-third of the currency in circulation was backed with gold, in practice billions of marks were circulating without any such security. By the summer of 1918, the President of the Reichsbank, Rudolf von Havenstein, was desperately worried about the insolvency of the Reich, since there was by that time a floating debt of over 51 billion marks.[5] The Reichsbank, like the Imperial Government, gambled on a German victory. Unlike the Kaiser, however, Havenstein remained at his post after the war was lost. A legally trained Prussian civil servant rather than a businessman, he retained the nationalistic attitudes which had conditioned his policy before and during the war, as did most of his senior colleagues. They were therefore unwilling to seek a solution to

* This is an American billion, or one thousand million.

inflation which might involve concessions to Germany's enemies. On the other hand, the French and the British were themselves deeply indebted to the USA and determined to make Germany pay for what they regarded as a war of aggression.

These factors, together with the political weakness of Republican governments after the Reichstag elections of 1920, made it difficult to tackle the problem effectively. The loss of the war, the need for high levels of public spending to overcome post-war social difficulties, shortage of capital in German industry and the pressure of reparations demands prevented a cure being found for inflation. There was also a steady flight of German capital abroad which successive governments were either unwilling or unable to control. Perhaps unfortunately, inflation did not increase steadily in the immediate post-war period; that might have concentrated politicians' minds on the problem of combating it. Although by the summer of 1920 the cost of living had risen to about thirteen times its pre-war level, there had actually been a check in inflation in the spring of 1920, and there was another in the winter of 1920/21.[6] Hopes could therefore be entertained that, with the mark actually rising against the dollar, the currency might stabilise itself as the economy recovered.

Such hopes proved vain, however. The Allied reparations ultimatum of May 1921 had brought home both to the German public and to the international money markets how precarious Germany's financial position was. Huge budgetary deficits were difficult to close because taxes tended to lose their value before they could be collected, and in any case there was much tax evasion, especially amongst the better-off. Although reparations payments accounted for less than half the budgetary deficit, they were enough of a psychological burden to inhibit German governments from taking serious steps to rectify the situation. The Western Allies, whose bickering over reparations at Paris had prevented a clear-cut settlement of the issue, were still unable to agree on a constructive compromise settlement. The British were determined not to let the French get the lion's share of reparations unless the Americans reduced Britain's debt obligations. The Republican administration in Washington refused to consider helping its debtors because it wanted to cut taxes in the USA.[7] With no international settlement of reparations being possible, and with Germany's political parties unwilling to shoulder the odium of serious retrenchment at home, the only way the German government could keep going was to print money. This encouraged the further decline of the German currency on the world markets.

In the initial stages the inflation apparently had some advantages. Cheap money meant that industrial production could be reorganised quickly on a peacetime footing. Real wages remained low and therefore unemployment could be mopped up fairly quickly. Industrial debts were reduced. The government, always a heavy borrower, also benefited. The national debt in Germany was virtually wiped out. This had a damaging effect on banks, however, whose reserves were seriously depleted. For many individual Germans the results were even more damaging. Patriotic citizens who had invested in War Loans after 1914 saw their value dwindle into insignificance. Unwittingly they had made a present of their money to the State. They did not blame the Imperial government which had borrowed the money, but the Republican regime which had presided over its devaluation. The same catastrophe befell all those who had fixed interest savings. Deposit accounts, insurance policies, debenture stocks – in other words, the staple investment areas for the cautious middle class – had all been undermined by the beginning of 1923.

However, it would be wrong to imagine that inflation harmed only the lower middle classes. Workers in the factories and the farms also found life very difficult in an inflationary situation. Cheap money certainly meant work – at least until the mark had ceased to have any value at all. But prices always raced ahead of wages. Hence, even though they were employed, the workers faced a steadily diminishing standard of living.

It was this situation which was grossly aggravated by Cuno's policy in the Ruhr. Passive resistance was phenomenally expensive. During the first six months of the Ruhr occupation the financial cost to Germany – ignoring lost production from the occupied area – was estimated at 827.6 million gold marks. Between January and the end of June 1923 the German treasury was actually paying out an average of a trillion (a million million) marks per month in inflated currency to support the Ruhr conflict.[8] By the summer of 1923 the downward plunge of the mark had become so sharply aggravated that its valuation ceased to have much meaning except to those speculators who were able to

deal in foreign currency. Indeed, fixed prices were often abandoned and figures either referred to foreign currency or to the
most recent quotations for the mark on foreign exchanges. Since
bank depositors spent their money as soon as they received it, the
normal machinery of credit began to dry up and bank reserves
were liquidated. Industrialists could no longer go on expanding
production, and unemployment began to add a new dimension to
the misery of the working class.[9]

Cuno's policy of passive resistance to the French received voci-
ferous support. But expressions of disgust at French action were
not at all the same as declarations of loyalty towards the Republic.
The extreme nationalists on the right and the Communists on the
left did not give up their hostility to the government in Berlin
simply because it was involved in a major crisis. Perhaps the most
consistent opponent of the Republic was Adolf Hitler. He argued
that Germany could never be strong while the Weimar system was
allowed to continue. The Germans should therefore concentrate
all their energies on destroying it. Only then could they hope to
challenge France. He liked to call the politicians in Berlin
'November criminals', a reference to the November revolution
of 1918. According to him, such people should be eliminated, and
there could be no question of forming a 'common front' with
them. Writing in the *Völkischer Beobachter*, he said:

> So long as a nation does not do away with the assassins within
> its borders, no external successes can be possible. While writ-
> ten and spoken protests are directed against France, the real
> deadly enemy of the German people lurks within the walls of
> the nation .... Down with the November criminals, with all
> their nonsense about a united front![10]

The Communists' attitude was not so very different, although
they did try to appeal to nationalist sentiment by attacks on
Poincaré. They argued that Germany could only hope to liberate
herself from Versailles by overthrowing capitalism and creating a
proletarian dictatorship. The Ruhr crisis was denounced as a
'nationalist swindle'. On 23 January *Die Rote Fahne* carried the
headline 'smite Poincaré and Cuno on the Ruhr and on the
Spree'.*[11]

*The Spree is the river on which Berlin stands.

Such subversive tendencies were aggravated by the policies of Cuno's government. The complete collapse of the mark increased working-class bitterness and insecurity. The Communist Party – hitherto largely unsuccessful in its search for mass support – began to make perceptible gains in membership and voting strength.[12] On the right the Patriotic Leagues, with their para-military character, grew more powerful and belligerent, actively supported by the German army.[13]

French invasion of the Ruhr caused von Seeckt to intensify the recruitment and training of formations sometimes referred to as the 'Black Reichswehr'. They stood in varying degrees of subor-dination to regular army officers. Generally speaking they received part-time training from the Reichswehr, for which some of them drew weapons from army depots. But many of the Patriotic Leagues – especially in Bavaria – had their own weapons in secret stockpiles. They were also careful not to put their members too directly under the army's control for fear of losing their political identity. This did not, however, prevent the Reichswehr chiefs from continuing to support them. Few army officers felt any more enthusiastic about the Republic than did the members of the Patriotic Leagues. General von Seeckt was concerned to maintain as effective discipline as possi-ble among all Germany's forces – whether clandestine or other-wise – but he did not exert himself to ensure their loyalty to the Republic.

So long as Cuno remained in office pressure for a right- wing coup was unlikely to become very serious. But by the beginning of August it was clear that his ministry could not continue. Unable to cope with the economic and social problems facing Germany, Cuno resigned.

On 13 August Stresemann formed his first cabinet. He did so as the leader of a coalition in which all parties accepting the Repub-lican Constitution were represented, from his own People's Party to the Social Democrats. Such broadly-based support made it possible for him to envisage radical measures to overcome both the inflation and Germany's difficulties with the French. But he faced severe pressure from the nationalist opposition, supported as it was by powerful interests in agriculture, industry and the army. Von Seeckt himself had no very high opinion of Stresemann, and the presence of the Social Democrats in the

Government outraged the Patriotic Leagues. Stresemann's position was somewhat strengthened by agreements between employers and trade unions to keep wages at least partly abreast of soaring prices and, more particularly, by a good grain harvest. The latter advantage, however, simply underlined the need for a drastic reform of the currency. German farmers were no longer prepared to sell their produce for worthless paper marks. Despite a plentiful stock of food, therefore, urban areas were threatened with hunger and the associated likelihood of civil disturbance.[14]

Stresemann was ready to give up passive resistance in the Ruhr but sought concessions from Poincaré in return. None was forthcoming. German hopes that British pressure might cause the French to yield also proved vain. Although the British government disliked the occupation of the Ruhr it was not prepared to rupture relations with France for the sake of the Germans. When this was finally made clear to Stresemann he prepared for the unconditional cessation of passive resistance.[15]

This important change of policy was publicly announced on 26 September. At once there was swift reaction in Munich. Claiming that it faced a threat to internal order, the Bavarian cabinet declared a state of emergency and appointed Gustav von Kahr – who had resigned as Prime Minister in 1921 – as commissioner with dictatorial powers.[16] This move caused consternation in Berlin since it seemed to undermine the authority of the central government. Von Kahr was known as a determined opponent of the Republican regime. Stresemann's cabinet reacted by announcing a state of emergency throughout the Reich, and entrusting Defence Minister Gessler with emergency powers to maintain law and order. It soon became apparent, however, that the Bavarians would not accept orders from Berlin whatever the source of their authority.

Nor was disloyalty confined to Bavaria. In the early autumn of 1923 the German government faced numerous threats to its sovereignty. Some were overt, and took the form of localised rebellions. Potentially more serious was the clandestine network of intrigue aimed at deposing the parliamentary regime in Berlin itself. Participants in such machinations included leaders of the Patriotic Leagues, nationalist politicians in both the National People's Party and the German People's Party, industrialists and army leaders.

The atmosphere in the Reichswehr was particularly disturbing from a Republican viewpoint. Since the previous January the army had been preparing for a possible war with France and had completely ignored the restrictions placed upon it by the Versailles Peace Treaty. The end of passive resistance was seen as yet another Republican capitulation to the enemy. In the words of one lieutenant-colonel, it was 'a new lost war'. He remarked bitterly that the army now had two duties: 'protection of the constitution, of a diseased system, and preparation of the war of liberation, which is prevented by the system...'.[17] This was a gross distortion of the facts, but it was a widely-held view in military circles.

The first open symptom of revolt came at the beginning of October when units of the 'Black Reichswehr' mutinied in Kustrin and Spandau – uncomfortably near Berlin. Led by a former participant in the Kapp Putsch called Major Buchrucker, the dissidents were quickly overpowered by regular Reichswehr units. Von Seeckt himself had no sympathy for undisciplined soldiery of the freebooting Freikorps type who formed the backbone of the clandestine military formations recruited during 1923. But no severe measures were taken against the mutineers. Buchrucker received a term of 'honourable imprisonment'.[18]

The Reichswehr was more enthusiastic when suppressing Communist subversion which was threatening in central Germany. The German Communist Party was at last preparing to embark on a new wave of revolutionary activity. It was being encouraged by the international Communist organisation, the Comintern. Partly as a result of domestic power struggles in Moscow, the Russian Communist leadership had decided that the time was ripe for their German comrades to seize power. Russian political and military specialists were sent to Germany to help organise the fight. Funds were collected in Russia to aid the German proletariat in its forthcoming struggle.[19] The leader of the German Communist Party, Brandler, was aware that his party was in no condition to launch such a dangerous adventure, but in face of his ebullient and experienced Russian comrades he quelled his doubts. On 23 October a half-hearted and botched attempt at a Communist rising took place in Hamburg. It was easily suppressed by the police authorities. From then on the Communist effort was to be concentrated in the two central

German states of Saxony and Thuringia, where the Land governments were headed by left-wing Social Democrats who accepted
Communist ministers into their cabinets. It was hoped to use
these states as a proletarian power base from which revolution
would spread over Germany. The Reich government in Berlin,
however, took prompt measures to scotch this threat. On 29
October, using its emergency powers, it deposed the government
in Saxony. This measure was implemented by the Reichswehr,
which also marched into Thuringia on 6 November. Opposition
in both states was overawed by an enthusiastic show of military
force. The KPD had suffered another humiliating reverse.

Such strong measures against the danger of left-wing subversion brought demands from the Social Democratic members of
Stresemann's cabinet that action should be taken to quell the far
more dangerous mutineers in Bavaria. The Social Democrats
were awkwardly divided between support for a strongly anti-
socialist Reich government, the survival of which was needed to
protect democracy, and anger over the manner in which their
party comrades in Saxony were being treated. On 2 November
they resigned from the cabinet. The SPD was not to share power
at Reich level again until 1928.[20] This Social Democratic gesture
did nothing to weaken the threat from the nationalist right in
Bavaria itself. Ever since the appointment of von Kahr as State
Commissioner in Munich the extent of Bavarian insubordination
had been growing more obvious.

The commander of the Bavarian section of the Reichswehr,
Lieutenant-General von Lossow, refused to obey instructions
from the Reichswehr Ministry and looked to von Kahr for author-
ity. Von Kahr himself was hoping for political changes in Berlin.
Neither he nor von Lossow was a Bavarian separatist. They
wanted an eventual restoration of the Wittelsbach monarchy in
Bavaria, but envisaged this as being within the framework of the
German Reich.

On 22 October the Bavarian Reichswehr took an oath of loyalty
to von Kahr's government. Two days later von Lossow explained
Bavarian policy to a gathering of staff officers, state officials and
paramilitary leaders. The Government's purpose, he said, was to
establish a new regime in Berlin – evidently by force. This would
have to take place within three weeks, but in the meantime he
urged the Patriotic Leagues to exercise discipline and restraint.[21]

The Bavarians were pinning their hopes on Nationalist groups in Berlin – and in particular on action by the head of the Reichswehr General von Seeckt. The leading Ruhr industrialist, Hugo Stinnes, a member of Stresemann's DVP, was enthusiastic for a dictatorship. He hoped it would put the clock back before November 1918, particularly in the field of labour relations.[22] Von Seeckt himself did indeed make efforts to overthrow Stresemann. He complained to Ebert that the army no longer had confidence in the Chancellor, and, when this had no effect, leaked news of his displeasure to some of Stresemann's rivals in the People's Party. Stresemann's position was shaken, but he remained in office. Von Seeckt was too cautious to do more, and the Bavarians were warned to avoid precipitate action.

Restraint was possible for von Kahr and von Lossow, but not for Hitler. He had been made leader of a union of paramilitary formations in Bavaria – the so-called *Kampfbund*. This included the most radical and impatient of the Nationalist Leagues. Hitler distrusted the official Bavarian leadership and its conservative allies in northern Germany. He rightly suspected that they were more concerned with restoring the ascendancy of the old ruling classes than with regenerating Germany along Völkisch lines. He realised that von Lossow wanted to use the Kampfbund to further his own plans, but would not give Hitler any very responsible part to play in the political developments which were expected to follow. The same suspicious attitude prevailed in the breast of General Ludendorff, whose great prestige was now attached to the Völkish wing of the nationalist movement in Bavaria.

Hitler decided he must take matters into his own hands. On the night of 8 November his SA men burst in upon a meeting at the Burgerbräukeller in Munich, where von Kahr was holding forth to a large and distinguished audience on the moral justification for dictatorship. By a mixture of bluff and threats Hitler persuaded von Kahr, von Lossow and Ludendorff to join him in establishing a new national government.

There is still some doubt about the motives of von Kahr and von Lossow at this moment. After the coup had failed they naturally claimed to have been acting under duress and to have deceived Hitler with their promises to support him. Actually it seems quite likely that they were carried away by the enthusiasm of their beer hall audience and the authority of General

Ludendorff. One of those present later compared the emotional scenes in the Burgerbräukeller with the Rütli oath in Schiller's *Wilhelm Tell*.[23] To von Kahr and von Lossow the differences between Hitler's objectives and their own were not very great in the short term – both wanted to overthrow the Berlin government. Hitler could always be restrained when the action was over. It was a dangerous mode of thought which was to reappear later with more tragic results.

The Putsch in Munich was short-lived. Its suppression was mainly due to the hostile attitude adopted by von Lossow's immediate subordinates in the Bavarian Reichswehr. The commander of the Munich garrison took steps to ensure that army units remained loyal to their officers, and that weapons were not distributed to Hitler's supporters. The State Police were ordered to secure communications centres. Von Lossow had to reverse these actions or disown Hitler. He chose the latter course. In the early hours of the morning von Kahr and von Lossow issued a statement condemning the Putsch.

On 9 November Hitler – encouraged by Ludendorff – made a last desperate bid for support by marching his paramilitary formations into the centre of Munich. The march was more of a demonstration than a military operation. Ludendorff and Hitler gambled on the reluctance of police and troops to fire on them. These were tactics similar to those used by Eisner's revolutionaries five years earlier.

At first they seemed to be succeeding; police cordons melted away and the crowds in the streets were friendly. But when the procession neared the centre of the city it passed through a narrow street leading past the former royal palace. There a more resolute detachment of Bavarian State Police barred the way. An exchange of fire took place. Hitler's neighbour in the march was mortally wounded and pulled Hitler to the ground as he fell. Others in the procession fell flat or scattered. Within minutes the demonstrators had fled and the Putsch was over.

The failure of the Putsch meant that the Republic was secure from internal subversion for several years to come. Indeed, Hitler drew the lesson that state power could only be achieved from within. Putsches were unlikely to succeed. The state of emergency was maintained throughout Germany for four months. It was administered by von Seeckt with perfect correctness. Although the Social Democrats still refused to support Stresemann as Chancellor and he was forced to resign on 23 November, a new coalition under the Centre Party leader, Wilhelm Marx, included him as Foreign Minister, a post he held until his death in 1929. He was thereby in a position to carry on the patient work of extricating Germany from her desperate international position.

The ability of Republican governments to withstand conspiratorial assaults increased the tendency among the monarchist and authoritarian opponents of the régime to make compromises with it. A year later German Nationalist ministers entered a Republican government. But popular faith in the Republican system – never very strong – had been badly, and in some cases permanently, shaken by the events of 1923. The collapse of the currency left behind it a legacy of resentment, especially among Germany's numerous lower middle class. The revaluation of the mark brought with it an acute shortage of credit, particularly damaging for farmers and small businessmen. Legal cases about debt repayments during the inflation dragged on for years and caused much bitterness. All these economic and financial difficulties were not without political effects. When the time came Hitler was to be the beneficiary.

Notes

1. Carsten, *Reichswehr*, pp. 154–5.
2. Heiber, *Die Republik von Weimar*, pp. 97–100.
3. Bullock, *Hitler*, p. 91. For details of the inflation of the mark in terms of the US dollar and of the retail price index see Feldman, *The Great Disorder*, pp. 5, 637, 643. See also Feldman, *Iron and Steel in the German Inflation, 1916–1923*, app. 1. For a discussion of the panic among the middle classes in Germany see Winkler, *Mittelstand, Demokratie und Nationalsozialismus*, pp. 76–83.
4. Feldman, *The Great Disorder*, p. 35.
5. Ibid., p. 49.
6. Kent, *Spoils of War*, p. 59, 118 ff.
7. Ibid., p. 182.
8. Feldman, *The Great Disorder*, pp. 669–70. See also Winkler, *Weimar, 1918–1933*, pp. 193–4.

9. See the figures for the percentage of unemployed trade unionists given in Appendix III, 4 of Angell, *The Recovery of Germany*, pp. 370–1. See also tables for unemployment in Germany and Hamburg respectively in Ferguson, *Paper and Iron*, pp. 123, 181.

10. Bullock, *Hitler*, pp. 91–2.

11. Angress, *Stillborn Revolution*, p. 295.

12. Ibid., pp. 359–61. Angress points out that such gains were probably not as great as some enthusiastic writers have suggested.

13. For a good discussion of the Bavarian Patriotic Leagues see Hofmann, *Der Hitlerputsch*, pp. 59–65.

14. Winkler, *Revolution*, pp. 609–10. See also Feldman, *The Great Disorder*, pp. 701–2.

15. Turner, *Stresemann*, p. 117.

16. Hofmann, *Der Hitlerputsch*, pp. 94–9. See also Deuerlein, *Der Hitlerputsch*, pp. 180–2. For Bavarian views on Stresemann's cabinet see ibid., pp. 159–61.

17. Carsten, *Reichswehr*, p. 164.

18. Ibid., p. 168. Also Gordon, *The Reichswehr*, pp. 233–4.

19. Angress, *Stillborn Revolution*, pp. 395–7, 418–19.

20. Winkler, *Revolution*, pp. 655–64.

21. Deuerlein, *Der Hitlerputsch*, pp. 257–8.

22. Winkler, *Revolution*, p. 617; Winkler, *Weimar, 1918–1933*, p. 212.

23. Hofmann, *Der Hitlerputsch*, p. 168; the observer was Professor Karl Alexander von Müller. For accounts of the events in the Burgerbräukeller see Bullock, *Hitler*, pp. 106–9, Hofmann, *Der Hitlerputsch*, pp. 150–69. Kahr's own account of the Putsch, which, although confidential, was designed to be seen by too many officials to guarantee absolute frankness, is printed in Deuerlein, *Der Hitlerputsch*, pp. 495–8. A very well-documented account is given by Gordon in his *Hitler and the Beer Hall Putsch*, although his judgements on some aspects of Weimar politics are controversial.

8 Towards Recovery

Having survived foreign occupation and internal subversion from the right and left, the Republic found its situation improving. Three important achievements marked the post-crisis era. The first, which had already been embarked upon when Hitler launched his abortive coup, was the stabilisation of the currency. The second was the Dawes Agreement, regulating Germany's reparations payments, and the third was the Locarno Treaty.

By the autumn of 1923 a new currency had become essential to Germany if serious unrest was to be avoided during the winter. For some time various schemes had been canvassed to overcome the problem. The government had to be particularly careful not to upset agricultural interests by its remedial measures, for if the farmers were dissatisfied food supplies might suffer. Hans Luther, the Food Minister, was especially insistent that urgent steps be taken to end the inflation. Largely as the result of his prompting, the Government accepted a scheme whereby a new currency should be based on land and industrial values. A loan was to be issued to the Reichsbank from a specially constituted authority, the Rentenbank. The loan was backed by a mortgage, first of all on agricultural property and then on industrial resources. The Reichsbank could issue Rentenmarks to the value of its loan holding. Rentenmarks were valued at one gold mark each. The old paper marks were to be gradually redeemed at their current value. The agrarian backing for the new currency was, of course, largely fictitious, because land is not convertible in the same way as gold. Nevertheless, since Germany lacked enough gold to launch a new bullion-backed currency, the psychological effect of the Rentenmark's paper mortgage helped to maintain its value. The restricted amount of the new currency available to the Reichsbank also prevented a slide towards inflation. Most important of all was the fact that the Government could no longer draw on unlimited currency credits from the Reichsbank but had to try to balance expenditure against income.[1]

The introduction of the new currency involved many problems and hardships. That the Rentenmark succeeded at all was largely due to the energy of Luther, who became Finance Minister at the beginning of October. Luther gave decisive support to the Rentenmark scheme and once it was under way prevented the pleas of vested interests from undermining it. He appointed a Currency Commissioner, Hjalmar Schacht, to deal with problems arising from the introduction of the new revaluation. The following summer the Rentenmark was replaced by the Reichsmark, which was to remain the German unit of currency until after the Second World War.

The stabilisation programme in Germany meant that economic life revived throughout the Reich, although dearer money caused a high level of unemployment. Fears that the Rentenmark would soon begin to be devalued proved groundless. On the other hand, the French began to experience financial troubles, and the franc to come under heavy pressure. Elections were held for the French Chamber and in May 1924 Poincaré was defeated. The new Prime Minister, Édouard Herriot, was more interested in conciliation than extortion. The French threat to Germany's integrity in the West ebbed away. It was also helpful that in January 1924 there had been a change of government in Britain, with Ramsay MacDonald taking over as leader of a Labour administration. MacDonald was more inclined to pursue a policy of conciliation towards Germany than his predecessors had been. There had therefore appeared a real chance of tackling the Republic's international and financial problems by negotiation and compromise.[2]

It was in this more favourable atmosphere that the discussion over the Dawes Plan took place. The work of an inter-Allied Committee chaired by two Americans, Charles Dawes and Owen D. Young, it approached the problem of German financial stability from a self-consciously businesslike standpoint. Wherever possible, political pitfalls were avoided. Nevertheless, the report had enormous political implications. Its major concern was to establish a scale of reparations payments which would not prevent Germany from stabilising her currency and balancing her budget.

On 9 April 1924 the committee submitted its recommendations. They were undoubtedly more practicable than any previously produced by a similar body. They involved firm

guarantees that the Germans would make regular annual payments, a controlled system of transfer which would protect
Germany's currency from threats of devaluation, and a loan
from the Western Powers to help Germany start payments and
initiate an economic recovery. If there was a weakness in the
scheme it lay in the firm economic optimism with which Dawes
and his colleagues regarded the future. Speaking of the potenti-
alities of Germany, Dawes wrote:

> The task would be hopeless if the present situation of Ger-
> many accurately reflected her potential capacity; the proceeds
> from Germany's national production could not in that case
> enable her to meet the national needs and to ensure the pay-
> ment of her foreign debts.
>
> But Germany's growing and industrious population; her
> great technical skill; the wealth of her material resources; the
> development of her agriculture along progressive lines; her
> eminence in industrial science; all these factors enable us to be
> hopeful with regard to her future production.

After referring to the large-scale renewal of plant which had
taken place in Germany after the war Dawes continued:

> Germany is therefore well equipped with resources; she pos-
> sesses the means for exploiting them on a large scale; when the
> present credit shortage has been overcome, she will be able to
> resume a favoured position in the activity of a world where
> normal conditions of exchange are restored.[3]

The success of the Dawes reparations scheme therefore
required a prosperous Germany. Indeed, the report envisaged a
continuous growth in Germany's economic strength and made
arrangements that future prosperity should benefit reparations
creditors as well as the Germans themselves. In one sense the
committee's reasoning was quite correct; Germany undoubtedly
had the physical capacity to increase production. It might perhaps have been asked whether the development of world trade
would allow her to utilise this capacity. Dawes and his colleagues
were not required to face that question, nor could they have been
expected to provide a realistic answer.

The Dawes scheme was criticised in Germany because it involved submitting to Allied controls over the central banking system and the railways. These would be supervised by committees consisting of Germans and Allied representatives. The railways were to be run for profits, part of which would go to repay a loan raised for reparations. The central bank's credit policy was to be controlled to ensure currency stability. The German government was to pledge certain revenues for the repayment of its debts, and German industry, which the Dawes Committee judged to have profited from inflation, was to bear a special debt of five thousand million marks for the benefit of Germany's reparations creditors.[4] These provisions were seen as a monstrous invasion of German sovereignty.

The German Nationalist Party campaigned against the Plan as a 'second Versailles'. But influential pressure groups within the party – agricultural and business interests and even the leaders of the Reichswehr – saw that the Plan would bring Germany great material advantages. In a crucial vote in the Reichstag on 28 August 1924 the Nationalists split on this issue and some of them voted for the implementation of the Plan, which was duly carried into effect.

By the beginning of 1925 the Nationalists were themselves represented in the cabinet – under the Chancellorship of Luther. They soon found a new target for their patriotic indignation.

The cause of their displeasure was a security pact which Stresemann was attempting to negotiate with Germany's western neighbours. This would involve a recognition of German frontiers in the West and membership of the League of Nations. The Nationalists regarded such moves as tantamount to treason. They had refused to accept the final loss of Alsace-Lorraine and demanded that the Allies must renounce what they described as the 'war-guilt lie'. As for the League of Nations, this had been bitterly unpopular in Germany ever since she had been kept out of it in 1919.

It was also feared that German relations with the Soviet Union would be damaged by entry into the League. The Russians regarded it with even more hostility than did the Germans. They feared German participation in League sanctions against Russia. The Reichswehr set its face firmly against any move which might weaken its ties with the Red Army. Stresemann managed to overcome all this opposition to his policy. To do so he relied on guile and diplomacy.

The Russians were mollified, if not entirely consoled, with a trade pact favourable to the Soviet Union and a successful German effort to interpret the Article on sanctions in the League Charter so that it was, in the words of the Russian Foreign Minister, Chicherin, 'really emasculated'.[5] The Nationalists were persuaded to stay in the German cabinet for domestic reasons – not the least of which was their desire to affect tariff policy – and by the hope that when any agreement was made public the blame for its shortcomings could be heaped on Stresemann, who would then have to resign. But Chancellor Luther, after a moment of doubtful loyalty to his Foreign Minister, decided to associate himself formally with Stresemann's policy and the Nationalist plan proved unsuccessful.[6] A conference was convened in the Swiss town of Locarno to negotiate the Western security pact.

For Luther and Stresemann it was a considerable diplomatic success. The nationalist pressures within his own country enabled Stresemann to reject French and British proposals which were unattractive to him. Hence he was able to obtain Anglo-French agreement for the interpretation of Article 16 of the League Charter in a sense which would absolve Germany from the responsibility to participate in joint action – whether economic, financial or military – against an aggressor. He was able to restrict the frontier guarantees contained in the final agreements to Germany's western boundaries with France and Belgium; the eastern frontiers were not accepted by Germany as final. He was able to restrict the most important negotiations to a charmed circle of Western nations from which France's allies in Eastern Europe – in particular the Czechs and the Poles – were excluded. This was to foreshadow events in the 1930s when the concept of a four-power consortium to settle European problems – the powers in question being Britain, France, Italy and Germany – culminated in the notorious betrayal of Czechoslovakia at Munich in September 1938. Stresemann himself expressed his satisfaction about this discomfiture of Germany's eastern neighbours when he told a delighted audience in Berlin:

Messrs Benes and Skrzynski* had to sit there in an adjoining room until we allowed them to come in. That was the position of states which had previously been so inflated in importance because they were the servants of others, and which were dropped the moment it seemed possible to make an agreement with Germany.[7]

The Locarno Agreements took the form of a Western non-aggression pact between France, Belgium and Germany, guaranteed by Italy and Great Britain. Arbitration agreements were signed between Germany and France and Belgium to ensure the peaceful settlement of future disputes. Germany concluded similar arbitration arrangements with Poland and Czechoslovakia. She did not, however, accept the finality of her frontiers with those countries. Stresemann claimed that legal opinion on the arbitration treaties held that Germany need feel no restriction on resorting to war in the East if the occasion arose.[8]

Stresemann's own motives in concluding the treaties have been the subject of much speculation – a good deal of it superfluous. Stresemann naturally presented himself to his diplomatic colleagues in the west as the champion of European rapprochement. The negotiations which culminated in the Locarno Treaties generated a good many public statements at international gatherings stressing the need for a new era of peaceful co-operation. In 1926 Stresemann himself was to be awarded the Nobel Peace Prize. After his death sections of his diaries and papers were published, and it was hardly surprising that the editors selected those which reinforced the picture of Stresemann the peacemaker, Stresemann the good European. With German defeat in the Second World War a great deal more documentary evidence became available – much of it in the files of the German Foreign Office. It became clear that, at the time when he was working for a détente in the West, Stresemann was also expressing strongly nationalist points of view over such questions as the future of Germany's eastern frontiers and the possible union with Austria. In addition, there could no longer be any

---

* Benes and Skrzynski were the Czechoslovakian and Polish representatives at Locarno. They were not allowed to participate in the major discussions. Benes was the President of Czechoslovakia in 1938.

doubt that he knew of the secret military arrangements between Berlin and Moscow. [9]

There was nothing particularly surprising in these revelations. The real difference lay in the climate of opinion before and after the Second World War. Stresemann had always been a German nationalist in the sense that he wanted to further German interests in the diplomatic sphere. His career in the war and after it had demonstrated this. He made few bones about the fact that it was German weakness, not a belief in pacific courses for their own sake, which forced him to make concessions over such matters as passive resistance in the Ruhr, reparations or the recognition of Germany's western frontier.

So far as Locarno was concerned, Stresemann believed that it would forestall a bilateral Anglo-French treaty, hasten the removal of Allied troops from the Rhineland, and create an atmosphere of détente in which Germany could rebuild her economic strength. By keeping a free hand in the east and maintaining his Russian connection, he could still hope for territorial adjustments *vis-à-vis* Poland. This does not mean that he was hypocritical in his attitude towards the Western Powers. It is unlikely that French or British statesmen really imagined that Stresemann, formerly of the Pan-German League, had been transformed into a fervent internationalist. They knew the German Foreign Minister as a tough negotiator who was well able to defend the interests of his country.

The fact was that the British and the French governments were willing to accept a *modus vivendi* with Germany, even if it did give the Reich a more favourable position than it had possessed since 1918. The cost of repressing Germany was high. Collaboration between the four Western Powers – France, Britain, Germany and Italy – might bring economic benefits to all. As for secret rearmament, Western observers were well aware that Germany had not fulfilled the Versailles disarmament clauses. They realised also that the extent of Germany's illegal rearmament could not pose a real military threat to her neighbours. Throughout the Weimar period the German army was hardly strong enough to fight the Poles, let alone wage war on France. Stresemann himself was ready to allow an increasing military power so long as the Reichswehr did not thereby jeopardise his own diplomatic manoeuvres. Despite friction with von Seeckt and his colleagues, the

Foreign Ministry was never baulked of its objectives by military obstruction.[10]

As for the League of Nations, Stresemann regarded this with no more enthusiasm than most of his countrymen. But he realised that Germany would be better able to defend her international interests from within the League than if she stayed outside it. When she was finally admitted to League membership in the autumn of 1926 he used this new platform at Geneva to air the grievances of German minorities under foreign rule – particularly those in Poland.*

The Germans had also harboured hopes that the League might be persuaded to consider more general questions affecting Germany and her former enemies. The first of these was disarmament, over which Germany demanded equality. The Western Powers must either disarm down to her level or let her rearm up to theirs. Although the League devoted itself with great assiduity to the problem of disarmament, no solution was ever found. On the surface the issue was technical; it was impossible to find a proper balance between powers of different sizes and geographical situations. Basically it was political – no German government was satisfied with Germany's restricted condition, and no French government was prepared to see the more numerous Germans achieve military equality with France.

Lastly, the German hope that Allied troop withdrawals would be more rapid after the Locarno agreements was only partly fulfilled. Although the Cologne Zone was evacuated and the Allied military control commission for the supervision of German rearmament ceased to function, Allied troops remained in the Rhineland. It was not until the summer of 1929 that their withdrawal was finally promised to the Germans, and by then the 'spirit of Locarno' was ebbing rapidly away.

German public opinion was not therefore immediately impressed with Locarno. There was a basic divergence between the German and the Anglo-French attitudes towards it. In London and Paris it was seen as the termination of a warlike period; the final establishment of European stability. Austen Chamber-

---

* Geneva was the seat of the League's headquarters. Stresemann actually showed sensible moderation in dealing with minority problems, but his successors were far less tactful.

lain, the British Foreign Secretary, described it as 'the real divid-ing line between the years of war and the years of peace'.[11]

To the Germans it was only the beginning of an era which would see the dismantling of the whole Versailles Treaty. This does not mean that the diplomats and Republican politicians in Berlin were preparing a new world war. It does not mean that Stresemann was a Nazi in striped trousers and a frock-coat. But it did mean that many Germans had still to face up to the realities of the post-war world. When these realities were compounded by a sudden economic crisis they fled into even wilder realms of fan-tasy conjured up for them by Adolf Hitler.

On the domestic front these were gloomy years for the parties of the Weimar coalition. Currency stabilisation and the Dawes Plan were not vote-catching achievements. Germany was still in the grip of economic hardship and national humiliation. Those bearing responsibility for the nation's affairs suffered for it polit-ically. Retrenchment led to cuts in jobs and services. Unemploy-ment was high, credit became expensive and taxes were raised. Farmers felt particularly aggrieved, and continued to do so throughout the Republic's short history. Agriculture was not overwhelmingly important from the economic viewpoint – it accounted for just over 16 per cent of Germany's net domestic product in the period 1925–29. Yet in 1925 30.5 per cent of the economically active population was engaged in agriculture broadly defined.[12]

During the war farmers had been subjected to a comprehensive system of state controls, and once peace was made the govern-ment was slow to remove them. It was only in the summer of 1921 that the sale of butter and milk was deregulated, for example, and the last price controls on agricultural products had only been formally abolished in June 1923. So farmers had not been able to benefit from a free market when their products were scarce. During the inflation period it was estimated that 4.5 billion marks worth of agrarian savings had been wiped out. After much of a good harvest in 1923 had been sold for worthless paper marks, farmers found themselves facing increased costs for fuel and fertiliser and severe increases in agrarian taxes, all of which had to be paid in the new hard currency. The result was that most of them became seriously indebted, a situation which was only bear-able as long as they could sell their own products at good prices.

In 1927, however, those prices began to drop, and an economic crisis struck agriculture two years before the great industrial depression engulfed Germany in 1929.[13]

The German Nationalists, who were associated with the landed interest in many parts of Northern and Eastern Germany, reaped the rewards of opposition by making substantial gains in Reichstag elections held in May 1924. The Social Democrats – who had actually left the Government in November 1923, but who were associated with republican policies – lost ground. They found themselves facing a serious rival in the competition for working-class allegiance. This was the German Communist Party, which collected 3.5 million votes – well over half the number given to the SPD. Henceforward the KPD was to be a dangerous magnet for working-class militants. It was especially attractive to the young. Its leadership presented a far more youthful and dynamic image than the ageing bureaucracy of the SPD.

Of the moderate parties, the Democrats and Stresemann's People's Party had also fared badly at the polls. But their defeat did not induce them to close ranks against extremism. Erich Koch-Weser, the new leader of the Democratic Party, spoke of the need to create a strong national middle and a national democracy,[14] but his party and Stresemann's DVP were suffering from such severe internal conflicts that no merger between them could be contemplated. In any case the DVP was more inclined to seek an arrangement with the German Nationalists, and Stresemann had not forgotten his treatment at the hands of the Democrats in the early days of the Republic. Hopes of a united liberal party opposed to socialism but loyal to the Republic were once again torpedoed.

New Reichstag elections in December 1924 scarcely changed the situation. In February the following year the Republican parties received another blow when Friedrich Ebert died. The presidential election which followed – the first popular vote for this office – brought success to Field-Marshal Paul von Hindenburg, the hero of Kaiser Wilhelm's army and an important contributor to the 'stab-in-the-back' theory.

Hindenburg's victory was not foreseen when the election campaign began. In the first round of voting he was not even a candidate. His former chief of staff, General Ludendorff, on the other hand, was persuaded by Hitler to stand for the racialist right, and received a derisory 1.1 per cent of the vote. Hitler was actually not displeased to witness the humiliation of a potential rival.[15] Since none of the Republican party politicians managed to win an overall majority in the first round of voting, the SPD and the Democrats decided to unite their forces behind the candidate of the Centre Party, Wilhelm Marx. The right-wing parties felt that only a man with geniuinely national appeal could defeat Marx, and they plumped for Hindenburg. Stresemann was dismayed at this decision, since he thought it would outrage foreign opinion. Had he pressed his objections, Hindenburg might have withdrawn, but the Foreign Minister chose to remain silent.

The field-marshal defeated Marx by a narrow margin. His cause was aided by the Communists, who persisted in running their own candidate despite the displeasure of the Comintern in Moscow. Nearly two million votes were wasted on their man, although it is not certain that they would otherwise have gone to Marx. It was also evident that there had been defections from the Democrats and Centre Party in favour of Hindenburg.[16] Lastly, the Roman Catholic Bavarian People's Party may well have affected the outcome decisively by supporting the protestant Prussian field-marshal instead of the Centre Party's candidate. This demonstrated that, in the BVP, 'even religious affiliation was over-shadowed by a deep-seated anti-socialist sentiment'.[17] Once again, Bavarian particularism had played a fateful role in the history of the Weimar republic.

The result was certainly not helpful for the Republic in the long run, although its immediate effects did not seem very dramatic. The field-marshal was greeted on his arrival in Berlin by crowds of admirers waving black, white and red flags – the colours of the old empire. Stresemann was shocked to find Hindenburg reading the the reactionary *Kreuzzeitung** when he made his first official visit to the President. But the Foreign Minister had nothing to complain of in the way business was conducted. A flurry of outraged foreign press comment – particularly in Paris – subsided when it was seen that Hindenburg's assumption of power was not accompanied by any sinister changes in German policy. Superficially his election implied a strengthening of state authority,

---

* Traditionally the newspaper of the German conservatives, especially the East Elbean landowners.

since the Presidency was now no longer an object of anti-Republican revilement except from the Nazis and the Communists.

Hindenburg's election can be seen as an attempt by the German people to flee from the responsibilities of parliamentary government back to the comforting safety of pre-war authority. Hindenburg represented order and security; commodities which the Republic had been unable to provide. The field-marshal was an old man unendowed with political talent. He was aptly described by his English biographer as 'The Wooden Titan'.[18] He accepted the Weimar Constitution and did not consciously set out to betray it. He was a great disappointment to those who had hoped to use him as a stalking horse for a monarchist restoration or some other form of dictatorship.

Yet Hindenburg never identified himself wholeheartedly with the Republic. He still felt bound by ties of loyalty to the Emperor Wilhelm II, whose irresponsible arrogance had not been diminished by his exile in Holland. The President tolerated many violently anti-Republican figures among his personal circle of friends, and although he resisted their more obviously subversive suggestions, their influence depressed and confused him. Had he possessed a more forceful personality he might have been able to win many of the more reasonable conservative elements over to positive collaboration with the new régime. As it was, his influence was largely negative; he refused to betray the Republic, but he did not rally the people to its banner.

This is not to suggest that popular support for the Republic was nowhere to be found. One of the most striking developments on the domestic scene in 1924 was the birth of a new Republican defence organisation, the *Reichsbanner Schwarz-Rot-Gold*. Despite the reluctance shown by Social Democratic leaders to encourage militant self-help among their own followers, the turbulent events of 1923 had provoked an active response among those who wished to protect German democracy.

The provincial governor of Magdeburg, a tough Social Democrat called Otto Hirsing, decided to establish a paramilitary force open to all those willing to demonstrate their loyalty in action. The Reichsbanner, as it was called, quickly mushroomed to success. Social Democratic Party locals formed the basis for its growth, but non-Socialists were also encouraged to join. Within a year the Reichsbanner could claim over a million members, and had become the most successful paramilitary formation in Germany. Its demonstrations and propaganda reached the remotest parts of the country, teaching the population to celebrate the foundation of their new Republic, honour its flag and its constitution. The Reichsbanner proved that Republicans could don uniforms, march in step and prepare to fight for their beliefs with as much enthusiasm as any Nationalist rivals.[19]

By the end of 1925 such enthusiasm did not seem misplaced. As the German economy began to revive under the impact of the Dawes Plan and as the country's international position showed obvious signs of improvement, it seemed that the Weimar Republic might be able to establish itself on a firmer foundation than had been possible in the difficult years after the revolution.

Notes

1. Schacht, *Stabilization of the Mark*. Also Luther, *Politiker ohne Partei*, pp. 156–68. For the implementation of the Rentenmark see Feldman, *The Great Disorder*, pp. 752–3.
2. Winkler, *Weimar, 1918–1933*, p. 260.
3. 'Reports of the Expert Committees appointed by the Reparations Commission, English Version', Cmd 2105, 1924 (London, HMSO, 1924), pp. 14–15, in *State Papers*, 1924, vol. XVII, pp. 844 ff.
4. Bergmann, *Reparationen*, pp. 285–9.
5. For a good account of the Russian opposition to Locarno see Freund, *Unholy Alliance*, pp. 213–44.
6. Turner, *Stresemann*, pp. 204–8, 217.
7. Stresemann's speech to the 'Landesmannschaften in Grosse-Berlin', 14 December 1925, *Akten zur deutschen auswärtigen Politik*, series B, vol. II, p. 752. Stresemann's account was exaggerated. The Czechs and the Poles signed the final protocol of the conference and were reassured by defensive agreements with France.
8. Cf. ibid. This interpretation was a very sophisticated one and did not accord with the spirit of the agreements or the wording of the preamble. But Stresemann himself was presenting the treaties to a nationalistically minded audience, and there is no reason to suppose he was particularly concerned about the military issue. On the other hand, he had been very careful not to commit Germany to an 'Eastern Locarno'. This latter possibility was most distasteful to the German

Foreign Office, which consistently resisted any suggestion of a détente in the East.
The terms of the Locarno Agreements are given in C. A. Macartney (ed.), *Survey of International Affairs 1925*, vol. II, pp. 439–52.

9. See Stresemann, *Vermächtnis;* Gatzke, *Stresemann* and 'The Stresemann Papers'; Thimme, *Stresemann.* For a good illustration of Stresemann's awareness of the Russo-German arms collaboration, see his letter to Gessler enclosing a report on a conversation about this between Trotsky and Brockdorff-Rantzau in June 1924, printed in Freund, *Unholy Alliance*, pp. 254–8.
10. Cf. Post, *The Civil–Military Fabric of Weimar Foreign Policy*, pp. 234–8.
11. Quoted in Macartney (ed.), *Survey of International Affairs 1925*, vol. II, p. 56. Kimmich, *Germany and the League of Nations*, pp. 133–7, 147–9.
12. James, *The German Slump*, p. 246. 'Agriculture' includes forestry and fishing.
13. For the continuation of wartime controls on agriculture, see ibid., p. 250, and Feldman, *The Great Disorder*, pp. 706–7. For the impact of the inflation and retrenchment policies see James, *The German Slump*, p. 253–9.
14. Jones, *German Liberalism*, p. 213.
15. Kershaw, *Hitler, 1889–1936*, pp. 268–9.
16. On the Hindenburg election see Dorpalen, *Hindenburg*, pp. 64–89; Turner, *Stresemann*, pp. 191–202.
17. Schönhoven, *Die Bayerische Volkspartei, 1924–1932* p. 126. See also Wiesemann, *Die Vorgeschichte der nationalsozialistischen Machtübernahme in Bayern, 1932/1933*, pp. 43–5.
18. Wheeler-Bennett, *Hindenburg*.
19. For an important study of the Reichsbanner see Rohe, *Reichsbanner*.

9 The Semblance of Stability: 1924–1929

In the three years which followed the Locarno Agreements Germany enjoyed internal peace and a stable relationship with foreign powers. Republican politicians were no longer under a constant threat of assassination. The number of right-wing para-military formations dwindled. The army began to show itself more amenable to civilian control. Even the German Nationalist Party, seeing no future in sterile opposition, tacitly compromised its monarchist principles in the quest for political power.

In foreign affairs the Germans achieved a modest success in the summer of 1927 when the Allies agreed to a reduction of 10 000 in their Rhineland occupation forces. At home the Reichstag managed to agree to a generous unemployment insurance law. This was a major piece of social legislation, even though it could only be self-financing if unemployment were stabilised at a relatively low level. That did not seem an unreal hope. By 1927 German production exceeded that of 1913. Foreign trade was larger in volume than before the war, although Germany's share of world markets had fallen and her import/export balance was unfavourable. Looking back on the grim situation in 1923 it seemed that Germany had experienced a remarkable economic recovery.

Superficially at least, the Republic had been granted a period of economic, political and diplomatic stability. How far had it managed to consolidate itself? In terms of electoral success there seemed real grounds for optimism. General elections held in May 1928 brought a clear victory for those parties which accepted the constitution. Extremists on the right and left gained less than 30 per cent of the votes cast. This figure included the supporters of the German Nationalist Party, which had participated in Republican cabinets and accepted – albeit with bad grace – the main lines of Stresemann's foreign policy in the post-Locarno period. The Nationalists lost thirty seats in the 1928 elections and the Social Democrats gained twenty-two. Socialist ministers entered the cabinet for the first time since 1923, and one of their number, Hermann Müller, became Reich Chancellor. President Hindenburg seemed quite willing to work loyally with the Social Democrats in his government. Indeed, he had a high opinion of Müller and compared him favourably with other Chancellors.[1]

Despite these signs of political improvement, the Republic had been unable to root itself very firmly in German society. Perhaps it was asking too much to expect it to do so in such a short space of time.

Economically the country still faced very serious problems. Its industrial and financial recovery had been deceptive in its rapidity. Although Germany seemed prosperous, the manner of achieving success had not been that envisaged by the authors of the Dawes Plan. They had intended that the German reparations burden should be sustained by a domestic tax surplus and by a favourable import/export balance. Hence Germany should really pay her way both at home and abroad. In fact, Germany's trade figures nearly always showed imports outrunning exports, while the national budget did not produce the sort of surpluses that had been hoped for. Indeed, during the years 1924-30 there was an overall deficit of nearly 1300 million Reichsmarks.[2] Hence the reparations payments made by Germany were really being financed by foreign loans. In addition, the capital needs of German industry could not find satisfaction in domestic profits or savings. Germany was still suffering from the loss of capital which had taken place during the wild post-war inflation. German industrialists were eager to re-equip their factories with new plant, but many of the funds for such enterprises had to be borrowed from abroad. The result was an unhealthy dependence on foreign capital for economic prosperity.

The Dawes scheme itself was to some extent responsible for this state of affairs. It had imposed restrictions on the German money market designed to prevent a repetition of Germany's inflation. The Reichsbank was prevented by the Dawes legislation from allowing its interest rate to drop below 5 per cent.[3] The bank itself was eager to prevent the mark slipping again. Although it had no effective power to stop private banks from lending money or borrowing it from abroad, its President, Hjalmar Schacht, was obsessed with the need to prevent Germany being dependent on foreign capital. To deter borrowing, German interest rates were therefore kept high, with the paradoxical result that the country became attractive to overseas investors. They could achieve as good or even better returns on capital lent on a short-term basis to Germany than they could from longer-term investments in their own countries. German indebtedness to foreigners rose sharply. The country even enjoyed a favourable balance of payments because of the loan funds pouring into it. But well over half of this debt was in the form of loans which could quickly be recalled if investors lost confidence in the Republic's economic prospects.[4]

Between 1926 and 1929 Germany's share of world industrial production was 2.7 per cent lower than that it had been in 1913. Her share of world exports also fell from 13.2 per cent in 1913 to 9.1 per cent in the years 1927–29. Critics of German industry have claimed that it was over-cartelised and too conservative in its attitudes, so that more modern industries were undercapitalised at the expense of older, less competitive branches. At the time businessmen claimed that wages were too high and profits too low, a view some historians have shared. This is a complicated question, about which it is unwise to generalise. But it should be remembered that Germany's industrial production and export performance exceeded those of Britain or France, and that within five years of stabilising the mark she was attaining remarkable export levels in sectors as varied as steel, chemicals, textiles and toys.[5] Nevertheless, this recovery was based on fragile foundations so far as its finances were concerned.

Lastly, it should be remembered that Germany's economic problems were to a considerable degree inherited from the Kaiser's war. To take one case in point, high levels of public spending are often pointed to as a cause of economic weakness, but much expenditure was rendered inevitable by the war. In the financial year 1929 1.35 billion Reichsmarks was spent providing pensions for war invalids and the dependents of those killed in the conflict. This was twice the amount spent on the relief of unemployment, and amounted to 18 per cent of the entire Reich government expenditure.[6]

If the Republic was economically vulnerable it had yet to develop institutions upon which it could rely unconditionally in times of crisis. The Reichswehr was a case in point. In the years

1924–28 the army certainly showed a greater willingness to collaborate with Republican politicians. Von Seeckt resigned in October 1926, and his successor General Heye was a less forceful officer. He even admitted that the army had been sometimes at fault in its relations with civilian authorities – something which would have been quite unthinkable during von Seeckt's period of office.[7]

The army made genuine efforts to improve its relations with Republican parties in the Reichstag. The Reichswehr regularised some of its clandestine payments for purposes forbidden under the Versailles Treaty. Its official budget rose by roughly 75 per cent between 1924 and 1928. Some apparently harmless items of expenditure were inflated and the surplus put to other uses. In addition, money was secretly made over to the army from other ministerial budgets, including the Reich Ministry of Transport. Previously funds set aside for confidential purposes had been known only to the army officers concerned, but by 1928 the Chancellor, the cabinet and two members of the Reichstag's budgetary committee were also informed so that awkward questions in parliament might be avoided.[8]

In December 1927 Defence Minister Gessler resigned and was replaced by General Groener, who had played such an important part in shaping the destinies of the officer corps after the November revolution.[9] A general himself, he was in a stronger position than Gessler *vis-à-vis* his military colleagues. He had no time for counter-revolutionary tendencies among his soldiers. On the other hand Groener was not a democratic general. He was willing to work with the Social Democrats, for example, because he no longer feared 'Marxism', having witnessed its impotence during the revolution. Communism now seemed to him to be the real enemy. Yet he would not tolerate socialist or pacifist criticism of the army, nor would he permit parliamentary pressure to restrict its activities. Collaboration with parliament was a one-way affair.[10]

Fundamentally the army had changed very little since 1919. The officer corps was overwhelmingly anti-Republican. Recruitment remained restricted very largely to men of nationalist or apolitical backgrounds, most of them from rural areas. At a regional level – especially in Prussia, where the Social Democrats controlled the Ministry of the Interior – relations with the civilian authorities were often strained.

Nor can it be claimed that other German institutions, such as the civil service and judiciary, developed anything approaching a Republican *esprit de corps* in these years of stability. Collaboration with the existing authorities was necessary because there was no alternative, but enthusiasm was lacking. In Germany's universities many of the students and their professors regarded the Weimar system with contempt. As the twenties wore on, so projects for the reform of the state to give it a more authoritarian form of government began to be heard. There was a general call for 'strong leadership', and this affected many political groups. By 1928 the Republic's four years of peace had not produced the impression of stability. One right-wing intellectual journal *Tat* summed up a widely-held attitude when it wrote: 'These times long for authority, they are tired of liberal ideals.'[11]

Much criticism was directed at the parliamentary system itself, and there can be no doubt that it suffered from serious defects. Most of these were due not so much to its liberal character as to the weakness of Germany's political parties.

As we have seen, these inherited a sectional or class character from the former German Empire, and attempts to widen their appeal had never been successful. The so-called Weimar Coalition of Centre, Democrats and Social Democrats had always been subject to tensions over class interest and religion. Hence the appeal of any single Republican party was necessarily limited, and there was no chance of it being entrusted with full responsibility for the nation's government.

The liberal parties, the DDP and the DVP, were divided against themselves on a number of issues. They could not unite on economic policy because, although they might have been expected to support the free market and private enterprise, they had to concern themselves about such special interest groups as civil servants or white-collar workers, to whom laisser-faire capitalism might not seem entirely attractive. At the same time they were deeply divided over constitutional issues concerning Republican institutions and democracy. When, in the autumn of 1924, some distinguished liberals, including the industrialist Carl Friedrich von Siemens, the former finance minister Eugen Schiffer and the historian Friedrich Meinecke, set up the Liberal Association (*Liberale Vereinigung*) to try to promote liberal unity, they received very little support from the DDP or the DVP.

Stresemann and his colleagues went out of their way to rebut arguments in favour of unity, claiming that liberalism and democracy were mutually exclusive concepts which had as little in common as liberalism and conservatism.[12] This illustrated an important legacy of Wilhelmine national liberalism which the DVP had inherited; a morbid fear of the masses in politics, masses whose 'tyranny' was supposed to threaten the individual. Clearly it would be difficult for many Democrats – let alone Social Democrats – to make common cause with politicians who held such beliefs. On the other hand, the right wing of the DVP was always hoping to link up with the German Nationalists (DNVP) in a 'bourgeois', and fundamentally anti-Republican, bloc. Although the Liberal Association did manage to bring Koch-Weser and Stresemann together at a large banquet for prominent liberals in February 1926, the differences between the two parties remained unbridgeable.

Even the Social Democratic Party, the most wholehearted defender of the Republican system, was torn between a desire to protect the interests of the working class and its responsibility for the safety of German democracy. In 1925 the party had adopted a new programme at its Heidelberg conference which largely returned to the hardline class-war orthodoxies of the pre-war era. This had been due to the influence of former Independents in the Party, especially Hilferding. It was part of the price paid for social democratic unity in 1922, and some on the right of the party thought it was too high. Friedrich Stampfer, the editor of the party's paper, *Vorwärts*, remarked: 'We must learn the art of *winning majorities*, keeping them and harnessing them to our political and economic purposes....'.[13]

Unfortunately such pragmatism was not consistently supported, largely because too many of the party faithful clung to Marxist doctrines of class conflict. When Paul Lobe, the Socialist Reichstag President (speaker), wrote in May 1927 that the real issue was not 'Republic versus monarchy' but 'capitalism versus socialism', he was stressing the divisions between Social Democracy and the bourgeois liberal parties.[14] Yet many of his colleagues, especially those with ministerial experience like the Prussian Premier, Otto Braun, believed that Social Democrats should do all they could to share administrative power so that the Republic could be governed by those who were emotionally attached to it.

There is nothing unusual, or particularly disgraceful, about the expression of material interests through political parties. But such sectional objectives cannot become the overriding concern of political leadership if government is to work effectively. As it was, the compromises and bargaining between coalition groups necessary before a government could hope to obtain parliamentary support made consistent policies on major issues difficult to achieve unless ministers treated parliament as of secondary importance. Instead of the Republican parties forming a united front when faced with critical problems, they often simply agreed to differ, leaving responsibility to be shouldered by their ministerial colleagues.

In the middle years of Republican development such an arrangement put Reich Chancellors in a very weak position *vis-à-vis* the coalition parties, since they had to agree to a series of concessions in order to hold their governments together at all. The support given to ministries by parliament was often tepid in the extreme. Although it was envisaged in the constitution that cabinets should command the confidence of a Reichstag majority, only two out of five were given a formal vote of confidence between 1924 and 1928. Two of the others received what was described as a 'declaration of acceptance' and the third had to make do with a statement that the Reichstag 'took note' of its existence.[15]

Under these circumstances it was not surprising that the gulf between the Reichstag and ministerial leaders grew wider, that the influence of the President became more important, and that the successes of government were attributed not so much to political parties, as to civil servants and to 'expert' ministers.

The weaknesses in the party system here described did not necessarily mean that Germany's parliamentary system was doomed to failure. Had the country been vouchsafed a longer period of economic and international stability, it is possible that more effective forms of parliamentary co-operation might have been found. But this is a matter for speculation. What is clear is that, even during an apparently calm interlude, the relationship between Reichstag parties, ministers and President was not developing in a manner designed to strengthen those forces in the

State which were loyal to the Republic. The stature of parliamentary institutions was being diminished in the public mind.

In the summer of 1928 such a forecast of doom for the parliamentary system would have seemed pessimistic. With the appearance of a Social Democratic Chancellor, Hermann Müller, Republican fortunes seemed to be on an upward curve. But the elections of that year had actually brought no real improvement in the parliamentary situation. The new Chancellor lacked the qualities to inspire his followers or to make a great public impact as a national leader. The Social Democratic Prime Minister of Prussia, Otto Braun, might have been a better choice. A decisive man, with a clear commitment to parliamentary democracy, he had little time for those on the left of the SPD who preferred Marxist rhetoric to the responsibilities of government. Had he been able to combine the offices of Prussian premier and Reich Chancellor he would have enjoyed a very powerful position, especially since the SPD had just made heartening gains in the Prussian Landtag elections. But the complexities of the Weimar party system would have caused problems at both levels. Braun did not want Stresemann's DVP in his Prussian coalition; the People's Party was pressing to gain entry. Relationships between the Catholic Centre and the DVP were also very poor at this time owing to the failure of attempts to achieve a *Konkordat* between the Reich and the Vatican, a failure the Centre blamed largely on the DVP. Then there was the suspicion felt in other German Länder towards Prussia and the centralising tendencies favoured by the SPD. Lastly, Braun was no friend of lavish military expenditure, and would not have been well received by the Reichswehr.

In any case, he was unpopular with left-wing colleagues in his own party, and even middle-of-the-road social democrats thought he would provoke conflict within the SPD. For them, the issue of collaboration with 'bourgeois' parties was a tactical question and not a fundamental matter of principle. Braun refused to be considered as leader of a national government. The respectable but ineffective Hermann Müller was appointed Reich Chancellor.[16]

The fact that president Hindenburg regarded Müller as his best Chancellor itself illustrates the strengths and weaknesses of the man. He was diplomatic and conscientious, but lacked the power of personality to bend others to his will. Within the SPD he was a conciliator, not a crusader. This was going to be unfortunate at a time when the party needed decisive leadership to hold it to its task of defending parliamentary government against growing threats from the left and right. Müller had to take office without firm pledges of support from a parliamentary majority, even though his ministry included men from all the major Republican parties. He was soon in the humiliating position of being forced to vote against the policy of his own cabinet by order of his party's Reichstag delegation. This occurred because the Government felt unable to honour a Socialist election pledge that the military budget would be cut; in particular, a controversial scheme to build armoured cruisers for the navy was allowed to go ahead by the government even though the SPD had waged a fierce election campaign against it.[17]

There were other dark spots on the horizon. The elections had been a severe blow to the German Nationalists, who were once again forced into opposition. There had always been conflicts between those in the Nationalist Party who wanted to concentrate on attacking the Republic, and those who were more interested in influencing the conduct of the government – particularly in economic affairs. After failure at the elections, the intransigent elements gained the upper hand. They were personified in the figure of Alfred Hugenberg, an industrialist turned newspaper proprietor. His views on the political course to be followed by the DNVP had already been summed up the previous year in a letter to von Westarp, when he remarked that no Nationalist could adapt himself to the Republican system. One who did, he claimed, 'becomes a genuine parliamentarian, and that is the same as a German Democrat...a cripple in his heart'.[18] Hugenberg refused to be a 'cripple'. He wanted a united, disciplined party, absolutely loyal to its leader. Not surprisingly, he felt himself called to exercise this leadership, and he had the means to obtain it.

In the autumn of 1928 the Nationalist Party was demoralised and short of funds. Hugenberg offered it financial aid and the propaganda machine which lay to hand in his own newspaper empire. The party felt it had little choice and, in any case, many welcomed a swing to the right. The former leader, Count von Westarp, had to yield, and Hugenberg took over. The policy of the DNVP now became one of strident and unrestrained opposition to the Republic.

The situation on the right of the political spectrum was even worse than it looked on the surface. The inflation and measures of retrenchment which had followed it had embittered many of the provincial German middle classes, especially farmers, small businessmen, self-employed craftsmen and others who felt themselves being ground down between the rapacity of big business and the power of trade unions. A substantial proportion of such people turned their backs on the established liberal or conservative politicians and began to vote for smaller, special interest parties, some of which were organised on a regional basis. Even between 1924 and 1928 the liberal parties and the DNVP had been losing support to such groups in Land elections. The multiplicity and contradictory aims of these groups illustrated the dangerous fragmentation which had occurred within Germany's respectable middle class. One party was established to demand the revalorisation of debts which had lost their value in the inflation. Others demanded cheap credit for farmers and protection for small shopkeepers against department stores. Anti-Semitism was either covert or openly expressed. The established parliamentary system was usually portrayed as corrupt, ruthless and incompetent.[19] The elections of 1928 were a high point of success for these smaller parties at Reich level. They achieved nearly fifteen per cent of the vote – more than the DNVP or the two liberal parties combined.

The small parties – the most noteworthy of which were the Economics Party (*Wirtschaftspartei*) and two farmers' parties – could not themselves pose a threat to the republic, but they were helping to break up the constituency which might otherwise have supported broadly-based 'people's parties' within the Republican system. They added to the numbers of those who rejected Weimar, even if they were not yet sure what to put in its place.

Most of these political disruptions were occurring amongst the protestant middle classes, but the Roman Catholic minority was not wholeheartedly loyal to the parliamentary system of Weimar either. The Bavarian People's Party still hankered after its own authoritarian form of particularism. Even the Centre Party, a bulwark of republican administrations in Reich and Prussia, was moving to the right. At the end of 1928 a change took place in its leadership. Marx, a former candidate for the Presidency who had headed more than one Reich coalition, retired. A Roman Catholic priest, prelate Kaas, was elected leader by a narrow majority. Kaas, who had close links with the Vatican, was less interested in political collaboration with Republican parties than in the defence of his religion. On the whole he found conservative social groups, especially those associated with the maintenance of law and order, preferable to atheist Social Democrats or free-thinking liberals. Colourless and an incompetent administrator, he was an unhappy choice for such an important political post at a crucial period in the Republic's history.[20] The Centre Party's parliamentary delegation came under the direction of a young ex-officer and financial expert, Heinrich Brüning. He saw himself as representing the 'front soldier' generation of 1914–18. He regarded the November revolution as a disaster, and was a staunch monarchist, although he did not necessarily advocate the restoration of Wilhelm II. These developments, within a party which had always been one of Weimar's most constant political supports, were to have important consequences.

The year 1928 did, however, seem to bring with it the prospect of further progress on the reparations question. In February 1929 a committee of experts – this time including Germans – met to discuss a final plan for reparations. It was headed by Owen Young, formerly Vice-Chairman of the Dawes Committee. After some heated negotiations, a Plan was produced whereby Germany would pay reparations until 1988. This suited the Americans and the French because 1988 was also the year in which France would complete repayment of war debts to the USA. Germany's annual payments would rise from 1.7 thousand million marks in 1930 to 2.4 thousand million in 1966. After that they would diminish. In return, Germany was to be financially independent. Controls over her railways and banking system were dropped. She was no longer to enjoy the protection of an Allied agent in the field of transfer. On the other hand, some provision was made for the postponement of one-third of any given annuity in case of emergency, and another third could always be paid in kind. As with the Dawes Plan, the Young scheme – put into its final form at the end of August 1929[21] – presupposed a period of general economic growth and stability. By the summer of 1929 signs were already apparent that such optimistic forecasts were unwarranted. Unemployment remained ominously high, and investment was falling.

In any case, the scheme aroused furious opposition from the German Nationalists. They felt that it set the seal on Germany's defeat. It seemed to mortgage the future for generations, and by establishing a final settlement, it would undermine the German will to destroy the Versailles Treaty. Even the promise given to Stresemann by the French at the end of August 1929 that the Rhineland would be evacuated in 1930 – five years ahead of schedule – did nothing to dampen their fury. It was not the terms but the whole concept of a settlement which they rejected.

Alfred Hugenberg eagerly took the lead in opposing the Young Plan. He coupled his assault on it with a campaign against the 'war guilt lie' and the whole Republican system. In July 1929 a committee was established to organise a right-wing front against the Plan. In it were represented Hugenberg's Nationalist Party, the Stahlhelm, the Pan-German League and Hitler's Nazi Party. The latter group was an unusual ally to be recruited into what was otherwise a socially conservative and backward-looking movement. But Hugenberg found Hitler's unrestrained assaults on the Weimar system attractive, and he thought that his dynamic oratory, together with the youth and enthusiasm present in the Nazi Party, would materially assist the Nationalist cause. Hugenberg, like others of his background and political persuasion, saw Hitler as a 'drummer' who would whip up popular support for a campaign controlled by his social superiors. It was a grievous miscalculation.

Hitler benefited greatly from the alliance; Hugenberg not at all. By association with the German Nationalists and their friends, the Nazis gained an aura of respectability they had lacked before. Even more important was the publicity given them by the Hugenberg press, which was far more widely read than the miserably unsuccessful Nazi papers. Hitler also came into contact with men of wealth and influence who could be of great material help to his party.

Hugenberg, on the other hand, simply increased the tensions within his own following which had already been growing as the result of his new tactics within the DNVP. The *Führerprinzip**

* Literally, 'leadership principle'.

demanded complete obedience to the leader's authority. Many local organisations, as well as some Reichstag members, were loath to submit themselves in this way and the alliance with Hitler aroused even more discontent among moderate sections of the Nationalist Party.

The campaign against the Young Plan culminated in December 1929 with a plebiscite which registered 5.8 million votes in favour of Hugenberg's anti-Young proposals. This was well short of the 21 million needed for success, but the campaign had ensured that the Young Plan was received in Germany, not as a triumph of Republican diplomacy, but as at best an expedient, at worst a national humiliation.[22]

Indeed, there were good reasons for nervousness about Germany's economic future if the Plan was implemented. The Plan had been accepted in principle at a conference in The Hague in August 1929, but it was not finally signed by President Hindenburg until the following spring. During the intervening months there had been a catastrophic change in the country's economic prospects. The optimistic assumptions which underlay the terms of the Plan were no longer compatible with reality. Hopes that somehow the boom of the previous two years might return were completely shattered by the Wall Street stock market crash in October 1929. Its impact on the Germans was bound to be disastrous. Loss of confidence engendered by the slump in America meant that surplus funds were no longer available for investment in Germany.

Even before the slump in America the German stock market had been declining. Unemployment had risen to an average of nearly two million in 1929. The Government was divided over measures to raise revenue.

On the issue of unemployment the German People's Party and the Social Democrats were naturally inclined to opposite points of view. Employers blamed the recession on high wages and high taxes; the trade unions argued that real wages were still low and that industrial profits should be ploughed back into industry. The unemployment insurance scheme set up in 1927 had placed a heavy burden on the State. It had not been assumed that unemployment would rise, and contributions were thus not high enough to meet the benefits which had to be paid out. The employers and their allies – especially the German People's

Party – thought that the burden ought to fall on those receiving benefits, while the trade unions fought for larger contributions from industry.

The People's Party itself had moved strongly to the right in 1929, a tendency that had been aided by Stresemann's failing health. Worn down by a kidney disease, he died on 3 October 1929. This was a severe blow for the Republic, but it is by no means clear that Stresemann could have kept his party from breaking with the Social Democrats even had he lived.[23] For their part, the Social Democrats showed little realisation of the nature of the crisis which faced them. They put loyalty to their class before loyalty to the Republican coalition.

The wrangling within the cabinet added strength to those in German public life who were demanding reform of the entire Weimar system. The cry for strong leadership grew more insistent. It found receptive ears in the Bendlerstrasse, where Defence Minister Groener and his chief political adviser, General von Schleicher, had decided that Müller's government would have to go. They wanted a cabinet which could be relied upon to protect the Reichswehr's interests in a time of crisis. They wanted to see the moderate element in the German Nationalist Party brought back into the Government at the expense of the Social Democrats. Above all, they envisaged a government which would not have to rely on the constantly shifting forces in the Reichstag. Instead, the emergency powers of the President would be invoked to impose ministerial authority on the nation.[24]

The final conflict came over financial policy. The Social Democrats and the People's Party were at loggerheads. The former were determined that the burden of sacrifice in a critical situation should not fall on the unemployed, whose dole payments were an obvious target for administrative economy. Ministers of both parties would have been ready for a compromise; their Reichstag colleagues preferred to make a break. An attempt by Chancellor Müller to enlist presidential aid was rejected by Hindenburg.[25] On 27 March 1930 Müller resigned. No other government ruled Germany on the basis of a parliamentary majority until Hitler took power with the intention of destroying German democracy.

Müller's fall has sometimes been seen as the termination of democratic government in Germany, and 27 March 1930 as the date on which the Republic really expired.[26] This might seem an unduly fatalistic view. There was nothing unusual in the appearance of a minority government, and the use of presidential decrees during an emergency had respectable precedents.[27] There were certainly strong tendencies among the non-socialist parties in favour of structural reforms in Germany which would strengthen the executive against parliament, and it was natural that at a time of crisis there should be a widespread yearning for stability. But this was far from being a rejection of constitutional government. None of those who played a part in engineering the fall of Müller's cabinet could have had any idea that their action would help to bring about the rise of Adolf Hitler.

In the spring of 1930 the Nazis did not seem a very serious danger, even though their party had sprung into prominence during the campaign against the Young Plan. They only held twelve seats in the Reichstag. As a bogey they could not be used to frighten politicians. The Communist Party, on the other hand, looked more formidable, especially to the Social Democrats, who were its main rivals for working-class support. Since 1928 the Communists, now largely controlled from Moscow, had been following a line of violent hostility towards the Social Democrats, dubbing them 'social fascists'. Unemployment naturally seemed to work in favour of the Communists. Many in the SPD felt that unless their party stopped seeing itself as a pillar of the Government, and began to act as a representative of the working class, it would lose its mass support. The threat from the right did not seem very frightening. Hugenberg's leadership was wrecking the German Nationalist Party; Hitler was still regarded with contempt.

On the right General von Schleicher believed that his intrigues would strengthen conservative forces in Germany while isolating the Hugenberg wing of the German Nationalist Party. The non-socialist parties in the coalition had become less and less happy about collaboration with 'Marxists', and they had no reason to feel that union to save democracy was imperative. The Weimar 'system' was judged to have failed. It was thought that a strong government based on presidential power would be needed to steer Germany through the crisis. This did not necessarily imply the end of constitutional government. Brüning, the new chancellor, was also no dictator. Yet he was no friend of Republican democracy either. He had tried hard to hammer out a compromise between the SPD and the People's Party, and it was not his fault that the Social Democrats, egged on by the trade unions, had rejected it. Nevertheless, once in power, he was determined to provide firm government which would strengthen the power of the executive in the Reich. He had formerly been willing to collaborate with the Social Democrats. Now he had to form a cabinet without them. His government included all the other parties of the former coalition, and representatives of some splinter parties on the right. Nevertheless, without the SPD the Government possessed no parliamentary majority.

In the summer of 1930 Brüning made it clear that he would press through a programme of financial retrenchment by the use of presidential decrees if necessary. Rejection by the Reichstag would be answered by a dissolution. The Social Democrats, who did not wish to face elections at that moment, would have been willing to make a compromise agreement with Brüning, but this would have endangered his new coalition. In any case, the real forces behind the new Chancellor – the President and the army – would not have tolerated such a shift to the left. Doubtless the Social Democrats erred in not paying enough attention to ominous nazi gains in Saxony's Land elections in June 1930, but they felt themselves to be in opposition to a conservatively inclined government and saw no reason to give way.[28]

Brüning pressed on with his programme, suffered defeat in the Reichstag as the result of Social Democratic opposition, and dissolved parliament. In September 1930, Germany faced a general election two years earlier than would normally have been the case. It was an election which brought small comfort to Brüning – his government parties could barely hold their own. But it was a triumph for another young German leader. Adolf Hitler's Nazis returned 107 members to the Reichstag. National Socialism was now a political force which could not be ignored.

Notes

1. Dorpalen, *Hindenburg*, p. 143.
2. The official figure was RM 1284 million. See Luke, *Stabilisierung*, p. 92.
3. Born, *Bankenkrise*, pp. 29–30.

4. Ibid., p. 18.

5. James, *The German Slump*, p. 122; Peukert, *The Weimar Republic*, p. 197; Mommsen, *Weimar Democracy*, pp. 298–30. For a discussion of the complexities of Germany's industrial economy in this period see James, *The German Slump*, ch. IV, pp. 111–61.

6. Bessel, *Germany after the First World War*, p. 276.

7. Carsten, *Reichswehr*, p. 267.

8. Ibid., pp. 273–5.

9. Ibid., pp. 24 ff.

10. Ibid., pp. 290–6.

11. Curt Hölzel, *Tat*, XX (1928), quoted in Dorpalen, *Hindenburg*, p. 164.

12. Jones, *German Liberalism*, pp. 232, 273.

13. Winkler, *Der Schein der Normalität*, p. 322.

14. Dorpalen, *Hindenburg*, p. 119.

15. Stürmer, 'Probleme der parlamentarischen Mehrheitsbildung in der Stabilisierungsphase der Weimarer Republik', p. 80. See also his chapter 'Parliamentary Government in Weimar Germany, 1924–1928', in Nicholls and Matthias, *German Democracy and the Triumph of Hitler*, pp. 59–77.

16. Schulze, *Otto Braun*, pp. 539–56, also Winkler, *Der Schein der Normalität*, pp. 529–38.

17. Winkler, *Weimar, 1918–1933*, pp. 339–40.

18. Quoted by Chanady in 'The Disintegration of the German National People's Party, 1924–1930', p. 81. The entire article, pp. 65–91, is illuminating on the tragic development of the German Nationalist Party at the end of the Republican era. See also Hiller von Gaertringen, 'Die Deutschnationale Volkspartei', in Morsey and Matthias (eds), *Das Ende der Parteien*, pp. 543–56.

19. The Economics Party did *not* want revalorisation of debt. The Revalorization and Construction Party (*Aufwertungs and Aufbaupartei*) and the People's Justice Party (*Volksrecht-Partei*), founded in 1926, favoured that. For the issue of smaller parties and political fragmentation see T. Childers, 'Interest and Ideology: Anti-system politics in the Era of Stabilization, 1924–1928', in Feldman (ed.), *Die Nachwirkungen der Inflation auf die Deutsche Geschichte, 1924–1933* pp. 1–19, and Jones, *German Liberalism*, pp. 235–7, 258–65, 302–3.

20. Ruppert, *Im Dienst am Staat von Weimar*, p. 356.

21. With some modifications owing to British opposition, Germany had to guarantee payment of a rather large part of the annuities unconditionally, and had to agree to pay part of the Allies' occupation costs. These did not, in any case, last very long. For a full discussion of the negotiation of the Young Plan see Kent, *Spoils of War*, pp. 268–9, 278–300.

22. See Bullock, *Hitler*, pp. 147–9; Bracher, *Auflösung*, pp. 290–1, 316–22.

23. For Stresemann's difficulties with his party in 1929, see Turner, *Stresemann*, pp. 250–1, 267.

24. For accounts of the crisis in the early months of 1930 see Bracher, *Auflösung*, pp. 287–389; Conze and Raupach, *Staats- und Wirtschaftskrise*, pp. 176 ff; Dorpalen, *Hindenburg*, pp. 163–78; Wheeler-Bennett, *Hindenburg*, pp. 336–49. The latter account was based on personal acquaintance with and information from many of the leading participants in the crisis. Although in some minor particulars it has been superseded by time, its main interpretations have been fully borne out by subsequent research.

25. Dorpalen, *Hindenburg*, pp. 175–6.

26. Heiber, *Die Republik von Weimar*, p. 218. See also Rosenberg, *A History of the German Republic*, pp. 300 ff., in which the Brüning era is described as the beginning of the triumph of counter-revolution.

27. In November–December 1923, for example.

28. See below, p. 179.

10 The End of the Republic

What of Hitler in the years of stability? He had experienced imprisonment and a return to political obscurity. But he had not been deflected from his purpose. His years in the wilderness had been well spent, building up the party machine which was to carry him to power.

During his trial for high treason at Munich in April 1924 he was allowed by nationally-minded Bavarian judges to launch a fierce attack on the whole Republican system. He did not attempt to excuse his role in the Munich Putsch. On the contrary, he gloried in it. His more respectable collaborators in the conflict with Berlin – von Kahr, von Lossow and von Seisser – were called as witnesses for the prosecution, and had to pretend that they were not responsible for what had happened. By contrast Hitler appeared as a fearless, honest leader willing to take the consequences for his actions:

'I alone bear the responsibility', he boasted, 'but I am not a criminal because of that. If today I stand here as a revolutionary, it is as a revolutionary against the revolution. There is no such thing as High Treason against the traitors of 1918.'[1] This brave stand made his former colleagues in the conspiracy look wretched indeed, and it was far more impressive than the behaviour of the leaders of the Kapp Putsch in 1920.

Hitler was sentenced to five years' imprisonment – the minimum possible for the charge on which he had been arraigned. Even then it was made clear that he would be released well before the end of his sentence. He was incarcerated at Landsberg, a small town west of Munich. His treatment was generous in the extreme; very different from the harsh conditions imposed on those Socialists and Communists who had been tried after the crushing of the Munich Soviet five years earlier.

It was in prison that Hitler dictated *Mein Kampf*. This book – part autobiography and part political treatise – was one of Hitler's main sources of personal income in the lean years which followed the Putsch. After his rise to political prominence in 1930 it became a best-seller. Max Amann, Hitler's business manager, was the publisher of the book, and credit with him served as Hitler's only bank account. Amann was to be well rewarded. In the Third Reich his Nazi publishing house came to control a lion's share of the German press.[2]

Mein Kampf was a long, rambling and badly written book which demonstrated that Hitler's gifts as an orator could not easily be turned to literary purposes. It contained many errors of punctuation, style and grammar which were only gradually eliminated in later editions. Changes in substance, however, were less noticeable and this bore witness to the relative consistency of Hitler's thought. In only one particular did he make any serious modification. A reference to 'Germanic Democracy' in the organisation of the Nazi Party was deleted, and replaced with a passage stressing the need for unconditional obedience to the Leader. This too was perfectly in keeping with Hitler's political behaviour from the very beginning of his career.[3]

Generally speaking the book mirrored Hitler's character and fundamental attitudes faithfully enough. His belief in the right of the strong to dominate the weak, his violent racialism, his fascination with the techniques of mass manipulation and his contempt for the masses themselves, all found lengthy – if unconvincing – expression.

He was released from prison in time for Christmas 1924. The Nazi Party was in a bad state after his absence, partly because he had deliberately refrained from appointing an effective deputy. Rivalries had appeared between different personalities and there were ideological conflicts within the Nazi movement. One of the most able and energetic Bavarian leaders, Gregor Strasser, had been conducting a successful campaign to build up the party's strength in north Germany. Working-class elements were more strongly represented in the North German Nazi movement than in Bavaria. North Germans were suspicious of the Roman Catholic South and resented the dictatorial attitude of the party headquarters in Munich. They disliked some of the more disreputable figures who seemed to be influential there, such as Hermann Esser and Julius Streicher.

By the beginning of 1926 these frictions had been compounded by arguments over policy. Some of the North German Nazis wanted more open attacks on capitalism and rejected parliamentary activity. They pressed for participation in the campaign being organised by Communists and Social Democrats to dispossess the former German royal houses. Hitler would have none of this. Although originally opposed to parliamentary tactics, he had decided that the party must keep to the paths of legality if it was to survive. He had no interest in social revolution for its own sake, and realised that such radical programmes would simply frighten the propertied classes. There followed a confrontation in which Hitler was victorious in every respect.

In February 1926 Strasser and his friends capitulated, being consoled with some changes in the personnel at party headquarters. One of Strasser's young sympathisers, an ambitious orator called Josef Goebbels, was completely won over to Hitler. He was later sent to Berlin to offset the influence of Strasserites there.

Hitler's victory ensured that the Nazi movement remained true to its Bavarian origin in both its ideology and its organisation. At a party congress in May 1926 its programme was declared immutable. This helped to muffle theoretical discussions which might deflect the party from its true purpose, the seizure of power.[4]

The next few years were difficult ones. Political stability and economic recovery were no help to Hitler's party, and in the Reichstag elections of 1928 it only won twelve seats. It was still most strongly supported in Bavaria – especially in the Protestant Franconian province, where the Nazis received over 8 per cent of the poll. But this was a very weak performance compared with that of the ruling Bavarian People's Party, and the Bavarian Social Democrats fared much better than the Nazis. The party seemed on its way to permanent obscurity.

Nevertheless, it possessed some advantages. The Nazis in the Reichstag had previously belonged to a heterogenous racialist grouping. Now they formed a disciplined party, totally loyal to Hitler. There was no rival to him on the extreme *Völkisch* wing of the political spectrum. His party was young – its age structure compared very favourably in this respect with all parties except the Communists. It was apparently classless. It had never been compromised by exercising power in the Republic, nor was it associated with monarchism. The Nazis could attack 'reaction' in their speeches with as much verve as when they castigated the Jews or the Marxists. Unlike the Communists they did not threaten property, nor were they controlled by a foreign power. On the contrary, a strident nationalism was a fundamental element in their appeal.

After 1928 this appeal began to find a more sympathetic hearing throughout Germany. The self-evident weaknesses in the parliamentary system damaged the authority of the Republican State. The defeat of the German National People's Party, and the subsequent divisions within it, made Hitler's movement seem at once both respectable and more effective. Above all, the growth in unemployment and economic uncertainty led to a radicalisation of public attitudes towards politics. Hitler was the most obvious beneficiary of Germany's new troubles.

As we have seen, his first great political opportunity came with the campaign against the Young Plan, when his alliance with Hugenberg's group enabled him to obtain publicity in the Nationalist press and to make contact with men of wealth and social position. The result of such contacts, and of a growth in party membership, was reflected in the new affluence of Hitler's party in Munich, where the Nazis moved into more imposing premises – the 'Brown House'. Money was also available for propaganda and the expansion of the SA.

The Nazis' radical propaganda methods made it possible for them to raise money from their own supporters. They did not confine their activities to election periods, but continued campaigning as hard as they could, regarding parliamentary elections simply as high points in a propaganda campaign against the Republican system. Nazi meetings were often held in provincial towns, where political activity was a rarity. They were noisy, exciting affairs which aroused a great deal of local interest. Those attending often had to pay an entrance fee, and there were cash collections carried out by the SA. Unlike the poorly-organised 'middle-class' parties of the right, the Nazis were able to tap their own activists and supporters for money, and were therefore less dependent on business interests than their apparently more respectable rivals.[5]

By the autumn of 1930 the Nazis were ready for greater triumphs. Their membership was rising; their finances in a healthier state than ever before. At local levels, the older liberal parties and smaller special interest groups no longer carried conviction with disenchanted citizenry eager for change. Gradually, opinion-forming members of provincial communities moved over to the Nazis in substantial numbers.[6] The parties of the right did not react sharply or speedily enough to this development. Often their newspapers treated the Nazis as well-meaning if boorish allies rather than as a danger to themselves, even though the Nazis were clearly contemptuous of their rivals. Obsessed with the desire to defeat 'Marxism' and Republican democracy, the parties of the right overlooked the threat from Hitler.

The Nazis organised special sections to appeal to particular interest groups – students, lawyers, doctors, teachers, self-employed craftsmen and small businessmen. They also made a concerted attempt to woo the German farmer, whose economic situation was becoming increasingly desperate. From the end of 1927 the NSDAP had begun to switch its main efforts from larger towns to the provinces and rural areas where discontent was rife and its activism could make a bigger impact. Then, in March 1930, Walther Darré, a racialist with a romantic vision of the peasantry as the backbone of the German Nordic *Volk*, published a Nazi agrarian programme. The Nazis told the farmers what they wanted to hear; that they represented a way of life which should be preserved, no matter what the economic situation. Rural life was morally superior to urban life and should be protected from the vicissitudes of a market economy.

In September 1930, armed with this message of hope to the farming community, benefiting from the newly radical atmosphere created by the slump and harping on national resentments which became stronger as Germany's domestic situation grew more hopeless, the Nazis won a resounding triumph at the polls. With over 18 per cent of the vote and 107 seats in the Reichstag they were the second largest party in Germany. The Social Democrats remained in first place, but on their left the Communists had also made big gains. The Centre Party had held its position, but all the other Republican groups had fared very badly. Hugenberg's DNVP had lost over two million votes – almost half its previous total – and its representation in parliament fell from 73 to 41. His Nationalists were now in a position of inferiority *vis-à-vis* Hitler's Nazis in the anti-Republican right.

The election showed that the Nazis had broken out of their older regional boundaries and had gained support throughout the country. In particular, it was noticeable that in those places where there had been most votes cast in the anti-Young referendum the Nazis produced the best election results some nine months later. In the eastern and northern areas of Germany as well as in Franconia, a mainly protestant province of Bavaria, they polled heavily. Schleswig-Holstein, a region of small farmers whose security was threatened by indebtedness and foreign competition, gave them their best result, with 27 per cent of the total vote.[7] The association with Hugenberg's anti-Young campaign and the appeal to the farmers had brought rich rewards. The Nazis also benefited from increased participation in elections provoked by the atmosphere of crisis. Together with an increase in the size of the electorate, this meant that four million more votes were cast in 1930 than in 1928. A high percentage of these went to the Nazis.

Chancellor Brüning faced a difficult situation after the September elections. His hopes of a Centre-Right victory were dashed, and it was clear that the new Reichstag would be even more difficult to work with than the old one. On the other hand, the two main opposition parties in the previous parliament – the Social Democrats and the German Nationalists – had fared much worse at the polls than Brüning's own coalition group. Arrangements with them seemed a real possibility.

This hope was justified in the case of the Social Democrats. The dramatic Nazi gains in the elections had come to them as a shocking surprise. They reacted with a sharpness which verged on panic. Whereas before the election they had seen German politics as an economic struggle between rich and poor, they now realised that the whole structure of their parliamentary Republic was in jeopardy. One result of this anxiety was a revival of enthusiasm for the Reichsbanner, which had tended to lose its militancy after the 1928 elections. Prominent Social Democrats now announced their adherence to it, and the Reichsbanner as a whole prepared to wage a much more vigorous battle against Hitler's SA.[8] Some leaders of the SPD wanted to make common cause with Brüning in the Government. Support for such a move came from industrial and banking circles, where it was feared that the extremist gains in the elections would damage Germany's international standing. But no coalition resulted.

Brüning could not move to the left without encountering the opposition of the President and the Reichswehr. Coalition with the Social Democrats would also have made collaboration with the

People's Party and the moderate Nationalist groups very difficult. In any case, Brüning was able to win the tacit support of the Social Democrats without taking them into his government. Their leaders agreed not to overthrow him in the Reichstag, and this meant that he could continue to rule by emergency decree without parliament intervening against him.[9]

There is, however, little evidence that Brüning had any intention of seeking coalition with the Social Democrats. His hopes rested on an accommodation with the right, which he needed to retain the confidence of Hindenburg and the army. Brüning's medium-term objective was to undermine the Versailles Treaty, especially its reparations and disarmament clauses. Ultimately he also hoped to be able to reform the German constititution to reduce the power of the Reichstag and the *Länder vis-à-vis* the executive, and possibly even to restore the monarchy, although not Wilhelm II.[10] To attain his foreign policy goals, Brüning was prepared to allow the German people to sustain considerable economic hardship. He felt it would be better that the Weimar system should take the odium for harsh measures which were needed to retrench the economy and force Germany's creditors – the former victor powers – to make concessions.[11] If the Germans tightened their belts and held firm, Brüning hoped to be able to dismantle the Versailles Treaty; in particular, reparations should be abolished. The ideal way of achieving all this would be by an enabling law such as the ones which had been used by Stresemann and Luther to help stabilise the mark. To achieve this Brüning would have to broaden the basis of his government's support.

He therefore continued to try to woo anti-Republican nationalists in the DNVP and the *Stahlhelm*. He was even prepared to enlist the collaboration of Adolf Hitler. In October 1930, Brüning told Hitler that the economic crisis would last 'four or five years' and that it would be unlikely that living standards could return to those of 1927/8 even if reparations were abolished. He indicated that his ultimate goal was the restoration of the monarchy in collaboration with the parties of the right. In foreign policy he would expect criticism from the Nazis, which would strengthen his hand when negotiating with the Western powers over the revision of the Versailles Treaty.[12] He only asked Hitler to assist him by agreeing with the government about the form this opposition should take. Hitler must have been delighted at the prospect of long-term economic misery; he certainly had no intention of helping Brüning's government to gain its objectives. The longer the crisis lasted, the more likely the Nazis would be to reap the benefits.

More serious attempts to win support for the Government from Hugenberg's Nationalists and the ex-soldiers' association, the Stahlhelm, proved just as disappointing. Hugenberg maintained an unyielding attitude. He demanded that, as a price for his collaboration, the Prussian government should be reconstructed to eliminate the Social Democrats. This was an unrealistic condition, since the Nationalist group in the Reichstag could in no way replace the voting power of the Social Democrats. The Stahlhelm seemed at first more amenable to Brüning's overtures, but their hatred of the Republican system got the better of them and they stayed aloof.[13]

Hindenburg regretted the failure of these right-wing groups to support Brüning, but he did not distance himself from them as a result. Their influence continued to be felt in the presidential palace, and in the ranks of the army. Although Hindenburg was loyal to Brüning throughout 1931, he and his military advisers disliked a situation in which they had to rely on the Social Democrats for the stability of their regime. As the year wore on and conditions grew more critical, an arrangement which would include the Nazis in a genuinely nationalist government seemed more and more attractive.

The root cause of the severe political stresses which troubled Germany was economic. The year 1929 had seen the beginning of the Great Depression. It continued to gather momentum in the years which followed. Share prices fell steadily and bank reserves dwindled. Germany, dependent as she was on foreign credits for her economic health, was especially vulnerable to a crisis of confidence which affected the whole world. Unemployment, already at crisis level in 1929, rose catastrophically as the slump grew worse. By February 1931 there were nearly five million registered unemployed and a year later the figure was well over six million. The crisis meant ruin for many small businessmen and farmers, and even threatened the security of larger concerns.

Brüning showed great courage in tackling these problems, but he was not able to offer the German people very much positive encouragement. His opponents dubbed him the 'Hunger Chancellor' and his policies did seem to involve sacrifice rather than hope. They also included a number of glaring anomalies made necessary by his attachment to the conservative forces around the President. Despite large cuts in government spending the military budget remained relatively high. The Reichswehr was too powerful to be treated like other departments of state.

Others to receive preferential treatment were large landowners in Eastern Germany. These were among the least efficient farmers in the country, and many of their estates were heavily mortgaged. The President, himself an East Prussian landowner, had always shown a lively interest in their welfare. The eastern provinces were Germany's wheat-growing areas, and in order to protect their home market heavy duties were placed on imported grain. While unemployment benefit was being cut, wages and salaries reduced and industrial prices forced down, the cost of bread and cereals was maintained at an artificially high level. Grain cost 250 per cent more in Germany than it could be purchased for on the world market. So the cost of living – especially for the poor – fell less sharply than the level of incomes. In addition, a financial burden was placed on German industry to provide cheap credit for the East Elbean farmers. This meant that one of the least efficient parts of the German economy was being propped up by an industrial sector which was itself desperately short of capital. Meanwhile, other sections of German agriculture – the smaller proprietors with mixed and dairy farms – were left relatively unprotected and had to pay an inflated price for their grain. The incomes from their farms fell spectacularly, and in desperation many of them turned to the Nazis for salvation.[14] It was a situation which prompted one distinguished economist to exclaim: 'I do not understand this policy. Do we want a social revolution?'[15]

Brüning certainly did not want a social revolution. His harsh policies were designed to shield Germany from worse catastrophe. The preferences given to the Eastern landowners and the military were unfortunate, especially since both groups were strongly opposed to the Republic which supported them. Nevertheless, it is difficult to believe that savings on these items alone could have righted the German economy.

The Depression posed agonising problems for all governments which had to grapple with it, and few of them survived the test.* Brüning, who had considerable experience of financial and economic matters, adopted methods of dealing with the crisis similar to those used in other countries. His policy was one of stringent economy and deflation. Owing to the fall in the national income caused by the slump, tax receipts were falling. Hence very severe measures had to be taken to reduce spending and raise taxes. In July 1930 new taxes were imposed and a special levy placed on people in public employment. By the end of the year there was still a deficit of 1200 million Reichsmarks. Brüning then started imposing price cuts on government contractors, and during 1931 public employees had their pay reduced by a total of 23 per cent. In January and December 1931 there were compulsory price cuts for cartelised industrial products. With the second of these reductions wages were pegged back to the level of January 1927. A National Price Commissioner was established to ensure that these measures bore fruit.

In the years which followed the Great Depression it became fashionable to attack such deflationary policies as counterproductive. There were apparently successful government spending programmes in Hitler's Germany and Roosevelt's America. The economic theories of J. M. Keynes seemed to prove that the way to defeat unemployment and recession was to increase purchasing power, even if this involved reducing the value of the currency and risking inflation.

Brüning was far too orthodox an economist to run such risks. It is as well to remember that Keynes's *The General Theory of Employment, Interest and Money* did not appear until 1936. Most informed opinion in 1930 would have supported Brüning's deflationary tactics. Trade union leaders as well as businessmen were agreed that there had to be cuts – they simply argued that the burden should fall on capitalists rather than the unemployed. It was believed that reductions in wages could produce proportionately heavier falls in prices, thus causing consumption to rise.[16] Inflation was seen as Germany's worst enemy; the memories of 1923 were still very much alive.

* To take the most obvious examples, President Hoover was defeated in the American election in 1932 and Ramsay MacDonald's Labour government collapsed in August 1931.

Brüning's policies may well have exaggerated the crisis and caused unemployment to rise more than was necessary. But a more ambitious course might have led to a complete collapse of the mark. There is no evidence that, even with a perfectly free hand, Brüning could have helped Germany to survive the depression by pursuing – in isolation from the rest of the world – a policy of reflation.

In any case, his hands were not free. Germany was in a special position economically because of her reparations debts. The Young Plan, created in an atmosphere of economic optimism, had put very specific restrictions on Germany's credit system. Under the agreement implementing the plan Germany had pledged herself to maintain the value of the mark. Whenever discreet hints were dropped in Washington and Paris that it might be necessary to revoke this pledge they were met with forthright and unyielding resistance.[17]

Brüning may certainly have exacerbated the crisis by pursuing his political objectives so obsessively. He was determined to end reparations, both because of their damage to the German economy and because he thought that success in foreign policy would win his government the popular support it badly needed. If the Allies were to be made to see that Germany could no longer continue meeting its obligations under the Young Plan, he would have to demonstrate that she was pursuing a policy of rigorous economy. He could not afford to indulge in work-creation schemes or other palliatives for unemployment lest his reparations creditors should claim they were not being given first priority. It was the old policy of 'fulfilment' carried to its most logical conclusion.

For Germany to reach a satisfactory settlement of her reparations difficulties there would have to be a willingness to make concessions among her former enemies. By the summer of 1929 Stresemann had managed to win considerable prestige in the West, and in Aristide Briand he had found a sympathetic French counterpart. But after Stresemann's death the situation deteriorated. His successor, Julius Curtius, was a less skilful diplomatist, and neither he nor Brüning showed the same understanding of French susceptibilities as Stresemann had done. Both were impatient to revise the Versailles treaty in Germany's interests, and to this end an energetically nationalist diplomat, Bernhard

Wilhelm von Bülow, was promoted to head the German Foreign Office in May 1930. As Germany's politics took a turn towards the right, so the public posture of Germany's leaders became more nationalistic. Coupled with the alarm created in Paris by Hitler's showing in the 1930 elections, this rendered financial concessions from the French, whose economy was less seriously affected by the world depression in 1931, more difficult to obtain. The atmosphere was further poisoned by a botched attempt by Brüning and Curtius to set up an Austro-German customs union in March 1931, a project which was rightly seen as a preliminary step towards *Anschluß* between the two countries. Facing united opposition from the British and the French, the outcome was an ignominious fiasco.[18] Brüning had not actually been the chief architect of the scheme, although he approved of it.

It should not be thought, however, that Brüning was in any way exceptional in putting nationalist foreign policy objectives at the forefront of his agenda. Throughout the period from 1929 to 1932, the political parties in Weimar vied with each other in their assertion of Germany's national rights and their condemnation of the iniquities of the Versailles Treaty. Not the least strident was the German Communist Party, which was supposedly committed to international socialist brotherhood. In the 1930 Reichstag elections it had attacked the SPD as voluntary agents of French and Polish imperialism.[19] When the Austro-German customs union scheme failed the government was not reproached for its tactless alienation of the French; rather it was blamed for being too weak towards Germany's enemies. Even the relatively conciliatory SPD avoided criticising Brüning's policy, not wishing to cast doubt on German rights to self-determination.[20]

The Chancellor's own major objectives lay in the field of reparations and armaments. Brüning hoped to win relief from the former and equality over the latter. Friction with the French did not help his cause, nor did the aggressive tone of German domestic politics. One historian had described Brüning's policy as 'an attempt to appear nationalist at home and conciliatory abroad'.[21] Unfortunately for the Chancellor, it was impossible to hide the resurgence of German nationalism from the eyes of the world, nor could his meagre successes in the field of foreign affairs appease domestic critics.

In fact, the year 1931 saw the end of reparations. The British government, worried by Britain's deteriorating trade figures, wanted to write off reparations and inter-Allied war debts. The gravity of the situation in Germany and Austria – where the leading private bank collapsed in May – caused the Americans to revise their policy. On 20 June President Hoover suddenly announced a moratorium on inter-Allied debts on condition that reparations payments were also suspended. This really ended German payments to the Allies. It did not, however, solve the country's immediate financial problems. The bankruptcy of a textile combine caused one of Germany's largest banks to close its doors. The government once again had to step in with emergency measures, including exchange controls.

Reparations were indeed dead, but the manner of their passing brought no kudos to Brüning. The moratorium was supposed to be temporary and came as a gift from America. It was not a diplomatic triumph for Berlin. The economic crisis remained and was growing worse. German diplomacy – affected as it was by the need to succour national pride – did not contribute to an atmosphere of international collaboration and confidence, without which the world's economic problems could not be overcome. The Germans did nothing, for example, to respond to French suggestions that 'a political moratorium' should accompany that on reparations. This would have involved the dropping of Germany's revisionist posture and reductions in her arms budget. But such measures would never have been tolerated, either by the government parties or by the Reichswehr.

Nevertheless, by the spring of 1932 Brüning's two major objectives seemed near to achievement. Reparations were suspended and there was every chance that they would never reappear. Negotiations at Geneva on the question of disarmament had revealed widespread willingness among the powers to give Germany the equal status she had been demanding for so long. Brüning afterwards claimed that in spring 1932 he had almost attained his goal.[22] It was a goal he never reached. At the end of May he was dismissed. His successors, von Papen and von Schleicher, reaped the fruits of his policies. At the Lausanne Conference in July 1932 Germany's creditors agreed to renounce almost 90 per cent of their former claims if their own war debts received similarly magnanimous treatment. In fact Germany never paid any more reparations at all. The following December Germany's equal status in the field of armaments was recognised by most of her former enemies.

It has been argued that if these concessions had been granted to Brüning before his fall he could have overcome Germany's political crisis. There is very little reason to believe this. His dismissal was not the result of diplomatic failures. Nor did subsequent successes over reparations and disarmament bring much comfort to the luckless Chancellors who followed him.

The immediate causes of Brüning's fall were entirely political. Not having received his mandate as Chancellor from the Reichstag and still less from the electorate, he was dependent on the goodwill of his real supporters – President Hindenburg and the army. By the beginning of 1932 this was a very unsure foundation upon which to base a government. General von Schleicher was disappointed that Brüning had not overcome the opposition of the Nationalists and had to rely on Social Democratic forbearance in the Reichstag. He wanted to see the Social Democrats ejected from their position of power in Prussia. So he began to feel that some sort of accommodation with the Nazis might be desirable. Hitler was only too willing to encourage this attitude, though he was careful never to compromise his own independence.

Brüning himself wanted no truck with Hitler. But his position was being undermined. Hindenburg – his mind burdened by the constant complaints of his Nationalist acquaintances – was beginning to lose confidence in the Chancellor. In March 1932 the President had to face re-election. Efforts by Brüning to persuade the Nationalist opposition to allow the old field-marshal to be returned unopposed failed. Hindenburg was unhappy about this. He refused to address public rallies on his own behalf. Brüning had to act as his spokesman, doing his best to create a 'Hindenburg myth' with which to enthuse the electorate for the president's re-election. But the field-marshal did not show him any gratitude.[23]

The presidential election campaign did indeed reveal an extraordinary reversal of political roles since the previous contest in 1925. Then it had been the parties of the right which had supported Hindenburg. The Weimar Coalition parties – Democrats, Centre and Social Democrats – had provided his most serious opposition. By 1932 the political landscape had been transformed. The Republican parties, together with the more cautious conservative groups represented in Brüning's government, campaigned for Hindenburg. The mass of his votes would come from the Social Democrats and the Roman Catholic Centre Party. His old supporters among the German Nationalists and the Stahlhelm had turned their backs on him. They ran their own candidate, the radically anti-Republican Duesterberg, who was second-in-command of the Stahlhelm. It was clear that Duesterberg was not going to be a powerful challenge to Hindenburg, and that most votes on the right would go to Hitler. The other serious candidate was Thälmann, for the Communist Party.

Hitler himself had hesitated before entering the battle. The Nazi Party was by no means invincible. It was not even the largest in the Reichstag. Hindenburg would be very difficult to beat. Nevertheless the party had been making impressive progress. Its membership was growing fast and the SA was mushrooming also. Nazi campaigns were reinforced by the paramilitary rowdiness of the SA, which had been put under the leadership of the swashbuckling, if sinister, soldier of fortune, Ernst Rohm. The SA did not itself seek to challenge the state by trying to seize power, but was used to intimidate opponents and create an atmosphere of insecurity. Since it mainly attacked communists and socialists, it was regarded by many middle-class people as a force protecting 'law and order'. In fact, it was deliberately furthering chaos. Communists and Nazis brawled enthusiastically with one another, knowing that the end result would be to weaken parliamentary democracy.[24] By the end of 1931 there were over 300 000 brown-shirted SA men available for demonstrations, marches and street fights. A growth in mass support also brought an increase in funds. Hitler's party had initially been regarded with suspicion by big business circles, but in the early months of 1932 Hitler wooed industrialists and financiers, claiming that his assaults on democracy were easily compatible with capitalism. Although Hitler was never the tool of any vested interest, and although the major industrialists' organisations did not give substantial funding to the Nazis, money did flow from various businessmen to important individuals in the party.[25]

Once the election campaign got under way the Nazis' propaganda machine, directed by Josef Goebbels, excelled itself. The SA crossed the country in lorries to march and countermarch

toured Germany to
and mass meetings.
rivals could match,
no means passive.
nt's stead, revealed
ven if he lacked the
had already set up
democracy. Based
he Reichsbanner, it
he President.

t was forced to go
he narrowly missed
their efforts and
as elected with 53
share from 30 per
rteen million votes,
opposition' to the Weimar
Republic had at last found an effective leader. Roughly speaking,
the basis of Hitler's support lay in the middle classes and the
provincial communities of Protestant Germany. Hindenburg
owed his re-election largely to the Social Democratic working
class and the Roman Catholics.

This was not a result to please either the President or the
Reichswehr. It reinforced the charge made by Hindenburg's
Nationalist critics that he had sold himself to the anti-German
forces of Marxism and the Pope. Brüning was the man held
responsible in the President's entourage for having put the old
field-marshal in such a false position.

It should be stressed that at this time there was no reason why
Hitler should have been regarded as an invincible force in
German politics. Indeed, the nation had, by its votes, shown
that it rejected dictatorship from the left or the right. The fact
that the Nazi leader had been unable to defeat an uncharismatic
octogenarian field-marshal hardly suggests that a majority of the
German people was yearning for a fascist dictatorship. Had the
President and the army leaders been determined to defeat Hitler
they could easily have done so. There were plenty of loyal Republicans ready to help them. The Reichsbanner had been organising
defence units to supplement the police in the event of a coup by
the SA. Braun, the Prussian Prime Minister, whose state's police

were a thorn in the flesh of Nazi and Communist troublemakers, suggested on several occasions that there should be a consolidation of Reich and Prussian authorities in Berlin. This would have strengthened the forces loyal to the constitution and identified the Social Democrats quite clearly with the Reich government. [26]

Von Schleicher and his friends wanted none of this. They were furious when the Social Democrats tried to present themselves as allies of the State. On 15 March Schleicher wrote to Groener complaining that the socialists were trying to associate him with their activities. Referring to the date of the second presidential ballot, he went on:

> I am really looking forward to 11 April – then it will be possible to talk to this lying brood with no holds barred.... After the events of the last days I am really glad that there is a counter-weight [to the Social Democrats] in the form of the Nazis, who are not very decent chaps either and must be stomached with the greatest caution. If they did not exist, we should virtually have to invent them. [27]

The victim of all this spleen was to be Chancellor Brüning.

Hindenburg, whose age was a serious handicap to his judgement, was told on all sides that Brüning had lost public confidence. He was disturbed when the Government drew up plans for a very moderate land reform in eastern Germany. These involved breaking up some of the more spectacularly bankrupt estates and making them available as smallholdings to the unemployed. It was denounced as 'agrarian bolshevism' by the landed interest. Meanwhile von Schleicher had become convinced that he could win Nazi agreement to support a right-wing government. In return they would have to be granted new Reichstag elections, and the repeal of a ban on the SA which Brüning's government had finally imposed after a long period of violence and provocation.

On 30 May Brüning was dismissed from office by Hindenburg. His replacement was Franz von Papen, a protégé of von Schleicher who lacked political experience and parliamentary support. The way was clear for Hitler to take another step in his bid for power. Papen was a very nationalistic member of the Centre Party, although the latter disowned him when he replaced

Brüning as Chancellor. He, too, hoped to restore the monarchy,[28] but unlike Brüning he had little respect for constitutional niceties or parliamentary government.

Brüning's fall was a real turning-point in the collapse of German democracy. Until then the rising Nazi tides had been contained. Now they could burst forth in a menacing flood. The fate of Germany was in the hands of General von Schleicher, who left the comparative obscurity of his military office and entered the new cabinet as Defence Minister.

Von Schleicher and von Papen had a plan of campaign according to which they would dissolve the Reichstag, raise the ban on the SA and eliminate the socialist-dominated government in Prussia. They believed that these measures would encourage the Nazis to support the regime. On the diplomatic front, concessions wrung from the forthcoming disarmament conference would – it was hoped – enable the Government to create a reserve military force into which the nationalist energies of the nation's youth could be channelled with safety.

The hopes pinned on 'taming' the Nazis proved vain. Hitler showed no gratitude when the Government, having dissolved the Reichstag, lifted the ban on the SA and forced Land authorities to give up their own local restrictions.[29] On the contrary, having obtained their concessions the Nazis became rapidly more obstreperous. Nevertheless von Papen pressed on with his action to destroy the Republican regime in Prussia. He saw this as a move to consolidate the power of the central government and to pave the way for a more authoritarian type of system in Germany, untrammelled by the rights of federal states.

Otto Braun's cabinet in Prussia was a vulnerable target. Landtag elections in April had destroyed its parliamentary support. The lifting of the ban in Hitler's storm troopers caused an immediate and alarming upsurge of violence. Murderous encounters took place, especially between Nazis and Communists. Deaths were frequent. Von Papen's own government was entirely responsible for this, but he preferred to blame that of Prussia. On 20 July he suppressed it, acting on presidential authority.

Politically von Papen's daring did him nothing but harm. The Nazis and the Communists were delighted; one of the main bulwarks of Weimar democracy had been destroyed. The Social

Democrats and Centre were indignant at the removal of their ministers. Governments in other large German states like Bavaria and Württemberg were seriously alarmed lest the same fate should befall them. In Prussia itself the Social Democrats had toyed with the idea of resistance. Many of the rank and file in the party, the Reichsbanner and the trade unions were bewildered and angry when their leaders surrendered to von Papen. The younger Social Democrats who formed the backbone of the Reichsbanner Defence Units (*Schufos*) had been eager to fight. It was also suggested that the Prussian police might be used to defend their own government.

Yet the leaders of the 'Iron Front' – including the Social Democratic ministers, the trade union officials and the Reichsbanner commanders – all had to agree that no effective resistance was possible.[30] There were more than 200 000 men in the *Schufos*, but they had had no proper military training or equipment. Against the Reichswehr, doubtless supported by the SA and the Stahlhelm, they could have had no chance. Even on moral grounds there was some doubt about their position. They would have been fighting for a government which had been defeated at the polls. Against them was ranged a presidential authority recently confirmed by massive popular vote.

It is certainly true that the Social Democratic Party and the 'Iron Front' had never prepared themselves for a civil war in which they would be the revolutionary factor. They were used to operating within the framework of the law, and when that framework began to collapse around them they lacked the ability to improvise resistance. The Social Democratic ministers in Prussia have been criticised for taking no steps to fight for survival after von Papen came to power, even though his intentions were clear. It is difficult to see exactly what could have been done. Von Papen did not take office until May, by which time the Prussian government was operating on a caretaker basis with no majority. To have organised Prussia for civil war while Brüning was Chancellor would have been criminally irresponsible.[31] In 1932 the Social Democratic Party had more members than in 1928. Many of its supporters would have been ready to fight to save German democracy. That they could not do so was only partly due to the weakness of their own leadership. Their real mistake lay in trusting Hindenburg to defend the constitution.

Hindenburg himself was not encouraged to protect parliamentary democracy by the army. The military leadership in Germany had always been concerned to overcome the problems which faced the Reichswehr as a result of the limitations put on it by the Versailles Treaty. The fact that General Groener was defence minister from 1927 until 1932 certainly made it easier to evade some of the financial restraints on rearmament, but the major area of concern was the limitation on the numbers of mobilisable reserves which arose from the prohibition of conscription. By 1931, Germany's reserves of trained military manpower going back to the Great War period were beginning to run down. Unless some substitute could be found, the army would be permanently weakened in the event of general war. The ultimate aim was the reintroduction of conscription. In the meantime the encouragement of paramilitary formations and the military training of youth were seen as stopgaps. This involved the army in the support of nationalist paramilitary organisations, including the Nazi SA. The Prussian government, in particular, tried to obstruct these activities, rightly fearing that they were helping to strengthen the enemies of the Republic. It was noteworthy that the Army showed no wish to co-operate with Republican paramilitary forces such as the Reichsbanner.

By 1932 the Reichswehr was determined to break the chains of Versailles, and plans for military expansion were being drawn up in the *Bendlerstrasse*. It was partly because Groener did not seem capable of implementing these plans that army leaders were happy to see him removed. Brüning's deflationary policies were causing severe difficulties for firms supplying military equipment. A government more friendly to industry would be preferable from the army's point of view. Friction with the Prussian government over paramilitary training and the banning of the SA also inclined them to welcome a change.[32] They willingly supported Papen in his coup against Prussia, a measure implemented by a Reichswehr general, von Rundstedt. The army's discontent with the Republic, and ultimately its willingness to accept Hitler as Chancellor, were not simply due to the reactionary views of the officer corps, but owed much to the belief that a modern, technically powerful army would not be created unless the old party system was abolished. As one historian has put it, 'the military did not simply participate in the overthrow of the Weimar Republic in pursuit of old goals'.[33] Some of the most 'forward-looking' officers were Nazi sympathisers.

On 31 July the Reichstag elections took place. As had been expected, they were a triumph for Hitler. His party received 13.7 million votes – 330 000 more than in the second ballot of the presidential elections four months previously. The Nazis had 230 seats in the Reichstag – by far the largest number ever attained by a single party. Their share of the poll was 37.4 per cent. They were the strongest party in all Protestant German electoral districts except Berlin, and in many of mixed religious character also.[34] Without the proportional representation system they would have gained even more seats, although even the most lopsided constituency system could hardly have given them an overall majority.

Von Papen's government had no cause to be happy with the results. The Chancellor had not been associated with any particular party, but the German Nationalists, the People's Party and the Nationalist splinter groups which had broken from Hugenberg were sympathetic towards his regime. Of these the Nationalists nearly held their ground, but still lost 300 000 votes. They returned thirty-seven deputies to the Reichstag. The People's Party and the smaller groups suffered a complete disaster. Their eagerness to appease anti-democratic and nationalist sentiment simply encouraged their supporters to go the whole hog and vote for Hitler. The Social Democrats and the Centre, who had openly opposed von Papen and the Nazis, fared better. The fact that the Communist Party polled more than five million votes scarcely made von Papen's position any more secure.

The only possible coalition in the new Reichstag seemed to be between the Nazis and the Centre Party. Together they would have commanded a majority. Negotiations took place between them but led to no result. Hitler was determined to receive the Chancellorship and wreak his vengeance on the 'Marxists'. President Hindenburg, on the other hand, set his face against both Hitler and a cabinet based on parliament. If the Nazis entered the Government it would be as subordinates in a presidential regime. During these months Hitler showed great political courage in refusing anything but the highest post. There were important men in his party, and most prominent being Gregor Strasser, who felt that the Nazi wave had reached its crest and that the time had come to taste the fruits of office. There was reason in this. Hitler's intransigence was beginning to alarm some of his wealthy business patrons. They found von Papen, who was sympathetic to industrial interests, more attractive than earlier Chancellors, and they detected ominous signs of social radicalism in the SA. Some of them cut their links with the Nazis and others became less generous.[35] In the party as a whole the frenzied activism of the previous months could not be maintained without tangible achievements.

The danger to the Nazis was demonstrated in the autumn of 1932 when von Papen, faced with a completely uncooperative Reichstag, dissolved it yet again. On 6 November Germans trooped to the polls once more. Electoral participation was still high, although not the astonishing 83 per cent registered in July. For the first time since 1928 the Nazis lost votes in a Reichstag election, their share of the poll falling from 37.4 per cent to 33.1 per cent. The German Nationalists, who had begun to stress their difference with the Nazis, gained nearly 800 000 votes, and the People's Party improved its position slightly, though it only returned eleven deputies. Von Papen could claim that he was making ground, despite the fact that his supporters were still a tiny minority. He and President Hindenburg were quite prepared to go on governing without parliament – a breach of the constitution – until they were ready to implement a complete programme of constitutional reform. Von Papen had drawn up a number of public works schemes which he hoped would ease the unemployment situation. If the army and the President kept their trust in him he might survive.

It was here that von Papen's political inexperience revealed itself. His unpopularity was so widespread that even his colleagues feared a civil war if the government openly violated the constitution on his behalf. Such fears had been increased at the beginning of November, when Nazis and Communists had collaborated to organise a transport strike in Berlin. Acts of sabotage and violence accompanied this extremist alliance. Upbraided by his wealthier sympathisers, Hitler replied that, unless he allowed his rank and file to take such action, they would desert to the Communists. Reichswehr commanders were alarmed lest their soldiers should have to fight the SA and the Communists. They thought the Poles might take the opportunity to attack Germany.

Their anxiety was almost certainly exaggerated. A partnership between Nazis and Communists would have been difficult to maintain and would have aroused fierce opposition from such disparate political elements as the Reichsbanner and the Stahlhelm. Nevertheless, von Schleicher, now convinced that von Papen was a liability, stressed the dark side of the military picture, and his cabinet colleagues agreed with him. Von Papen resigned.

On 2 December von Schleicher himself became Chancellor. It was an exposed position which he had not coveted. Power without responsibility had been his goal. In one important respect he was even weaker than von Papen. His relations with the President had grown cooler since the previous spring. Von Papen had quite replaced him in Hindenburg's favour.[36]

Von Schleicher was an ingenious man who did not lack courage. Having failed once more to negotiate with Hitler, he attempted to create popular support for his government by cutting across normal party lines. Gregor Strasser, still regarded as Hitler's main rival within the Nazi Party, had previously indicated that he might be willing to break with his chief and take office under another Chancellor. Von Schleicher also tried to appeal to the trade unions with schemes of work creation. He envisaged projects for compulsory youth training and cheap labour for farmers. Had he remained in office, he was even prepared to consider nationalising the coal and steel industry.[37]

Imaginative though these ideas were, they quickly collapsed in practice. Strasser was forced to resign his offices in the Nazi Party on 8 December. Some trade union leaders were impressed by Schleicher's attention to work creation. At least one SPD politician, Otto Braun, seemed willing to compromise with Schleicher to save the state from Hitler. But Schleicher would not contemplate open collaboration with the SPD, and suggestions in the press that trade unions might work with him aroused a furious reaction amongst the Social Democratic rank and file.[38] Schleicher hoped that if he bargained hard enough he could tame the Nazis by getting them to accept a subordinate position under his leadership. If they refused, he would to ask the President to dissolve the Reichstag and govern without it – in breach of the constitution. However, in January 1933 Hitler was able to exploit a *Land* election in the tiny state of Lippe, a protestant and largely rural region in which the Nazis were bound to perform well.

They were able to concentrate all their energies on mobilising support amongst an electorate of only 100 000. On 15 January they achieved what was actually a fairly modest victory, winning 39.5 per cent of the vote. The Goebbels propaganda machine presented this as a great triumph, attempting to restore party morale after the disapponting Reichstag elections the previous November. The Nazis still faced serious financial problems, however, and there were ominous signs of disaffection within the SA. On 20 January Nazi negotiators seemed willing to postpone calling the Reichstag until the spring of 1933, thus giving the government a breathing space. Had Schleicher accepted this it is possible that the stresses within an already disaffected Nazi movement might have intensified. But he was eager to press for a clear-cut settlement on his terms. Hitler, for his part, stubbornly refused to contemplate supporting a government in which he was not Chancellor. Schleicher was therefore forced to ask Hindenburg for power to govern unconstitutionally – something which had been refused to von Papen on Schleicher's own advice.[39]

The President had no desire to take such a risk for Schleicher. Besides, it was not necessary. Von Papen was confident he could control Hitler. Egged on by his conservative entourage, and particularly by his son, Oskar von Hindenburg, the President agreed to call Hitler into office provided he was surrounded by conservative ministers. Papen also misled Hindenburg into believing that the Centre Party might be persuaded to support Hitler's cabinet, thus giving it a majority in the Reichstag.[40] Schleicher had to resign, and greatly feared that Papen would be his successor. Reichswehr leaders thought that this might lead to a civil war in which the overwhelming majority of the nation would be against the government. Their apprehensions soon disappeared. On 30 January 1933 Hitler became Reich Chancellor.

His appointment was quite unnecessary. His government, in which Alfred Hugenberg of the DNVP was the only other party leader, had no majority in the Reichstag. The Nazis could not have threatened the state if they had been denied power. Their movement was waning. A further period of frustration might have finished them off. It was perhaps for this reason that Hitler became attractive to men of property in Germany. If his mass support ebbed away the beneficiaries would either be the democratic Weimar parties or the Communists. The dream of national resurgence based on an authoritarian regime would then have been destroyed.

In any case, von Papen and his friends thought they could manage the Nazis. Hitler's men had only two major posts in the Reich government, those of the Chancellor and Minister of the Interior. Von Papen was deputy Chancellor and Reich Commissioner in charge of Prussia, and had the ear of the President. A general, Blomberg, headed the Defence Ministry. Hugenberg was Minister of Economics and Food, and Seldte, the Stahlhelm leader, Minister of Labour. There seemed little danger that the Nazis would overwhelm their colleagues.

Within a month Hitler had demonstrated how complacent von Papen had been. Having made a show of negotiating for a coalition with the Centre, Hitler persuaded his colleagues to dissolve the Reichstag for a third general election. He promised them that he would not change the complexion of his cabinet even if he won. The election campaign was conducted under quite unfair conditions, because the authority of the state was at Hitler's disposal. Göring had been appointed Prussian Minister of the Interior, and thus controlled police power in almost two-thirds of Germany. He recruited 50 000 'auxiliary police', most of whom were Nazi storm troopers. The regular police were purged and ordered to protect Nazis and Nationalists against 'Marxist' attack.

On 27 February the Reichstag in Berlin was set on fire by a young Dutchman of extreme left-wing opinions. Using this as a pretext to claim that Germany was threatened by a Bolshevik coup, Hitler issued a presidential decree 'for the Protection of the People and the State'. For many years this was to be one of the main foundations of Nazi tyranny. It swept away constitutional safeguards against arbitrary arrest and the suppression of free speech.[41] A wave of arrests followed. Hitler's opponents believed that the Reichstag fire had been a Nazi plot. This now seems unlikely, but the issue is not an important one. The Nazis had made preparations to take emergency action before the fire, and, had it not occurred, other excuses would have been found.[42]

The Reichstag elections on 5 April did not give Hitler an absolute majority, despite the enormous pressure exerted on the electorate. But with almost 44 per cent of the vote, and in coalition with Hugenberg's Nationalists, Hitler could command a simple majority in the Reichstag. The opposition to him was completely incapable of offering effective resistance. The Centre Party had already shown itself willing to collaborate with Hitler, and its leader, prelate Kaas, now desired only to safeguard the religious freedom of German Catholics.[43] The parties of the moderate right had already been destroyed as an electoral force in the summer of 1932. The Communists were arrested or forced into hiding. Only the Social Democrats tried to put a brave face on defeat. When, on 23 March 1933, Hitler presented the Reichstag with an enabling law empowering him to rule by decree, the Social Democrats were the one group to vote against it. With that last gesture of defiance, their Weimar Republic was finally interred. Hitler was the master of Germany.

Notes

1. Bullock, *Hitler*, p. 115.
2. See Hale, *The Captive Press*, pp. 27–8 and *passim*.
3. For the various versions of *Mein Kampf*, see Hammer, 'Die deutschen Ausgaben von Hitlers "Mein Kampf"', pp. 161–78. Also Maser, *Hitler's 'Mein Kampf'*, pp. 69–70.
4. For accounts of Hitler's policy at this time see Bullock, *Hitler*, pp. 130–40; Kershaw, *Hitler, 1889–1936*, pp. 257–79; and Noakes, 'Conflict and Development in the NSDAP 1924–27'. Strasser's beliefs are set out in Stachura, *Gregor Strasser and the Rise of Nazism*, pp. 44–55.
5. Turner, *German Big Business and the Rise of Hitler*, pp. 114–24.
6. Interesting comments on this process are in R. Koshar, 'Contentious Citadel. Bourgeois Crisis and Nazism in Marburg/Lahn, 1880–1933', in Childers (ed.), *The Formation of the Nazi Constituency, 1919–1933*, pp. 25–32.
7. Milatz, *Wähler und Wahlen*, pp. 112, 125–6. For the social basis of Hitler's new electoral support see Broszat, 'National Socialism, its Social Basis and Psychological Impact', in Feuchtwanger (ed.), *Upheaval and Continuity*, pp. 136–51. Also Winkler, *Mittelstand, Demokratie und Nationalsozialismus*, and 'From Social Protectionism to National Socialism', pp. 7–13.
8. Rohe, *Reichsbanner*, pp. 360–5.
9. Dorpalen, *Hindenburg*, p. 207; Bracher, *Auflösung*, pp. 370–1.
10. The extent to which Brüning was working for the restoration of the monarchy is controversial. There is no doubt he was a very loyal monarchist, but it is also clear that this issue was not given a high

priority in his day-to-day handling of policy, which has been described as 'crisis management'. A strong denial of the importance of monarchism in Brüning's regime is presented by Andreas Rödder: 'Dichtung und Wahrheit. Der Quellenwert von Heinrich Brünings Memoiren und seine Kanzlerschaft'. For a balanced discussion of this issue see Patch, *Brüning*.

11. H. Brüning, *Memoiren 1918–1934*, pp. 145–50. For Brüning's views on a restoration of Kaiser Wilhelm II see ibid., p. 453.
12. Ibid., pp. 191–7.
13. Berghahn, *Stahlhelm*, pp. 155 ff.
14. Born, *Bankenkrise*, p. 53.
15. Ibid., p. 54. The commentator was Lujo Brentano.
16. See, for example, Schorr, *Adam Stegerwald*, pp. 188–9. Stegerwald was Minister of Labour and a Catholic Trade Unionist. For a fuller discussion of this issue see Chapter 11.
17. Bennett, *Germany and the Financial Crisis*, pp. 11–12.
18. Patch, *Brüning*, pp. 123–4, 153–6.
19. Winkler, *Weimar, 1918–1933*, p. 386.
20. Ibid., p. 406.
21. Bennett, *Germany and the Financial Crisis*, p. 306.
22. See Brüning, 'Ein Brief', pp. 10–11.
23. Patch, *Brüning*, pp. 231–47.
24. R. Bessel, 'Violence as Propaganda: the Role of the Storm Troopers in the Rise of National Socialism', in Childers, *The Formation of the Nazi Constituency, 1919–1933*, pp. 131–45. For Nazi/Communist violence, especially in Berlin, see Rosenhaft, *Beating the Fascists?*
25. Bullock, *Hitler*, pp. 196–9. Turner, *German Big Business and the Rise of Hitler*, p. 156. Also see below, p. 178.
26. Braun, *Von Weimar zu Hitler*, p. 277.
27. Carsten, *Reichswehr*, pp. 339–40.
28. See the contribution of W. Pyta to Rödder, 'Reflexionen über das Ende der Weimarer Republik', p. 96.
29. Bracher, *Auflösung*, pp. 544–52; Vogelsang, *Reichswehr*, p. 221.
30. Rohe, *Reichsbanner*, p. 431. Höltermann, the Reichsbanner leader, favoured resistance as a gesture, but accepted the judgement of his Reichsbanner colleagues that the situation was hopeless.
31. For a discussion of these problems, see Matthias and Morsey, *Das Ende der Parteien*, pp. 127–45, and Rohe, *Reichsbanner*, pp. 432–5. See also Schulze, *Otto Braun*, pp. 745–54.
32. See Bennett, *German Rearmament and the West, 1932–3*, in particular pp. 51–70. Also M. Geyer, 'Professionals and Junkers: (German Rearmament) and Politics in the Weimar Republic', in Bessel and Feuchtwanger, *Social Change and Political Development in Weimar*

Germany, pp. 108–10. For Groener's carefully planned armament schemes see Deist, *The Wehrmacht and German Rearmament*, pp. 12–18.

33. Geyer, 'German Rearmament', p. 123.
34. Milatz, *Wähler und Wahlen*, p. 142. For a fuller discussion of Nazi support see Chapter 11.
35. Dorpalen, *Hindenburg*, p. 365. Also Wilhelm Treue, 'Der deutsche Unternehmer in der Weltwirtschaftskrise 1928–33', in Conze and Raupach (eds.), *Staats-und Wirtschaftskrise*, pp. 123–4.
36. Dorpalen, *Hindenburg*, pp. 395–7.
37. Vogelsang, *Reichswehr*, pp. 346–9, 381.
38. Winkler, *Der Weg in die Katastrophe*, pp. 817–19, 830. Also Schulze, *Otto Braun*, pp. 773–6.
39. For the Lippe elections and the possiblity of extending the Reichstag's recess until the spring, see Turner, *Hitler's Thirty Days*, pp. 63–5, 104–7. For Hitler's intrigues with Papen, see Kershaw, *Hitler, 1889–1936*, pp. 417–23.
40. Turner, *Hitler's Thirty Days*, p. 151.
41. Bullock, *Hitler*, p. 263.
42. Bracher, Sauer and Schulz, *Machtergreifung*, p. 82.
43. Aretin, 'Prälat Kaas, Franz von Papen und das Reichskonkordat von 1933', pp. 254–79. For the Centre attitude see Matthias and Morsey, *Das Ende der Parteien*, pp. 355–67. Many Centre Party members feared a new *Kulturkampf* if they voted against the law.

11 Hitler's Success and Weimar's Failure: Political Ineptitude or Economic Necessity?

Hitler had exploited his chances with great skill. Yet he had been remarkably fortunate in the turn of events since 1929. Under the pressure of the economic crisis parliament virtually abdicated responsibility for the nation's affairs to a Chancellor ruling with the support of the President and the army. Brüning's decision to call a Reichstag election in 1930 gave Hitler the opportunity to demonstrate his mass appeal, and rendered the re-establishment of parliamentary government virtually impossible. This left the Republic dependent upon a military, bureaucratic and business establishment which had no emotional loyalty towards it.

Such a regime could not arouse mass enthusiasm in Germany. It deliberately refrained from associating itself with militant Republican elements such as the Reichsbanner. The *Parteihader* (party squabbles) of the Weimar system were regarded with distaste, even by those who did not wish to act unconstitutionally. Brüning hoped for a limited monarchy, and von Papen for a corporate State dominated by the propertied classes. Von Schleicher had dreams of a national concentration headed by the army, in which organised Labour would participate and political parties disappear. It is difficult to see how – even if Hitler had not been called to power – the Weimar Republic could have reverted to its former democratic system.

The failure of German democracy after the First World War cannot be attributed to any single cause. Three explanations have commonly been given: that the German revolution was not sweeping enough and did not create institutions loyal to the new regime; that the Versailles Peace Treaty saddled the Republic with impossible burdens; and that the Weimar Constitution was impracticable.

The first of these explanations has some force, but it remains difficult to envisage what form a really radical revolution in Germany would have taken. Only the most extreme elements in the labour movement could have carried it through in 1919, and, as events showed, they lacked mass support. This was just as well, since socialist experiments would have been economically disastrous. Democratisation was certainly necessary, but difficult to implement. So far as the peace treaty is concerned, its demoralising impact on German public opinion was more important than its physical effects. Within ten years of the treaty Germany seemed to have made a remarkable economic recovery, and her international standing was being restored under Stresemann's guidance. Doubtless the financial aspects of the peace settlement contributed to the economic disaster which overwhelmed Germany from 1929 to 1933. But other countries – among them many of the victor powers – experienced an almost equally catastrophic recession. As for the constitution, it is difficult to see how any parliamentary system can be made proof against the electorate.

The Republic was never able to build up a stable block of parliamentary supporters. There is no doubt that it inherited many political weaknesses from the old Wilhelmine Empire. The Reichstag parties showed little enthusiasm for the acceptance of government responsibility. They remained closely associated with sectional or class interests. It was particularly unfortunate that no powerful Republican party appeared which could appeal to Germany's Protestant middle class. German liberalism had been divided and demoralised in the era of Bismarck and Wilhelm II. It was never able to consolidate itself under the Republic.

The parties which adapted best to the new situation were those representing the social outsiders in the German Empire – the Roman Catholic Centre and the Social Democrats. This increased the resentment of those who had felt themselves to be the backbone of the nation before 1918. In particular, the Social Democrats were pictured as revolutionaries, and their spokesmen sometimes encouraged this impression by talking in terms of class war. Fear of 'Marxism' was increased by the disturbances – the extent of which was commonly exaggerated – in the November revolution. It grew stronger after the humiliation of the peace treaty and the very real hardships caused by inflation. When the economic depression created an atmosphere of internal crisis the bourgeois parties lost their voters to Hitler, while the Roman Catholic Centre and the Social Democrats put up far stiffer resistance to the Nazi challenge.

Germany's political problems were exacerbated by the conflict of generations after 1918. The older parties appeared to have learned nothing from the experience of the war. In the SPD, trade union and party functionaries seemed concerned with problems more relevant to 1914 than to the 1920s. The same was true of the socially superior leadership of the German Nationalist Party. The youth of the country was frustrated both intellectually and professionally by this age bottleneck, and herein lay one of the most effective appeals of the Nazi and Communist parties. Youth – rather than totalitarianism – was their most striking common factor.

This does not mean, of course, that those who voted for Hitler were necessarily young. Electoral studies have shown that the basis of the Nazi constituency was very much more complex than has sometimes been imagined. Indeed, the elderly seem to have been even more willing to support Hitler than young voters. Middle-class pensioners, who feared for their future existence if the economic crisis were not overcome, were very likely to vote for the NSDAP.[1] The association of the Nazi movement with one type of person or social group, the lower middle classes, for example, is an oversimplification. It was sometimes suggested that only the 'small man', or petit bourgeois, supported Hitler, leaving the working classes to vote for Marxist parties and the wealthier sections of the community to back conservative parties like Hugenberg's DNVP. However, it has always been absurd to imagine that Weimar parties could be sliced into neat socio-economic categories – SPD, working class; Democrats, lower middle class; DVP, urban, upper middle class; DNVP, conservative landowners. In the Ruhr, for example, leading businessmen might be associated with the Stresemann's DVP, whereas nationalist schoolteachers and even industrial workers might support Hugenberg.

A closer look at electoral statistics makes it clear that the 13.7 million people who voted for the Nazis in their most successful free Reichstag election – in July 1932 – cannot be pigeon-holed neatly in terms of social class, or even gender. The picture of the Nazi movement which emerges from modern research is not fundamentally different from that of earlier historians. But some misconceptions have been eliminated.

The first point to notice is that National Socialism has been confirmed as a provincial rather than a metropolitan phenomenon. The tendency to vote Nazi varied inversely with the size of the community. The proportion of voters choosing Hitler in large towns was substantially lower than in small towns or villages. Some small communities in protestant parts of Germany registered Nazi votes of well over 80 per cent. This does not mean, of course, that there were not substantial numbers of Nazi voters in big cities also, but the proportion there was lower. So far as the class composition of these voters is concerned, the middle class was very strongly represented among them, but not necessarily the lower middle class. A study of voting in major cities like Berlin and Hamburg suggests that it was in the most affluent suburbs that the highest Nazi vote was to be found, whereas areas which might be designated 'lower middle class' returned about average results for Hitler.[2] What does seem to be clear is that the Nazis were likely to do worst in working-class districts in larger cities.

Substantial numbers of workers certainly did vote for Hitler in the early 1930s. Yet it should be remembered that the so-called 'working-class' parties, the KPD and the SPD, had never encompassed all the working population of industrial Germany. The Roman Catholic Centre appealed to many of them, and in areas like the Ruhr there had always been a strong nationalist vote, in part a reaction by Protestant workers to the strength of the Catholic Centre and to Polish immigration.[3] Workers who had voted National Liberal before 1914, or for the 'National opposition' to Weimar thereafter, were likely to turn to Hitler once his bandwagon was rolling. It also seems likely that some Nazi voters came from the ranks of the SPD. The fact remains, however, that the combined vote of the Social Democratic and Communist parties rose in absolute numbers from 12.4 million in 1928 to 13.2 million in July 1932. Although this was a decline of about 4 per cent in the *proportion* of the votes cast, it does not really suggest that supporters of this socialist camp were leaking away in huge numbers to swell Hitler's following.

One older generalisation which has been amply borne out by recent research is the importance of the confessional factor in German electoral behaviour. Although the NSDAP began its career in Munich, the capital of predominantly Roman Catholic Bavaria, its appeal was markedly stronger in Protestant communities than in Roman Catholic ones, irrespective of their social composition. This was evidently because Germany's Roman Catholic minority felt its interests best served by its own confessionally based political parties, as well as by its trade unions, farmers' co-operatives, youth groups and women's organisations. The result was that the Roman Catholic political parties withstood the Nazi onslaught at the polls with considerable success. If we compare the 1928 Reichstag elections with those of July 1932 we can see that the combined share of the vote given to the Centre and the Bavarian People's Party actually rose from 15.1 per cent to 15.7 per cent. This does not mean, of course, that no Roman Catholics voted for Hitler. Many did, but their numbers were disproportionately lower than those of Protestant voters.[4]

Sometimes it has been suggested that Hitler's movement was particularly attractive to women. In fact, women did not vote for the Nazis in larger proportions than men, and before 1932 they were less likely to support the Nazis than were male voters. Women in Weimar had been inclined towards the more moderate parties, especially those with a Christian character. Nevertheless, by 1932 Hitler's party was attracting millions of female voters, despite its aggressively anti-feminist attitude and the fact that it was run by obviously chauvinistic men. One explanation was that the Nazi message to women – that their place was in the home looking after their children – was common to conservative parties, including the Catholic Centre. Since most women's jobs outside the home were of a menial and exhausting kind, the prospect of a decent family life was not without its attractions. There were successful professional women in Germany, but their numbers were limited and they could count on little popular support.[5]

The study of the Nazi electoral appeal after 1929 reinforces the view that National Socialism presented itself, and was seen by its supporters, as a broadly-based movement of the nationalist right. Attacks on Versailles and tirades against Marxism were the salient feature of Nazi propaganda. These pleased those sections of the middle classes in such places as Saxony, where memories of a Marxist coalition in 1923 were still vivid and where, according to one observer, most of them 'view the suppression of Social Democracy as the be-all and end-all of politics'.[6] There were, to be sure, also fulminations against what was vaguely described as 'reaction' and attacks on international stock-exchange capitalism – often a euphemistic description of Jewish business interests. Such rhetoric did not inhibit the more socially conservative groups in Germany from accepting Hitler as a possible saviour. This was not surprising, since farmers, officials, small businessmen and professional people did not regard themselves as 'capitalists' and often blamed 'big business' for their own economic difficulties. Indeed, one major explanation for Weimar's weakness had always been the lack of understanding shown by most Germans for the concept of free-market capitalism. The banking crisis in the summer of 1931 reinforced public suspicion of capitalist machinations. Brüning himself was attracted by the idea of a planned economy and made speeches attacking 'abuses of capitalism', even though he denied any plan to abolish private enterprise.[7]

The political complexion of Nazi support can be illustrated by comparing the areas from which Hitler received most votes in 1932 with those from which Hindenburg drew his strength in the presidential election of 1925. Then he was elected as the candidate of the right against Marx of the Centre Party. By 1932 he had to rely on his erstwhile opponents for re-election, and the districts which had previously supported him polled strongly for Hitler.

There was, of course, a good deal of vote-switching within the electorate. Thus some left liberals might well have voted for the Social Democrats after 1929, and doubtless some former SPD voters drifted to the Communists or the Nazis. This does not alter the main contours of Nazi support, however. The Nazi party certainly appealed to a variety of people in German society. It made seductive, if often contradictory, promises to farmers, officials, the free professions, shopkeepers, artisans, students and workers. It has been described as a 'catch-all' party, offering something to most sections of the community, which was more evenly distributed amongst all social and demographic strata than any other German party. The notable exceptions to this vulnerability were the Roman Catholics and the industrial proletariat. Hitler's appeal was most successful in protestant, provincial Germany, and amongst those who had previously supported parties to the right of Social Democracy.[8]

One has to ask whether the rise of Hitler could have been stopped by the actions of his opponents in the period 1930–33. Certainly it is clear that Hugenberg, the leader of the DNVP, must bear a large burden of responsibility for inviting Hitler's party to participate in his campaign against the Young Plan, a campaign which gave the Nazis such welcome publicity. Hugenberg's folly was compounded by that of many on the right in the years which followed. Big business interests, which regarded National socialism with reserve owing to its often stridently anti-capitalist rhetoric, were not averse to enlisting Nazi support against the parties of the left. In the presidential campaign of 1932, for example, Hindenburg did not receive wholehearted backing from conservative industrialists who had helped to elect him in 1925. Paul Reusch, the head of the most important Ruhr industrial association, instructed newspapers under his control to avoid personal attacks on Hitler during the election campaign.[9] Although big business did not generally finance Hitler's party before he became Chancellor, it worked against the supporters of democracy, and must therefore be counted as yet another obstacle to Republican consolidation.

At a Land and municipal level, parties of the right were often willing to work together with the Nazis against the threat of 'Marxist' subversion, despite open Nazi contempt for 'bourgeois' rivals. In 1932 nearly all parties to the right of the Social Democrats – including the Roman Catholic Centre and Bavarian People's parties – were willing to contemplate coalitions with the Nazis, even though they did not want Hitler to be Chancellor. It is therefore almost justifiable to talk of a 'self-destruction' of parliamentary democracy so far as the non-socialist parties are concerned.

But what of the left-wing parties? How effective were they in opposing Hitler? Here again the picture is not as bright as it might be. The Communists, whose masters in Moscow's Comintern had laid down a particularly intransigent line since 1928, pursued a policy of attacking democratic parties in general and the Social Democrats in particular. The latter were described as 'social fascists'. Communist tactics were entirely negative and disruptive, their aim being to destroy 'sham' parliamentary democracy and replace it with a proletarian dictatorship. Even supposing this had been a desirable objective, the KPD had no real strategy for achieving it, but relied for its policy on instructions from Moscow. After Hitler had come to power, communists like Walter Ulbricht continued to attack the SPD and only changed their tune when the Comintern adopted a new policy in 1935.

So far as the SPD was concerned, its commitment to the Republican system was unqualified. Nevertheless, in the spring and summer of 1930 it put the sectional interests of its trade union supporters before the smooth functioning of parliamentary government. Despite ominous Nazi gains in Land elections in Saxony in June 1930,[10] the SPD still voted together with the Communists, the DNVP and the Nazis to throw out Brüning's package of economic reforms, thereby helping to ensure that the Reichstag would be dissolved and an election held. When the results of that election were announced, one SPD commentator referred to them as a colossal and shattering surprise, and exclaimed:

> The first lesson of the elections of 14 September is this, we must get to know this unknown people among whom there are eleven million Nazi and Communist voters.[11]

It might be felt that this admirable resolution came a little late in the day.

After the 1930 elections the SPD tolerated Brüning's government and allowed it to rule using the emergency powers vested in the president by Article 48 of the constitution. Without this SPD restraint, Brüning could not have carried on, because the Reichstag could have rescinded his emergency decrees. Since it did not oppose Brüning's measures, the SPD had to bear the odium for government policy without actually being able to shape it. It is open to question whether it might not have been better if the Social Democrats had forced the issue in the autumn of 1930, when the shock of the election results might have encouraged collaboration between the more moderate politicians against the extremes of right and left.

Nevertheless, the SPD was the one mass party in the Weimar Republic which unequivocally defended the parliamentary system against Hitler. Its leadership may have lacked flexibility. Its ability to appeal to the young, and especially to the unemployed, was limited. But its role in Weimar was an honourable one.[12]

Although, as we saw in Chapter 9, the political future of the Republic had not looked promising before the American stock market crash of 1929, there is no doubt that the atmosphere of crisis induced by the great depression contributed very much to Hitler's electoral successes, and to the willingness amongst conservative circles to contemplate replacing Weimar with a regime at least supported by the Nazis. The intensity of the depression was very severe in Germany – more so than in France or Britain, for example. The question then arises: could this economic disaster have been avoided, or at least ameliorated? Did Brüning's deflationary policies in 1930–32 so exacerbate the crisis that Hitler's triumph was inevitable and if so, could other policies have been adopted?

As we have mentioned above,[13] Brüning apparently had few options open to him. The arrangements which had been made for stabilising the currency in 1923/4 and the Dawes Plan agreements prevented the German government devaluing its currency and severely limited its opportunities to expand credit. Even though the Young Plan had restored German economic sovereignty, the obligations under the plan seemed to preclude a policy of cheap money. Furthermore, in the period before 1930, economic experts in Germany had been becoming increasingly worried about the unsound character of Germany's finances. There was particular concern about budget deficits at Reich and Land level, to say nothing of supposedly profligate spending – and borrowing – by city governments, such as that of Cologne, where Konrad Adenauer was mayor.*[15] By 1930 the rise in unemployment was putting intolerable strains on the funding of unemployment benefit, and even the Social Democrats agreed that retrenchment would have to take place.

Some historians have drawn the conclusion that the real causes of the crisis with which Brüning was faced when he took office at the end of March 1930 were to be found in the years 1924–29. They refer to this period as the 'crisis before the crisis'.

According to one view, political systems can only work effectively if there is enough economic growth to satisfy the needs of

---

* Adenauer was reputed to have a salary 'somewhere between that of the Reich Chancellor and the Lord God, but nearer the latter's'. He certainly received more *in toto* than the Reich Chancellor.[14]

competing interests, and Weimar was a period of economic stag-
nation, or at least inadequate growth. This would not have mat-
tered in a *laisser-faire* economic system, where conflicts of interest
would have been effectively settled by market forces and the state
itself need not have been involved. As it was, clashes of interest
between capital and labour, for example, became politicised,
firstly through abortive attempts to steer the economy by means
of the corporatist Central Working Association (ZAG) of employers and unions, and then as a result of state arbitration in labour
disputes from 1924 onwards. Similarly, economic fluctuations
could be blamed – however unjustly – on political causes, such
as the burden of reparations, redistributive taxation or high social
spending. It has been noted that the two leading parties in the
Weimar system, the Social Democrats and the Roman Catholic
Centre, were fundamentally unsympathetic to free-market
capitalism, and were not therefore likely to be able to pursue
consistently growth-orientated economic policies.[16] They were
more interested in wealth distribution than wealth creation.

Explicit in some of these critical accounts of Weimar's economic
performance is a comparison with the 'economic miracle' in West
Germany after 1948, when Ludwig Erhard freed the German
economy from wartime controls and introduced his 'social market' policy which led to a period of sustained economic growth.
The Federal Republic undoubtedly benefited from the prosperity
associated with Erhard's measures. It should, however, be
pointed out that comparisons between the two Republics can be
misleading. In post-Second-World-War Germany the Federal
Republic was established after the worst period of dislocation
and humiliation was over, the odium for it having been borne
by the occupying powers. The integration of the Federal Republic
into the Western alliance and the European Communities, and
the support the German recovery received from the United
States, created a very different environment to that which was
faced by Weimar. Furthermore the political institutions and climate of opinion in West Germany after 1948 were much more
positive than those which pertained in the 1920s.

To take up one particular point; neither the Centre nor the
Social Democrats dismantled free-enterprise capitalism in the
Weimar Republic. From 1924 until 1929 the German economy
functioned on a freer market basis than was true of the period

1948–54, when there were still controls on trade and foreign exchange. If anything, the market in Weimar was stifled by cartel-isation, a characteristic particularly of German heavy industry, and one which 'liberal' business interests fiercely defended. Social spending was certainly higher than it had been before the First World War, but then in the early 1950s the Federal Republic's social welfare expenditure took up a higher proportion of the national income than was the case in neighbouring countries.[17] It should also be pointed out that, in the Weimar period, liberal parties which appealed mainly to the protestant electorate were not themselves at all clear about a commitment to unrestrained competition and free trade. Nationalism was a far stronger ele-ment in their programme, and this encouraged a protectionist attitude to the economy.[18]

Nevertheless, it cannot be denied that Weimar's economic per-formance was more feeble than that of its West German successor. Its critics have blamed this on the circumstances created by the German revolution and the inflation which had been tolerated by republican governments. After 1923, trade unions pitched their wage demands very high, since they were used to wage increases being eroded by inflation. Employers were inhibited in their resistance to union pressure by the system of state arbitration in labour disputes which, so it is claimed, led to wage rises beyond what capitalists could happily afford. The high levels of taxation and public spending on welfare purposes discouraged savings; certainly the rate of savings remained low after 1924 by compar-ison with the post-1948 period.

This unhealthy situation led to an increase in unemployment, which rose to over two and a half million in the severe winter of 1928/9, and was in turn a further burden on the nation's finances. Well before the stock market crash in the USA there was a serious shortage of capital in Germany, although it should be pointed out that the stock market boom on Wall Street made loans to Ger-many less attractive for foreign investors. The crash itself simply confirmed a drying up of US investment and was bound to lead to a catastrophic slump. The only 'cure' for this had to be drastic deflation – the 'purging' of the economy of excess labour costs by wage cuts or sackings. Not until this 'cure' had been undergone could German industry emerge, leaner, fitter and more pro-fitable, to resume growth.

It should be noticed that the protagonists of this thesis [19] do not suggest that there could have been a solution to Weimar's economic problems, given the political framework within which her leaders were operating. The trade unions were bound to try to defend the interests of their members, whose real wages had fallen sharply during the hyperinflation of 1923. As for public spending, cuts imposed as the result of the stabilisation programme had already caused much bitterness among public employees and more draconian measures would have been politically impossible.

One point arising from this argument cannot, however, be overlooked. Trade unions, hitherto regarded as a bulwark of republican democracy, now appear, albeit unwittingly, as agencies of its destruction.[20] Redistributive taxation and high social spending are also identified as culprits in the creation of a hopeless situation. Furthermore, it is clear that, if the real sickness of Weimar's economy is to be located in the years of so-called stability, 1924–29, it is unreasonable to blame the governments which led Germany in the years which followed for their inability to cure that 'sickness'. This leaves us with the question: was there anything which could have been done after 1929 to shield Germany from the worst consequences of the depression?

The protagonists of the 'crisis before the crisis' theory answer this question in the negative. In their view, Brüning's neglect of reflationary measures was not just due to his obsession with foreign-policy goals, let alone to any lack of economic training, but simply to the fact that no other course of action was open to him. There was, to use a popular phrase, no alternative.

To have pursued a policy of devaluing the mark or creating government credits would have violated Germany's obligations towards her reparations creditors and conjured up the spectre of a renewed inflation. There is no doubt that at first even trade unions – and certainly most of the political parties – firmly rejected measures which might risk a return to the galloping inflation of the pre-1923 era.[21]

As for schemes of public investment designed to ameliorate unemployment and to create a 'starting mechanism' (*Initialzündung*) to get the market system back to life, these are dismissed as being either totally inadequate to solve the problem or likely to 'crowd out' the small amount of private investment which would otherwise have been available. Brüning could therefore do nothing but attempt to balance the books by drastic measures of retrenchment, and try to persuade the Western Powers that reparations would have to be abolished.

It must be said straight away that these are serious arguments, based on careful assessment of economic data. Not all historians, however, find them particularly convincing. So far as the 'sickness' of Weimar's economy after the end of inflation in 1924 is concerned, there is no doubt that real wages do seem to have risen during this period, but that is hardly surprising given the low levels to which they fell in 1923. So far as low levels of investment are concerned, it has been pointed out that comparisons in this respect are usually made with the pre-war years 1910–13. Yet these were not typical of Germany's economic performance. If a longer perspective is used, from 1850 to 1913, the average level of investment as a share of the net domestic product was 11.6 per cent, as against 10.5 per cent in the 1925–29 period; hardly a dramatic difference.[22] Furthermore, wage to income ratios were unusually low in 1913, amd therefore make the share of wages in 1928 look high. Recent studies of industrial wage levels do not suggest that they were a cause of economic weakness in 1924–28. Since Germany's export performance was strong in 1924–29, and since demand for labour was also rising, there seems little reason to claim that high wage settlements were making Germany uncompetitive.[23] Germany does not seem to have been much worse off than her Anglo-Saxon competitors so far as the level of industrial wages was concerned, although some years were better than others.

What is difficult to deny is that there were two unnecessary political burdens placed on the German economy in these years. The first was the decision in 1927 by the Reich Finance Minister, Heinrich Köhler of the Centre Party, to raise civil service salaries by up to 33 per cent. This infuriated industrial trade unions, and had an immediate effect on wage bargaining.[24] The second burden was the imposition by the Reichsbank of unnecessarily high rates of interest, apparently as the result of a nationalist feeling of hostility towards foreign investors harboured by Reichsbank president Hjalmar Schacht.[25] Schacht's behaviour became more erratic as the economic crisis broke; his hostility to the Republican system manifested itself when he attacked the Young Plan and later supported the Harzburg front. By that time he had resigned his duties at the bank, but he was happy to resume them, and to become Minister of Economics, under Adolf Hitler.

It is true that labour relations in heavy industry were not smooth, but the fault might be seen to lie as much with the employers as with the trade unions. The employers' associations in the Ruhr abandoned the eight-hour day as soon as they could and were happy to see the demise of the ZAG. They complained bitterly about high wages and government arbitration awards, but such complaints are so obviously self-interested that they should not be taken completely at face value. In 1928 the iron and steel employers in the Ruhr contributed to Germany's industrial diffi- culties by organising a lock-out of workers to obstruct an arbitra- tion award, a measure which aroused widespread indignation, even outside the ranks of social democracy.[26]

In fact Germany's economic performance does not seem to have been so desperately unsuccessful in 1924–29, especially when compared with those of France and Britain. Even though Germany was not able to recover her pre-war trade balance, exports rose strongly, increasing by 40 per cent between 1925 and 1929. In the year 1929/30 exports of finished goods exceeded the highest pre-war level. Machine-tool exports were a third higher than in 1913.[27] To outside observers Germany seemed to have made a dramatic resurgence by 1928; in 1929 the economist James W. Angell published *The Recovery of Germany*, lauding her industrial achievement. As for wages, there does seem to have been a certain 'stickiness' about wages in Germany which obstructed rapid wage cuts when market forces appeared to demand them. But this was common to most developed coun- tries, where workers were no longer prepared to be treated as inferior beings. Given the extraordinary intensity of the crisis, it seems unlikely that this 'stickiness' factor was crucial in generat- ing such massive unemployment.

What is clear is that, already before the slump, many in govern- ment and financial circles *believed* that drastic measures had to be taken to 'cleanse' Germany's economy. Leading advocates of this view could be found in the Reichsbank, where first Hjalmar Schacht and then, after Schacht's resignation in March 1930, Hans Luther were determined to curb the borrowing activities of Germany's municipal administrations and Land governments.

Luther was an enthusiastic centraliser, who clearly wanted to use the economic crisis as a means of reducing the independence of both the Länder and the cities.[28]

Brüning fully supported him. Subsidies to Bavaria, Prussia and other Länder were cut, forcing them to increase local taxes and cut public services. It was believed that such measures would make Germany's finances leaner and fitter, and make her invulnerable to outside pressure. In the short run, at least, they simply reduced purchasing power and exacerbated unemployment.

Here we should pause to notice that the impact of the slump in Germany was exceptionally harsh. Despite a fear of inflation, unemployment itself posed a tremendous problem for states and municipalities, because the cost of relief had to be met from the public coffers in one way or another. Unemployment, which had apparently become a way of life for many Germans by the end of 1932, brought with it serious privation; whole families were wandering across Germany in search of work, begging for food. Insofar as working-class 'solidarity' had been a source of support for the Republican system, it was shattered by the impact of unemployment.[29] Trade unions could only look after their employed members, who wanted to keep their jobs safe from unskilled or underpriced competition.

It could be argued that this was of little consequence, since the natural home of the unemployed was the Communist Party, which actually proved incapable of threatening the state. But quite apart from the disruptive role played by the KPD in the last years of the Republic, and its usefulness to the Nazis as a bogey with which to frighten the propertied classes, it should be pointed out that unemployment did not only affect organised labour. Germany suffered a higher proportion of white-collar unemployment than most other Western European countries, and the slump affected the livelihood of independent craftsmen, shopkeepers, small businessmen and farmers. Many people in these groups were threatened by, or succumbed to, bankruptcy.

Furthermore, the emergency measures used by Brüning to cut salaries, prices and public expenditures at all levels damaged the interests of many Germans well beyond the confines of the Marxist left. Even industrialists, who supported the cuts in wages and public spending, were angry when price reductions were imposed on them by government decree. They were soon complaining that labour was being pampered by the government and that taxes on business were too high.[30]

So far as possible alternatives to Brüning's policies are concerned, it is certainly true that none of the reflationary schemes put forward in 1930–32 was entirely convincing, nor did they enjoy strong political support. The most serious argument in favour of Brüning's policy is indeed that any suggestion of government laxity in financial matters might have led to a run on the mark, and that this could have left the state facing bankruptcy.[31]

Nevertheless, numerous voices were raised questioning the wisdom of constant cuts, and by no means all of them were on the far left.[32] J. M. Keynes himself, who was very well known and widely read by German economists, had already put forward alternative proposals to deflation by the end of 1930. The liberal German economist Wilhelm Röpke, a sturdy opponent of collectivism, advised a Reichstag-sponsored commission of enquiry into unemployment that measures should be instituted to rekindle the economy and break out of the vicious circle of deflation. He was angry when Brüning took no notice of these recommendations.[33] Other suggestions for relaxing the deflationary squeeze came from within the Finance ministry itself and the Economics ministry, an institution which was largely ignored during the crisis. No notice was taken of these warning voices. Between December 1930 and the end of 1932 the amount of money in circulation fell from RM 5 billion to 3.7 billion – a cut of over 25 per cent. Even the most hardbitten financial experts realised this would have disastrous consequences.

In September 1931 the State Secretary in the Reich Finance Ministry, Schäffer, was talking of the need to increase the money supply, but Luther rejected this suggestion, saying that they needed a political solution to reparations and a restructuring of the Reich first. Schäffer remarked: 'Can we justify neglecting a proper and effective solution which will bring social reassurance and political calm, simply on tactical grounds?' The answer appeared to be that they could. By December 1931 even Luther had decided that the purse strings had to be loosened, but only if it could be done without attracting public attention. He noted in his diary that Brüning's response was to claim that Germany 'must plunge more deeply into misery'. So far as the possibility of purchasing foreign loans in return for concessions over reparations was concerned, Brüning resolutely refused to compromise. Schäffer suggested getting an agreement to a five-year moratorium, but Brüning insisted that reparations must be completely abolished. When Schäffer protested at the reckless nature of this policy, Brüning sneered that the German people always collapsed just as they were about to win a victory. This was a reference to his obsession with German defeat in 1918.[34] Even in the spring of 1932 Brüning was insisting that there could be no concessions to the French in order to ameliorate the financial situation in Germany. His policy was dominated by the desire to dismantle Versailles, and until that was achieved the Germans would have to continue on their harsh deflationary course.[35]

It is obvious that Brüning sincerely believed in his deflationary policy and would contemplate no other. Was he wrong? Here there can be no certainty. What recent discussions have made clear is that the facile belief popular after the Second World War that the depression itself could have been 'cured' by deficit spending is untenable. This does not mean, however, that a different type of policy adopted by the German government from 1930 to 1932 might not have been able to ameliorate the situation created by the slump. If time could have been gained, Hitler might have been unable to keep the centrifugal forces within his heterogenous movement from breaking apart. We should not forget that the Nazi tide was beginning to ebb by the autumn of 1932 and Hitler's supporters were showing signs of disillusionment.

Were there, then, alternatives? A simple answer might seem to be that Hitler himself produced such an alternative. Three years after his accession to power the German economy was booming. Unemployment was reduced so drastically that labour shortages became a problem. Was not this the result of government expenditure – cleverly disguised by Schacht, who had become Economics Minister as well as president of the Reichsbank? Not so, claim Brüning's supporters. The slump had 'bottomed out' in late summer 1932 and the economy had been cleansed by deflation. Hitler simply took advantage of a natural cyclical upswing. Full employment and the rearmament boom were unhealthy developments which inevitably led to another economic crisis at the end of the Second World War.[36] Brüning, therefore, did the right thing. He was just unlucky.

The latter point is certainly true; the earlier one more questionable. Germany's economy actually remained very weak in 1933, and had it not been for work-creation schemes introduced by Papen and Schleicher, investment overall would have fallen. There can be no confidence that another downward twist in the economic spiral – bringing with it major plant closures – would not have occurred. For a 'purged' economy the German Reich looked very sick in 1933. There is also the point that if the slump was naturally over one would expect Germany's neighbours to have recovered too. Yet in the years 1933–34 other European countries and the USA had far higher rates of unemployment than Germany.[37] This suggests that the measures taken by Schacht and Hitler were actually effective.

Assuming, however, that Hitler's policies could not have been adopted by a parliamentary government, can we envisage measures which might have eased the situation enough to have saved the Republic? It has been argued with some force that in the construction sector, which was especially badly hit by cuts in public spending, a policy of even fairly limited expansion would have had a considerable impact on unemployment, especially considering the multiplier effects of such a programme outside those sectors directly affected by it.[38] Unemployment in construction was particularly high during the slump, at times reaching levels of 90 per cent in the building industry.

In answer to those who claim that there was simply no money for such programmes, Brüning's critics can point to the large-scale financial assistance given by his government to the East Elbean landowners, including the so-called Junkers. If any sector of the German economy was sick in Weimar Germany it was the grain-producing agricultural sector east of the Elbe. With inadequate communications, a poor climate, inferior soil and unprogressive farming methods, the rye producers of Prussia's eastern provinces were a burden on the economy. Not only did they consume subsidies at a time of capital shortage. They also distorted the agricultural market by raising the price of fodder imports for more efficient mixed farmers in other parts of the country. Their plight, at least, could not be blamed on high wages, since their labourers were desperately poor. Brüning was quite willing to suspend his policy of retrenchment when the interests of the landowners were at stake. In 1930 he declared that his government viewed 'the recovery of eastern agriculture as the basis of the national and political salvation of the German east'. At a time when cuts were devastating so many other areas of economic activity, state funds were being poured into completely uneconomic Junker estates, whose owners responded with ever more radical denunciations of the Republican system. By the end of 1931 most of these landowning interests were bitterly hostile to Brüning and many were supporting the Nazis.[39]

The Reichswehr budget had also proved remarkably resistant to cuts in the depression period.[40] The fact was, as we have seen in the last chapter, that the dependence of Brüning's government on the President limited his possible responses to the crisis in such a way that a truly market- orientated policy was not possible. This puts the question of alternatives in a different light, for it becomes apparent that the constraints on Brüning were as much political as economic, and came more from the right than the left.

All in all, the 'no alternative' case must be regarded as powerful but not proven. What *is* clear is that Brüning had no intention of seeking an alternative, and that, had he done so, his power base – Hindenburg and his entourage and the army leadership – would probably not have supported him.

The policy Brüning followed, doubtless with great courage and patriotism, was designed to free Germany from the shackles of Versailles, and reform the Reich to strengthen the central power *vis-à-vis* the Länder and the executive *vis-à-vis* parliament. Ultimately he hoped to restore the monarchy, although this was not an immediate aim of his policy, and he may have exaggerated it when looking back on his chancellorship.[41] He lacked the flexibility of mind to realise how dangerous the policies he was implementing would be in the medium term. By the time his goals were achieved, Hitler was the leader of the largest party in Germany, and the kind of political solution Brüning strove for was impossible.

The Germans certainly faced a serious economic crisis in the years 1929–33, and no government could have avoided that. Only the Germans, however, experienced a fundamental change in their political system as the result of that crisis. It seems both illogical and unnecessary to attribute this to the *economic* weaknesses of Weimar before 1929. In the case of the USA, for example, the slump had just as severe effects as in Germany. The American economy in the 1920s may have had its weaknesses, but it is not usually regarded as 'sick', and it was certainly not burdened by over-mighty trade unions or excessive social spending. Its president, Herbert Hoover, was the embodiment of robust free-enterprise capitalism.

The real German problem lay in the political structure of Weimar and the decisions of its political leadership. Instead of trying to ameliorate the crisis to save the Republican system, many officials, businessmen and politicians were only too happy to exploit the crisis to change that system. Most of them did not intend to help Hitler into power. By their actions, however, they undoubtedly did so. As the former left-liberal journalist Anton Erkelenz wrote in December 1931:

> The Republic and the Republican parties which are all sacrificing themselves to secure the state and the Republic, are being forced by the deflationary policies of the government to work for Hitler.[42]

It was a prophetic and tragic remark.

Notes

1. Childers, *The Nazi Voter*, p. 87; pp. 165, 228. Jürgen Falter has cast doubt on the strong correlation between youth and the increase in Nazi votes, 1930–33. Nevertheless, he confirms that there does seem to be a positive relationship between younger voters and Nazi success. Certainly the Nazi Party could cultivate a youthful image. See J. Falter, 'The National Socialist Mobilization of New Voters: 1928–33', in Childers (ed.), *The Formation of the Nazi Constituency, 1919–1933*, pp. 226–7.

2. Hamilton, *Who Voted for Hitler?*, pp. 90, 118–19. Unemployed blue-collar workers were much less likely to vote Nazi than unemployed white-collar workers. See J. Falter, 'Unemployment and the Radicalization of the German Electorate 1928–1933', in Stachura (ed.), *Unemployment and the Great Depression in Weimar Germany*, p. 204.

3. See K. Rohe, 'Political Alignments and Re-alignments in the Ruhr, 1867–1987; Continuity and Change of Political Traditions in an Industrial Region', in Rohe (ed.), *Elections, Parties*.
4. Childers, *The Nazi Voter*, p. 258–61, Falter, 'Mobilization', p. 209.
5. See Helen Boak, 'Women in Weimar Germany. The "Frauenfrage" and the Female Vote', in Bessel and Feuchtwanger, *Social Change and Political Development in Weimar Germany*, pp. 155–73; also Winkler, *Frauenarbeit im 'Dritten Reich'*, pp. 20–5.
6. Lapp, *Revolution from the Right*, p. 224.
7. Patch, *Brüning*, pp. 178–80.
8. See the admirable concluding chapter in Childers, *The Nazi Voter*, pp. 262–9. Also the contributions to Childers's *Nazi Constituency* relating to Nazi appeals to special interests, in particular, Z. Zofka on peasants, M. Kater on doctors and J. Caplan on civil servants. See also J. Falter, 'The First German Volkspartei: The Social Foundations of the NSDAP', in Rohe, *Elections, Parties*, p. 80. For an interesting study of Nazi *membership* which stresses the party's appeal to all social strata, see Mühlberger, *Hitler's Followers*, pp. 202–9.
9. Turner, *German Big Business and the Rise of Hitler*, pp. 236–7; also Koszyk, *Deutsche Presse, 1914–1945*, pp. 196–7.
10. Winkler, *Der Weg in die Katastrophe*, pp. 172–8.
11. Ibid., p. 201.
12. For a convincing discussion of this point see Pyta, *Gegen Hitler und für die Republik*, pp. 502–20. See also Albrecht, *Albert Grzesinski*, pp. 349–59.
13. See above pp. 153–4.
14. James, *The German Slump*, p. 88.
15. Ibid., p. 21.
16. K. Borchardt, 'Wirtschaftliche Ursachen des Scheiterns der Weimarer Republik', in Erdmann and Schulze (eds.), *Weimar, Selbstpreisgabe einer Demokratie, Eine Bilanz Heute*, p. 219.
17. Hockerts, *Sozialpolitische Entscheidungen im Nachkriegsdeutschland*, pp. 196, 430–1.
18. See my chapter on Ludwig Erhard and German Liberalism in Jarausch and Jones, *In Search of Liberal Germany*.
19. The architect of this fruitful line of enquiry is Knut Borchardt, whose views are now sometimes described as the 'Borchardt thesis'. They are set out in 'Wirtschaftliche Ursachen des Scheiterns der Weimarer Republik' and 'Zwangslage und Handlungsspielräume der Wirtschaftspolitik. Zur Revision des überlieferten Geschichtsbildes', both reprinted in Borchardt, *Wachstum, Krisen, Handlungsspielräume der Wirtschaftspolitik*, pp. 183–205 and 165–82, respectively. See also

K. Borchardt, 'A Decade of Debate about Brüning's Economic Policy', in von Kruedener (ed.), *Economic Crisis and Political Collapse*, pp. 99–151.

20. This point is made in the stimulating critique of Borchardt by J. Lee, 'Policy and Performance in the German Economy, 1925–35; a Comment on the Borchardt Thesis', in Laffan (ed.), *The Burden of German History, 1939–1945*, p. 132.

21. Büttner, 'Politische Alkternativen zum Brüningschen Deflationskurs. Ein Beitrag zur Diskussion über "Okonomischen Zwangslagen" in der Endphase von Weimar', pp. 224, 248–9. Also G. Schulz, 'Inflationstrauma, Finanzpolitik und Krisenbekämpfung in den Jahren der Wirtschaftskrise, 1930–1933', in Feldman, *Nachwirkungen*, p. 264.

22. Voth, 'Wages, Investment and the Fate of the Weimar Republic', p. 273.

23. Ibid., pp. 278–9; see also Balderston, *Origins and Course of the German Economic Crisis*, pp. 401–4.

24. James, *The German Slump*, pp. 218–19. The Roman Catholic trade unions were as angry as their social democratic counterparts.

25. Voth, 'Wages, Investment...', pp. 280–1; Nicholls, *Freedom with Responsibility*, p. 37.

26. Weisbrod, *Schwerindustrie in Der Weimarer Republik, Interessenpolitik zwischen Stabilisierung und Krise*, p. 426.

27. W. Fischer, 'Die Weimarer Republik unter den weltwirtschaftlichen Bedingungen der Zwischenkriegszeit', in Mommsen, Petzina and Weisbrod, *Industrielles System und politische Entwicklung in der Weimarer Republik*, pp. 42–3. Also cited in Lee, 'Policy and Performance', p. 134.

28. James, *The German Slump*. See, for example, pp. 79–82, 103.

29. Winkler, *Der Weg in die Katastrophe*, pp. 40, 116–19.

30. Büttner, 'Alternativen', pp. 246–8. Generally speaking, industrial interests did not have much direct influence over Brüning's government. Insofar as they supported it, they seem to have been grudging and critical. See James, *The German Slump*, pp. 181–4; Turner, *German Big Business and the Rise of Hitler*, pp. 227–8; G. Schulz, 'Inflationstrauma', p. 288.

31. Balderston, *Origins and Course of the German Economic Crisis*, pp. 406–9.

32. Büttner, 'Alternativen', pp. 222–9.

33. Nicholls, *Freedom with Responsibility*, pp. 51–6.

34. Büttner, 'Alternativen', p. 216. The quotations from Schäffer and Luther are in Schulz, 'Inflationstrauma', p. 266 and 263, respectively.

35. Patch, *Brüning*, pp. 256–7.
36. Lee, 'Policy and Performance', p. 138. For a critical discussion of Nazi 'achievements' in the economic sphere, see James, *The German Slump*, pp. 342–419.
37. Lee, 'Policy and Performance', p. 139.
38. Ibid., p. 138.
39. See above, p. 152. Also Carsten, A *History of the Prussian Junkers*, pp. 166–78. The quotation from Brüning is on p. 167.
40. H. Mommsen, 'The Breakthrough of the National Socialists as a Mass Movement in the Late Weimar Republic', in Laffan, *The Burden of German History, 1939–1945*, p. 126.
41. For a discussion of the significance of Brüning's monarchism, see the introduction to Patch, *Brüning*, pp. 1–13. There can, however, be no doubt that Brüning was emotionally committed to the monarchy.
42. Büttner, 'Alternativen', p. 251.

Chronological Table

1918	28/29 September	The German High Command advises the Kaiser to establish a parliamentary cabinet and sue for peace.
	1 October	Prince Max of Baden appointed Chancellor.
	23 October	President Wilson's Third Note implying that peace could not be negotiated unless the Kaiser abdicates.
	28 October	Naval mutinies begin in Kiel.
	7/8 November	Bavarian monarchy overthrown and a republic declared in Munich.
	9 November	Republic declared in Berlin. Ebert heads first Republican government – a coalition of Majority and Independent Social Democrats. The Kaiser flees to Holland.
	11 November	Erzberger concludes an armistice with Marshal Foch.
	16–20 November	Congress of Workers' and Soldiers' Councils in Berlin. Votes to hold elections for a National Assembly.
	29 December	Independent Social Democrats leave the Government.
	30–31 December	Foundation of the German Communist Party in Berlin.
1919	5–12 January	Spartakist rising in Berlin.
	15 January	Rosa Luxemburg and Karl Liebknecht murdered by government forces.
	19 January	Elections for the National Assembly.
	6 February	National Assembly meets at Weimar.
	7 April	Bavarian Soviet Republic proclaimed in Munich.
	1 May	Bavarian Soviet suppressed by Reichswehr and Bavarian Freikorps.
	28 June	Treaty of Versailles signed.
	11 August	The Constitution of the German Republic formally promulgated.

	21 August	Friedrich Ebert takes the oath as President.
	September	Hitler joins the German Workers' Party in Munich.
1920	24 February	Hitler announces new programme of the National Socialist German Workers Party (formally German Workers' Party).
	13 March	Kapp Putsch. Ebert and ministers flee to Stuttgart.
	17 March	Collapse of Putsch.
	24 March	Defence Minister Noske and army chief Reinhardt resign. Gessler and von Seeckt take their places.
	6 June	1st Reichstag election. SPD wins 102 seats, USPD 84, DNVP 71, DVP 65, Centre 64, DDP 39, BVP 21, KPD 4.
1921	21 March	Plebiscite in Upper Silesia.
	27 April	Reparations Commission sets German debt at 132 thousand million gold marks.
	5 May	Allied ultimatum delivered in London requiring German compliance with conditions about disarmament, reparations and war criminals.
	26–29 July	Hitler becomes undisputed leader of the Nazis.
	26 August	Erzberger assassinated.
1922	16 April	German–Soviet Agreement signed at Rapallo.
	24 June	Assassination of Rathenau.
	18 July	'Law to Protect the Republic' passed by the Reichstag.
1923	10 January	Germany declared in default on reparations payments.
	11/12 January	Franco-Belgian forces occupy the Ruhr and the German government declares passive resistance.
	Summer 1923	Inflation of currency completely out of control.
	13 August	Stresemann becomes Chancellor.
	26 September	Passive resistance ended. Von Kahr declares state of emergency in Bavaria and establishes himself as State Commissioner.
	27 September	Ebert declares state of emergency throughout Germany. Gessler given full powers under Article 48 of Constitution.

	1–3 October	Buchrucker Putsch suppressed at Kustrin.
	29 October–6 November	Socialist/Communist governments suppressed in Saxony and Thuringia.
	2 November	SPD ministers in Berlin resign.
	8/9 November	Hitler Putsch in Munich.
	15 November	First Rentenmark notes issued.
	23 November	Stresemann resigns as Chancellor but continues to serve as Foreign Minister.
1924	13 February	President Ebert declares end of state of emergency.
	1 April	Hitler sentenced to five years' fortress arrest.
	4 May	2nd Reichstag election. SPD wins 100 seats, DNVP 95, Centre 65, KPD 62, DVP 45, Racialists 32, DDP 28, BVP 16, Landbund 10, Economics Party 10.
	9 August	London Conference protocol accepting the Dawes Plan for reparations payments.
	7 December	3rd Reichstag election. SPD wins 131 seats, DNVP 103, Centre 69, DVP 51, KPD 45, DDP 32, BVP 19, Economics Party 17, Racialists 14, Landbund 8.
1925	28 February	President Ebert dies.
	27 April	Hindenburg elected President.
	5 October	Locarno Treaty initialled.
1926	24 April	German–Soviet Non-aggression pact.
	8 September	Germany elected to the League of Nations.
	9 October	Von Seeckt resigns as head of the Reichswehr. Succeeded by Heye.
1927	31 January	Allied Control Commission withdrawn from Germany.
1928	30 January	Defence Minister Gessler resigns. Groener becomes Minister of Defence.
	20 May	4th Reichstag election. SPD wins 153 seats, Centre 62, DNVP 73, KPD 54, DVP 24, DDP 25, Economics Party 23, BVP 16, Nazis 12, Landvolk 10, Farmers' Party 8, Landbund 3.
1929	7 June	Young Plan drawn up in Paris.
	6–31 August	First Hague Conference on Young Plan. Agreement on evacuation of Rhineland.

3 October
Stresemann dies.

1930	30 March	Brüning appointed Reich Chancellor.
	14 September	5th Reichstag election, SPD wins 143 seats, Nazis 107, KPD 77, Centre 68, DNVP 41, DVP 30, Economics Party 23, DDP 20, BVP 19, Landvolk 19, German Farmers' Party 6, Landbund 3.
1931	20 June	President Hoover suggests Moratorium on reparations and War Debts.
	13–14 July	DANAT Bank closes its doors. 'Bank holiday' in Germany.
1932	10 April	Hindenburg re-elected President.
	13 April	SA and other Nazi paramilitary formations suppressed.
	13 May	Groener resigns post as Defence Minister.
	30 May	Brüning resigns. Von Papen Chancellor.
	16 June–9 July	Lausanne Conference on reparations.
	17 June	Ban on SA lifted.
	20 July	Von Papen deposes Prussian government.
	31 July	6th Reichstag election. Nazis win 230 seats, SPD 133, KPD 89, Centre 75, DNVP 37, BVP 22, DVP 7, DDP 4, Economics Party 2.
	6 November	7th Reichstag election. Nazis win 196 seats, SPD 121, KPD 100, Centre 70, DNVP 52, BVP 20, DVP 11.
	17 November	Von Papen resigns.
	2 December	Von Schleicher appointed Chancellor.
1933	28 January	Von Schleicher resigns.
	30 January	Hitler appointed Chancellor.
	27 February	Reichstag fire.
	28 February	Decree to Protect the German People and the State.
	5 March	8th Reichstag election. Nazis win 288 seats, SPD 120, KPD 81, Centre 74, DNVP 52, BVP 18, DVP 2.
	23 March	Enabling Act passed through Reichstag.

Bibliography

Scholars of German history are fortunate in the availablity of a wealth of documentary material in the Federal and *Land* archives. The unification of Germany has opened up new possibilities of research and most documentation relating to Reich authorities in the Weimar period has been centralised in the Federal archives in Berlin.

Many important documentary collections have been published as aids to scholarship. On the politics of Weimar Governments scholars are indebted to Professor K. D. Erdmann and the Historische Kommission bei der Bayerischen Akademie der Wissenschaften for the documentary publication *Akten der Reichskanzlei: Weimarer Republik* (Boppard um Rhein, Harald Boldt Verlag), 1968–, a multi-volume publication.

A very useful set of documents is that edited by Michaelis, Schraepler and Scheel, *Ursachen und Folgen. Vom deutschen Zusammenbruch 1918 und 1945*, Volumes 1–8 (Berlin, Dokumenten Verlag, 1958–).

On the history of the Nazi party in Weimar, the first volume of the collection of documents on *Nazism, 1919–1945*, edited by Jeremy Noakes and Geoffrey Pridham, is particularly helpful.

On the collapse of the Empire and the German Revolution the books by Professor E. Matthias and Professors Matthias and Morsey contain sources of great value for the light they cast on the reform movement in the German Reichstag before November 1918. These are:

E. Matthias, *Der Interfraktionelle Ausschuss 1917–1918*, 2 vols. (Düsseldorf, Droste, 1959).

E. Matthias and R. Morsey, *Die Regierung des Prinzen Max von Baden* (Düsseldorf, Droste, 1962).

Das Kriegstagebuch des Reichstagsabgeordneten Eduard David, 1914 bis 1918, ed. E. Matthias and S. Miller (Düsseldorf, Droste, 1966).

Die Reichstagsfraktion der deutschen Sozialdemokratie, 1898–1918, ed. E. Matthias and E. Pikart (Düsseldorf, Droste, 1966).

In addition, Deist, *Militär und Innenpolitik, 1914–1918*, is very informative on the domestic role of the military in Germany during the war.

The memoirs of Prince Max von Baden should still be consulted, as should Arnold Brecht's fascinating autobiography, which adds to our knowledge of the confused and difficult situation in the Chancellery on the eve of revolution. Good accounts of the German revolution are given by F. L. Carsten in *Revolution in Central Europe*, and A. J. Ryder in *The German Revolution of 1918*. Very helpful is Wolfgang Mommsen's contribution to the admirable collection of essays edited by Richard Bessel and Edgar Feuchtwanger, *Social Change and Political Development in Weimar Germany*.

The flavour of the revolution and the success of Majority Socialist attempts to moderate it comes out well from C. B. Burdick's and R. H. Lutz's *The Political Institutions of the German Empire*, a book of documents on the revolutionary period. Fuller documentation is now available in German; the most authoritative publication is *Die Regierung der Volksbeauftragten, 1918–19*, ed. S. Miller and H. Potthoff with an introduction by Erich Matthias. The introduction has been separately published under the title *Zwischen Räten und Geheimräten* (Düsseldorf, Droste, 1969).

A good short selection of documents on the Revolution is that by Gerhard A. Ritter and Susanne Miller, *Die Deutsche Revolution 1918–1919 Dokumente*.

Eberhard Kolb's history of the Workers' Councils remains one of the most illuminating books on the working-class movement in this period. Ulrich Kluge has also produced a well-documented volume describing the Soldiers' Councils. The histories of the USPD by David Morgan and Robert Wheeler have deepened our understanding of the German Left and its reactions to the crisis years, 1918–20.

On the foundations of the Republic Professor Bracher's early chapters in *Die Auflösung der Weimarer Republik* and his general reflections in *Deutschland zwischen Demokratie und Diktatur* deal very effectively with the problems presented by the Weimar constitution, and by the nature of Germany's civil service, political parties and officer corps. For English readers, *The German Dictatorship* has useful introductory chapters on the rise of the NSDAP and the collapse of Weimar. On the important question of the reform of the bureaucratic system in Prussia, Wolfgang Runge's *Politik und Beamtentum im Parteienstaat* gives a good picture of the extent of which the Prussian civil service was Republicanised and the difficulties faced by reforming ministers in achieving this end.

For an illuminating and scholarly description of the position of officials in Weimar the reader is referred to Jane Caplan's *Government without Administration*.

On the army there is a very large bibliography, but Professor Carsten's history of the Reichswehr remains outstanding. New insights into military policy have been produced by Edward Bennett, Wilhelm Deist and Michael Geyer. Sir John Wheeler-Bennett's *Nemesis of Power* remains a classic indictment of military interference in German politics, and its main conclusions have been reinforced by the documentary evidence which has appeared since it was written. Important information on the organisation of secret reserve formations in Prussia, as well as on the political ideas of General Schleicher, are to be found in Thilo Vogelsang's *Reichswehr, Staat und NSDAP*. Hans Meier-Welcker's biography of Seeckt contains much interesting detail.

As far as particular political parties are concerned, the German Social Democrats have found a worthy historian in Heinrich Winkler, whose monumental three volumes, *Arbeiter und Arbeiterbewegung*, are of great importance. Professor Morsey's analysis of the Centre Party remains very valuable, although it only takes the story up to 1923. He has, however, published the protocols of the Centre's parliamentary delegation, 1926–33. The liberal parties have also received the benefit of a very effective treatment in Larry Jones's *German Liberalism and the Dissolution of the Weimar Party System, 1918–1933*, which will remain a standard work for many years. Nevertheless, for an understanding of the German People's Party, Henry Turner's *Stresemann and the Politics of the Weimar Republic is* still essential reading. A good idea of the tensions within the German National People's Party emerges from Hertzmann's *DNVP*, but much more work needs to be done on this subject. The situation has improved as far as left-wing parties are concerned. Apart from the histories of the USPD mentioned above, Hermann Weber's monumental study *Die Wandlung des Deutschen Kommunismus* has provided much valuable information on the KPD, and the early years of the Communist Party received a detailed and balanced treatment from Werner Angress in his *Stillborn Revolution*.

Two of the paramilitary formations which played such an important part in Republican political life have received illuminating and scholarly treatment in Karl Rohe's *Reichsbanner* and Volker Berghahn's *Stahlhelm*. The Nazi Party can best be understood by reading about its real creator in Alan Bullock's *Hitler: A Study in Tyranny*, and Ian Kershaw's *Hitler, 1889–1936: Hubris*. Werner Maser's *Die Frühgeschichte der NSDAP* gives an interesting and detailed account of the party's early struggles in Bavaria. The best short description of the nature of National Socialism in Martin Broszat's *Der Nationalsozialismus*. Extremely helpful are Ian Kershaw's *The Nazi Dictatorship* and *The Hitler Myth*.

On the making of Peace 1918–19 Alma Luckau's *The German Delegation at the Paris Peace Conference* remains very important, though sadly difficult to obtain. Klaus Epstein's biography of Erzberger is informative on the armistice and the critical negotiations leading up to the German acceptance of the Versailles Treaty. German attempts to stress the transformed nature of German politics in order to attract the Entente are illustrated in H. Holborn's chapter in Craig and Gilbert, *The Diplomats*. The extent of their failure can be read in vol. xii of *Foreign Relations of the United States. The Paris Peace Conference*. German–Russian relations are particularly well served for the early part of the Republic's history by G. Freund's *Unholy Alliance*. The military relationships are set out in Professor Carsten's *Reichswehr*. The foreign policy of the Stresemann era is illuminated by John Jacobsen's *Locarno Diplomacy*.

The collapse of the Republic is best studied in Professor Bracher's *Auflösung der Weimarer Republik* and, with W. Sauer and G. Schulz, *Nationalsozialistische Machtergreifung*. The volume on the demise of Germany's political parties, *Das Ende der Parteien*, by Professors Matthias and Morsey, is also essential. Professor Conze has some challenging comments on the Brüning Government in his chapter in Conze and Raupach (eds.), *Die Staats-und Wirtschaftskrise des Deutschen Reiches 1929–33*, while E. W. Bennett presents a critical picture of Brüning's foreign policy in *Germany and the Diplomacy of the Financial Crisis*. Readers are also referred to the second volume of Professor Schulz's *Zwischen Demokratie und Diktatur*. For the tangled intrigues leading to Hitler's appointment as Reich Chancellor, see Henry A. Turner, *Hitler's Thirty Days to Power, January 1933*.

The social and economic problems which bedevilled Weimar have been the subject of careful scrutiny. The works of Gerald Feldman, Carl-Ludwig Holtfrerich, Hans Mommsen, Bernd Weisbrod and Peter-Christian Witt have furthered our understanding of inflation, taxation policies and industrial pressure groups. On the economic crisis which engulfed Weimar, Harold James's *The German Slump* and Theo Balderston's *Origins and Course of the German Economic Crisis* are admirable, and the work of Knut Borchardt has opened up important perspectives and stimulated debate.

The victory of National Socialism has attracted many writers, but mention should be made of local studies which throw light on the nature of the support for Hitler. Heberle's analysis of Nazi growth among the farming communities of Schleswig-Holstein remains a classic of its kind, but Jeremy Noakes's work on Lower Saxony and Geoffrey Pridham's book on Bavaria have added a great deal to our knowledge of the mechanics of Nazi expansion and the nature of the party's appeal. Roloff's description of the Nazi victory in Brunswick illustrates the stages by which bourgeois parties lost their voters to the Nazis. W. S. Allen stresses the conflict between classes in his study of a small town in the Weser valley. The Nazi Party itself is described by Dietrich O. Orlow in the first volume of his history. The attraction of National Socialism for craftsmen and small businessmen is described by Professor Winkler in his *Mittelstand Demokratie und Nationalsozialismus*. Professor M. Brozat's chapter in *Upheaval and Continuity* (ed. E. J. Feuchtwanger) is also highly illuminating on the social basis of Nazi support. Detlev Mühlberger's study of Nazi membership, *Hitler's Followers*, emphasises the socially heterogenous nature of those who joined the party.

On the whole question of elections and electoral movements Milatz's study *Wähler und Wahlen in der Weimarer Republik* remains important. Much detailed work has been done on the Nazis' electoral support. Thomas Childers has made particularly outstanding contributions, and there is much to interest the reader in the writings of Jürgen Falter, Ian Hamilton and Michael Kater.

Leading figures in the Weimar Republic have not always found it easy to attract adequate biographers, but the gaps are being filled. Hagen Schulze's biography of Otto Braun is admirable. Kotowski's biography of Ebert stops at the end of the First World War. Rathenau has been sensitively and sympathetically treated by Count Harry Kessler and James Joll. Andreas Dorpalen's political biography of Hindenburg is a most useful and thoughtful book. Brüning has been sensitively treated in the scholarly biography by William L. Patch. The best studies of all have been reserved for Hitler himself: Alan Bullock and Ian Kershaw have produced masterpieces of biography which cover the Weimar period.

Heinrich August Winkler has produced an authoritative account of Weimar's political history in *Weimar, 1918–1933*. The fullest general history of the Weimar Republic in English remains that by Erich Eyck, *A History of the Weimar Republic*. This is good when dealing with parliamentary politics, foreign policy and constitutional questions. Social and economic issues are given less detailed consideration, although Eyck still has a good many sensible things to say about them.

Useful one-volume histories by German historians which have been translated into English are those by Eberhard Kolb and Hans Mommsen, and Detlev Peukert's account is particularly interesting for its discussion of cultural influences on German society during the Weimar period.

The following list of books and articles is selective. Books mentioned in this brief survey, and others of particular importance, are marked with an asterisk. The place of publication is London unless otherwise stated. For more detailed information the reader is referred to the bibliographical appendices published in the *Vierteljahrshefte für Zeitgeschichte*.

1   Publications of Documents and Other Source Materials

C. B. BURDICK and R. H. LUTZ, *The Political Institutions of the German Revolution* (Stanford and London, Stanford U.P., 1966).

W. DEIST, *Militär und Innenpolitik, 1914–1918* (Düsseldorf, Droste, 1970).

Foreign Relations of the United States. The Paris Peace Conference 1919, vol. XII (USGPO, Washington, DC, 1947).

J. HOHLFELD (ed.), *Dokumente der deutschen Politik und Geschichte vom 1948 bis zur Gegenwart* (Berlin, Dokumenten-Verlag/Dr Herbert Wendler, 1951–).

Geh. Justizrat HÖLFRON (ed.), *Die Deutsche Nationalversammlung im Jahre 1919 in ihrer Arbeit für den Aufbau des neuen deutschen Volksstaates* (Norddeutscher Buchdruckerei und Verlagsanstalt, Berlin, n.d.).

E. KOLB and R. RÜRUP, *Der Zentralrat der deutschen sozialistischen Republik*, 19.12.1918–8.4.1919 (Leiden, E. Brill, 1968).

C. A. MACARTNEY (ed.), *Survey of International Affairs 1925*, Vol. II (Oxford U.P., 1928).

P. MANTOUX, *Les Délibérations du Conseil des Quatre* (Paris, Editions du Centre National de la Recherche Scientifique, 1955).

E. MATTHIAS, *Der Interfraktionelle Ausschuss 1917–1918*, 2 vols. (Düsseldorf, Droste, 1959).

E. MATTHIAS and S. MILLER (eds.), *Das Kriegstagebuch des Reichstagsabgeordneten Eduard David, 1914 bis 1918* (Düsseldorf, Droste, 1966).

E. MATTHIAS and R. MORSEY, *Die Regierung des Prinzen Max von Baden* (Düsseldorf, Droste, 1962).

E. MATTHIAS and E. PIKART (eds.), *Die Reichstagsfraktion der deutschen Sozialdemokratie, 1898–1918* (Düsseldorf, Droste, 1966).

H. MICHAELIS, E. SCHRAEPLER and G. SCHEEL, *Ursachen und Folgen. Vom deutschen Zusammenbruch 1918 und 1945 bis zur staatlichen Neuordnung Deutschlands in der Gegenwart* (Berlin, Dokumenten-Verlag, 1958–).

S. MILLER and H. POTTHOFF (eds.), *Der Regierung der Volksbeauftragten, 1918–19*, 2 vols. (Düsseldorf, Droste, 1969).

R. MORSEY (ed.), *Die Protokolle der Reichstagsfraktion und des Fraktionsvorstands der Deutschen Zentrumspartei, 1926–1933* (Mainz, Grünewald, 1969).

JEREMY NOAKES and GEOFFREY PRIDHAM, *Documents on Nazism, 1919–1945* (Cape, 1974).

——*Nazism 1919–1945. A Documentary Reader*, Vol. 1, *The Rise to Power, 1919–1934* (Exeter U.P., 1983).

GERHARD A. RITTER and SUSANNE MILLER (eds.), *Die Deutsche Revolution, 1918–1919 Dokumente* (Frankfurt/M., Fischer Verlag, 1968).

H. ROTHFELS, M. BEAUMONT, A. BULLOCK and H. M. SMYTHE (eds.), *Atkten zur deutschen auswärtigen Politik 1918–1945, Series B, 1925–1945*, vol. I, I (Göttingen, Vandenhoeck & Rupprecht, 1966).

LEO STERN, *Die Auswirkungen der grossen sozialistischen Oktober-Revolution auf Deutschland*, 4 vols. (E. Berlin, Rütten & Loening, 1959).

ALBERT TYRELL, *Fürer Befehl... Selbstzeugnisse aus der 'Kampfzeit' der NSDAP Dokumentation und Analyse* (Düsseldorf, Droste, 1969).

2 Biographies, Memoirs, Diaries and Works Containing Source Materials

THOMAS ALBRECHT, *Für eine wehrhafte Demokratie: Albert Grzesinski und die preussiche Politik in die Weimarer Republik* (Bonn, Dietz, 1999).
*PRINZ MAX VON BADEN, *Erinnerungen und Dokamente* (Stuttgart, DVA, 1927).
EMIL BARTH, *Aus der Werkstatt der deutschen Revolution* (Berlin, Hoffmann, 1919).
*OTTO BRAUN, *Von Weimar zu Hitler* (Hamburg, Nord-deutsche Verlagsanstalt, 1949).
*ARNOLD BRECHT, *Aus Nächster Nähe. Lebenserinnerungen eines beteiligten Beobachters 1884–1927* (Stuttgart, DVA, 1966).
U. VON BROCKDORFF-RANTZAU, *Dokumente und Gedanken um Versailles* (Berlin, Verlag für Kulturpolitik, 1925).
HEINRICH BRÜNING, *Memoiren 1918–1934* (Stuttgart, DVA, 1970).
*KLAUS EPSTEIN, *Matthias Erzberger and the Dilemma of German Democracy* (Princeton U.P., 1959).
*OTTO GESSLER, *Reichswehrpolitik in der Weimarer Zeit* (Stuttgart, DVA, 1958).
D. J. GOODSPEED, *Ludendorff. Soldier: Dictator: Revolutionary* (Hart-Davis, 1966).
*WILHELM GROENER, *Lebenserinnerungen, Jugend, Generalstab, Weltkrieg* (Göttingen, Vandenhoeck & Rupprecht, 1957).
D. GROENER-GEYER, *General Groener, Soldat und Staatsmann* (Frankfurt/M., Societäts-Verlag, 1954).

Adolf Hitler

*ALAN BULLOCK, *Hitler: A Study in Tyranny* (Penguin, 1962).
—— *Hitler and Stalin. Parallel Lives* (HarperCollins, 1991).
JOACHIM C. FEST, *Hitler* (Frankfurt/M., Propyläen, 1973).
A. HITLER, *Mein Kampf* (Jubiläumsausgabe, Munich, Zentralverlag der NSDAP, 1939).
—— *Hitler's Secret Conversations 1941–44* (New York, Signet, 1961).
*IAN KERSHAW, *Hitler, 1889–1936: Hubris* (Allen Lane, 1998).
WERNER MASER, *Hitler*, trans. Peter and Betty Ross (Allen Lane, 1973).

HERMANN RAUSCHNING, *Hitler Speaks* (Butterworth, 1939).
ROBERT G. L. WAITE, *The Psychopathic God, Adolf Hitler* (New York, Basic Books, 1977).

Hindenburg

*A. DORPALEN, *Hindenburg and the Weimar Republic* (Princeton U.P., 1964).
W. GÖRLITZ, *Hindenburg: Ein Lebensbild* (Bonn, Athenäum-Verlag, 1953).
W. HUBATSCH, *Hindenburg und der Staat. Aus den Papieren des Generalfeldmarschalls und Reichspräsidenten von 1878 bis 1934* (Göttingen, Berlin, etc., Musterschmidt, 1966).
J. W. WHEELER-BENNETT, *Hindenburg. The Wooden Titan* (Macmillan, 1936).

WILHELM HOEGNER, *Der Schwierige Aussenseiter. Erinnerungen eines Abgeordneten, Emigranten und Ministerpräsidenten* (Munich, Isar, 1959).
*JAMES JOLL, *Intellectuals in Politics: Three Biographical Essays* (essay on Rathenau) (Weidenfeld & Nicolson, 1960).
H. KESSLER, *Walther Rathenau. His Life and Work* (Gerald Howe, 1929).
GEORG KOTOWSKI, *Friedrich Ebert. Eine politische Biographie* (Wiesbaden, Franz Stein, 1963).
DAVID LLOYD GEORGE, *The Truth about Reparations and War Debts* (Heinemann, 1932).
HANS LUTHER, *Politiker ohne Partei. Erinnerungen* (Stuttgart, DVA, 1960).
HANS MEIER-WELCKER, *Seeckt* (Frankfurt/M., Bernard & Graefe, 1967).
O. MEISSNER, *Staatssekretär unter Ebert–Hindenburg–Hitler* (Hamburg, Hoffmann & Campe, 1950).
R. MÜLLER, *Vom Kaiserreich zur Republik* (Vienna, Malik Verlag, 1924).
J. P. NETTL, *Rosa Luxemburg*, 2 vols. (Oxford U.P., 1966).
GUSTAV NOSKE, *Von Kiel bis Kapp* (Berlin, Verlag für Politik und Wirtschaft, 1920).
——*Erlebtes aus Aufstieg und Niedergang der deutschen Sozialdemokratie* (Offenbach, Bollwerk Verlag, 1947).
FRANZ VON PAPEN, *Memoirs*, trans. B. Connell (André Deutsch, 1952).
*WILLIAM L. PATCH, *Heinrich Brüning and the Dissolution of the Weimar Republic* (Cambridge U.P., 1998).
HERMANN PÜNDER, *Politik in der Reichskanzlei. Aufzeichnungen*, ed. Th. Vogelsang (Stuttgart, DVA, 1961).
F. VON RABENAU, *Seeckt. Aus Seinem Leben 1918–1936* (Leipzig, Hase & Koehler, 1940).

WALTHER RATHENAU, *Tagebuch 1907–1922*, ed. H. Pogge von Strandmann (Düsseldorf, Droste, 1967).

HJALMAR SCHACHT, *The Stabilization of the Mark* (Allen & Unwin, 1927).

—— *My First Seventy-Six Years* (Wingate, 1965).

PHILIPP SCHEIDEMANN, *Der Zusammenbruch* (Berlin, Verlag für Sozialwissenschaft, 1921).

—— *The Making of the New Germany. The Memoirs of Philipp Scheidemann*, 2 vols., trans. J. Mitchell (New York, Appleton, 1929).

HELMUT J. SCHORR, *Adam Stegerwald. Gewerkschaftler und Politiker in der Ersten Deutschen Republik* (Recklinghausen, Kommunalverlag, 1966).

*H. SCHULZE, *Otto Braun oder Preußens demokratische Sendung, Eine Biographie* (Berlin/Frankfurt/Vienna, Propyläen, 1977).

*CARL SEVERING, *Mein Lebensweg*, 2 vols. (Cologne, Greven, 1950).

P. D. STACHURA, *Gregor Strasser and the Rise of Nazism* (Allen & Unwin, 1983).

GUSTAV STRESEMANN, *Vermächtnis des Nachlasses in drei Bänden*, 3 vols., ed. H. Bernhard (Berlin, Ullstein Verlag, 1932–3).

EARL OF SWINTON, *Sixty Years of Power* (Hutchinson, 1966).

ANNELISE THIMME, *Gustav Stresemann* (Hanover and Frankfurt/M., Worldeutsche Verlags-Anstalt, 1957).

H. TROTNOW, *Karl Liebknecht. Eine politische Biographie* (Cologne, Kiepenheuer & Witsch, 1980).

*HENRY A. TURNER, *Stresemann and the Politics of the Weimar Republic* (Princeton U.P., 1963).

3 Secondary Works

L. ALBERTIN and W. LINK (eds.), *Politische Parteien auf dem Wege zur parlamentarischen Demokratie in Deutschland, Entwicklungslinien bis zur Gegenwart* (Düsseldorf, Droste, 1981).

*W. S. ALLEN, *The Nazi Seizure of Power. The Experience of a Single German Town 1930–1935* (Eyre & Spottiswoode, 1966).

ALFRED ANDERLE, *Die Deutsche Rapallo-Politik* (E. Berlin, Rütten & Loening, 1962).

JAMES W. ANGELL, *The Recovery of Germany* (Yale U.P. and Oxford U.P., 1929).

*WERNER T. ANGRESS, *Stillborn Revolution. The Communist Bid for Power in Germany 1921–1923* (Princeton U.P., 1963).

WILLIBALT APELT, *Geschichte der Weimarer Verfassung* (Munich, Biederstein, 1946).

G. AXHAUSEN, *Organisation Escherich. Die Bewegung zur Nationalen Einheit* (Berlin, Weicher, 1921).

*THEO BALDERSTON, *The Origins and Course of the German Economic Crisis, 1923–1932* (Haude & Spener, Berlin, 1993).

*EDWARD W. BENNETT, *Germany and the Diplomacy of the Financial Crisis* (Harvard U.P., 1962).

——*German Rearmament and the West, 1932–3* (Princeton U.P., 1979).

*V. R. BERGHAHN, *Der Stahlhelm. Bund der Frontsoldaten* (Düsseldorf, Droste, 1966).

V. R. BERGHAHN and M. KITCHEN, *Germany in the Age of Total War* (Croom Helm, 1981).

CARL BERGMANN, *Der weg der Reparationen. Von Versailles über den Dawesplan zum Ziel* (Frankfurt/M., Frankfurter Societäts-Druckerei, 1926).

A. J. BERLAU, *The German Social Democratic Party 1914–1921* (New York, 1949).

*RICHARD BESSEL, *Germany after the First World War* (Oxford, Clarendon Press, 1993).

*R. BESSEL and E. FEUCHTWANGER, *Social Change and Political Development in Weimar Germany* (Croom Helm, 1981).

W. BESSON, *Württemberg und die deutsche Staatskrise 1928–1933* (Stuttgart, DVA, 1959).

GEORGES BONNIN, *Le Putsch de Hitler à Munich en 1923* (Paris, Les Sables D'Olonne, 1966).

*K. BORCHARDT, *Wachstum, Krisen, Handlungsspielräume der Wirtschaftspolitik des 19. und 20. Jahrhunderts* (Göttingen, Vandenhoeck & Rupprecht, 1982).

*KARL ERICH BORN, *Die deutsche Bankenkrise 1931* (Munich, Piper, 1967).

*K. D. BRACHER, *Die Auflösung der Weimarer Republik. Eine Studie zum Problem des Machtverfalls in der Demokratie*, 4th edn. (Villingen, Ring Verlag, 1964).

——*Deutschland zwischen Demokratie und Diktatur* (Berne/Munich/Vienna, Schutz Verlag, 1964).

*——*Die Deutsche Diktatur: Entstehung Struktur Folgen des Nationalsozialismus* (Köln, Kiepenheuer & Witsch, 1969). [English translation: Jean Steinberg, *The German Dictatorship: The Origins, Structure and Effects of National Socialism* (Weidenfeld & Nicolson, 1971).]

*——,W. SAUER and G. SCHULZ, *Die Nationalsozialistische Machtergreifung*, 2nd edn. (Cologne/Opladen, Westdeutscher Verlag, 1962).

C. BRESCIANI-TURRONI, *The Economics of Inflation. A Study of Currency Depreciation in Post-War Germany, 1914–1923* (Allen & Unwin, 1937, republished 1968).

W. L. BRETTON, *Stresemann and the Revision of Versailles* (Stanford U.P., 1953).

*M. BROSZAT, *Der Nationalsozialismus. Weltanschauung, Programm und Wirklichkeit* (Stuttgart, DVA, 1960).

*——*Der Staat Hitlers* (Munich, DTV, 1969).

*JANE CAPLAN, *Government without Administration, State and Civil Service in Weimar and Nazi Germany* (Oxford U.P., 1988).

*F. L. CARSTEN, *The Reichswehr and Politics 1918–1933* (Oxford U.P., 1966).

*——*Revolution in Central Europe, 1918–1919* (Temple Smith, 1972).

——*A History of the Prussian Junkers* (Aldershot, Scolar Press, 1989).

*T. CHILDERS, *The Nazi Voter, The Social Foundations of Fascism in Germany, 1919–1933* (Chapel Hill/London, North Carolina U.P., 1983).

*——(ed.), *The Formation of the Nazi Constituency, 1919–1933* (Croom Helm, 1986).

NORMAN COHN, *Warrant for Genocide: The Myth of the Jewish World-conspiracy and the Protocols of the Elders of Zion* (Eyre & Spottiswoode, 1967).

*W. CONZE and H. RAUPACH (eds.), *Die Staats- und Wirtschaftskrise des Deutschen Reiches 1929–33* (Stuttgart, Klett, 1967).

GORDON A. CRAIG, *The Politics of the Prussian Army 1640–1945* (Oxford U.P., 1955).

——and FELIX GILBERT, *The Diplomats* (Princeton U.P., 1953).

WILFRIED DAIM, *Der Mann, der Hitler die Ideen gab* (Munich, Isar, 1958).

*W. DEIST, *The Wehrmacht and German Rearmament* (Macmillan, 1981).

ERNST DEUERLEIN, *Der Hitlerputsch, Bayerische Dokamente zum 9 November 1923* (Stuttgart, DVA, 1962).

PIUS DIRR, *Bayerische Dokamente zum Kriegsausbruch und zum Versailler Schuldspruch* (Munich, Mühlthaler, 1922).

HANS-PETER EHNI, *Bollwerk Preussen? Preussen-Regierung, Reich-Länder-Problem und Sozialdemokratie, 1928–1932* (Bonn/Bad Godesberg, Verlag Neue Gesellschaft GmbH, 1975).

MODRIS EKSTEINS, *The Limits of Reason: The German Democratic Press and the Collapse of Weimar Democracy* (Oxford U.P., 1975).

WOLFGANG ELBEN, *Das Problem der Kontinuität in der deutschen Revolution 1918–1919* (Düsseldorf, Droste, 1965).

K. D. ERDMANN, *Adenauer in der Rheinlandpolitik* (Stuttgart, Klett, 1966).

——and HAGEN SCHULZE (eds.), *Weimar, Selbstpreisgabe einer Demokratie, Eine Bilanz Heute* (Düsseldorf, Droste, 1980).

JOHANNES ERGER, *Der Kapp-Lüttwitz-Putsch* (Düsseldorf, Droste, 1967).

FRITZ ERNST, *The Germans and Their Modern History*, trans. C. M. Pruch (New York/London, Columbia U.P., 1966).

T. ESCHENBURG *et al.*, *The Road to Dictatorship: Germany 1918–1933*, trans. L. Wilson (Wolff, 1964).

*ERICH EYCK, *A History of the Weimar Republic*, 2 vols. trans. H. P. Hanson and R. G. L. Waite (Harvard U.P. and Oxford U.P., 1962 and 1964).

J. FALTER, Th. LINDENBERGER and S. SCHUMAN, *Wahlen und Abstimmungen in der Weimarer Republik* (Munich, C. H. Beck, 1985).

GOTTFRIED FEDER, *Der Deutsche Staat auf Nationaler und Sozialer Grundlage. Neue Wege im Staat, Finanz, und Wirtschaft* (Munich, Deutsch-völkische, Verlags-Buchhandlung, 1923).

*GERALD D. FELDMAN, *Army, Industry and Labour in Germany, 1914–1918* (Princeton U.P., 1966).

——*Iron and Steel in the German Inflation, 1916–1923* (Princeton U.P., 1977).

*——*The Great Disorder. Politics, Economics and Society in the German Inflation, 1914–1924* (New York and Oxford, Oxford U.P., 1993).

GERALD D. FELDMAN *et al.* (*eds.*), *The German Inflation Reconsidered: A Preliminary Balance* (Berlin, de Gruyter, 1982).

——*The Experience of Inflation: International and Comparative Studies* (Berlin, de Gruyter, 1984).

——*Vom Weltkrieg zur Weltwirtschaftskrise* (Göttingen, Vandenhoeck & Rupprecht, 1984).

——*Die Nachwirkungen der Inflation auf die deutsche Geschichte, 1924–1933* (Munich, Oldenbourg, 1985).

NIALL FERGUSON, *Paper and Iron, Hamburg Business and German Politics in the Era of Inflation, 1897–1927* (Cambridge U.P., 1995).

EDGAR J. FEUCHTWANGER, *From Weimar to Hitler, 1918–1933*, 2nd edn. (Macmillan, 1995).

——(ed.), *Upheaval and Continuity: A Century of German History* (Wolff, 1973).

CAROLE FINK, AXEL FROHN and JÜRGEN HEIDEKING (eds.), *Genoa, Rapallo and European Reconstruction in 1922* (Cambridge U.P., 1991).

*OSSIP K. FLECHTHEIM, *Die Kommunistische Partei Deutschlands in der Weimarer Republik* (Offenbach, Bollwerk Verlag, 1948).

GEORG FRANZ-WILLING, *Die Hitlerbewegung. Der Ursprung 1919–1922* (Hamburg/Berlin, Decker, 1962).

G. FREUND, *Unholy Alliance* (Chatto & Windus, 1957).

H. W. GATZKE, *Stresemann and the Rearmament of Germany* (Baltimore, Johns Hopkins U.P., 1954).

PETER GAY, *Weimar Culture. The Outsider as Insider* (Secker & Warburg, 1969).

M. GEYER, *Aufrüstung oder Sicherheit, Reichswehr in der Krise der Machtpolitik, 1924–1936* (Wiesbaden, Steiner, 1980).

HAROLD J. GORDON, *The Reichswehr and the German Republic 1919–26* (Princeton U.P., 1957).

HAROLD J. GORDON Jr., *Hitler and the Beer Hall Putsch* (Princeton U.P., 1972).

CHRISTOPH GUSY, *Die Weimarer Reichsverfassung* (Mohr Siebeck, Tübingen, 1997).

ORON J. HALE, *The Captive Press in the Third Reich* (Princeton U.P., 1964).

BRIGITTE HAMANN, *Hitlers Wien. Lehrjahre eines Diktators* (Munich, Piper, 1996).

I. F. HAMILTON, *Who Voted for Hitler?* (Princeton U.P., 1982).

W. HARTENSTEIN. *Die Anfänge der Deutschen Volkspartei* (Düsseldorf, Droste, 1963).

*R. HEBERLE, *Landbevölkerung und Nationalsozialismus. Eine Soziologische Untersuchung der politischen Willensbildung in Schleswig-Holstein 1918–1932* (Stuttgart, DVA, 1962).

HELMUT HEIBER, *Die Republik von Weimar* (Munich, DTV, 1966).

HERBERT HELBIG, *Die Träger der Rapallo-Politik* (Göttingen, Windhoeck, 1958).

A. HERMANS and T. SCHIEDER (eds.), *Staat, Wirtschaft und Politik in der Weimarer Republik. Festschrift für Heinrich Brüning* (Berlin, Duncker & Humblot, 1967).

LEWIS HERTZMANN, *DNVP. Right-wing Opposition in the Weimar Republic* (Nebraska U.P., 1963).

G. HILGER and A. G. MEYER, *The Incompatible Allies, German–Soviet Relations 1918–1941* (New York, Macmillan, 1953).

HANS GÜNTHER HOCKERTS, *Sozialpolitische Entscheidungen im Nachkriegsdeutschland. Alliierte und deutsche Sozialversicherungspolitik 1945 bis 1957* (Stuttgart, Klett-Cotta, 1980).

WILHELM HOEGNER, *Die verratene Republik, Geschichte der Deutschen Gegenrevolution* (Munich, Isar, 1958).

H. H. HOFMANN, *Der Hitlerputsch, Krisenjahre Deutscher Geschichte* (Munich, Nymphenburger Verlag, 1961).

*C-L. HOLTFRERICH, *Die deutsche Inflation, 1914–1923. Ursachen und Folgen in internationaler Perspektive* (Berlin, de Gruyter, 1980).

W. HORN, *Führerideologie und Parteiorganisation in der NSDAP, 1919–1923* (Düsseldorf, Droste, 1972).

RICHARD N. HUNT, *German Social Democracy 1918–1933* (New Haven, Yale U.P., 1964).

JOHN JACOBSEN, *Locarno Diplomacy. Germany and the West, 1925–1929* (Princeton U.P., 1972).

*H. JAMES, *The German Slump, Politics and Economics 1924–1936* (Oxford U.P., 1986).

K. H. JARAUSCH and L. E. JONES, *In Search of Liberal Germany, Studies in the History of German Liberalism from 1798 to the Present* (Oxford, Berg, 1990).

*L. E. JONES, *German Liberalism and the Dissolution of the Weimar Party System, 1918–1933* (Chapel Hill/London, North Carolina U.P., 1919).

M. KATER, *The Nazi Party: A Social Profile of Members and Leaders, 1919–1945* (Oxford, Blackwell, 1983).

ANTHONY KAUDERS, *German Politics and the Jews, Düsseldorf and Nuremberg 1910–1933* (Oxford, Clarendon Press, 1996).

B. KENT, *The Spoils of War: The Politics, Economics and Diplomacy of Reparations, 1918–1932* (Oxford U.P., 1989).

I. KERSHAW, *The Nazi Dictatorship, Problems and Perspectives of Interpretation* (Arnold, 1985).

——*The Hitler Myth, Image and Reality in the Third Reich* (Oxford U.P., 1987).

——(ed.), *Why Did German Democracy Fail?* (Weidenfeld & Nicolson, 1990).

J. M. (LORD) KEYNES, *The Economic Consequences of the Peace* (Macmillan, 1920).

CHRISTOPHER M. KIMMICH, *Germany and the League of Nations* (Chicago/London, Chicago U.P., 1976).

MARTIN KITCHEN, *The Silent Dictatorship: The Politics of the German High Command under Hindenburg and Ludendorff, 1916–1918* (Croom Helm, 1976).

*ULRICH KLUGE, *Soldatenräte und Revolution. Studien zur Militärpolitik in Deutschland 1918/19* (Göttingen, Vandenhoeck & Rupprecht, 1975).

*EBERHARD KOLB, *Die Arbeiterräte in der deutschen Innenpolitik, 1918–1919* (Düsseldorf, Droste, 1962).

——*Die Weimarer Republik*, 2nd revised edn. (Munich, Oldenbourg, 1988). [English translation: *The Weimar Republic* (Unwin Hyman, 1988).]

KURT KOSZYK, *Deutsche Presse, 1914–1945, Geschichte der Deutschen Presse III* (Berlin, Colloquium Verlag, 1972).

G. KROLL, *Von der Weltwirtschaftskrise zur Staatskonjunktur* (Berlin, Duncker & Humblot, 1958).

A. KRUCK, *Geschichte des Alldeutschen Verbandes 1890–1939* (Wiesbaden, Steiner, 1954).

JÜRGEN BARON VON KRUEDENER, *Economic Crisis and Political Collapse. The Weimar Republic 1924–1933* (Oxford, Berg, 1990).

M. LAFFAN (ed.), *The Burden of German History, 1939–1945, Essays for the Goethe Institute* (Methuen, 1988).

BENJAMIN LAPP, *Revolution from the Right. Politics, Class and the Rise of Nazism in Saxony, 1919–1933* (Humanities Press, Atlantic Highlands, 1997).

W. Z. LAQUEUR, *Russia and Germany. A Century of Conflict* (Weidenfeld & Nicolson, 1965).

—— *Weimar: A Cultural History, 1918–1933* (Weidenfeld & Nicolson, 1974).

ERNST LAUBACH, *Die Politik der Kabinette Wirth, 1921–22: Historische Studien Heft 402* (Lübeck/Hamburg, Matthiesen Verlag, 1968).

G. LEWY, *The Catholic Church in Nazi Germany* (Weidenfeld & Nicolson, 1964).

W. LIEBE, *Die Deutschnationale Volkspartei* (Düsseldorf, Droste, 1956).

*A. LUCKAU, *The German Delegation at the Paris Peace Conference* (New York, Columbia U.P., 1941).

*ROLF E. LUKE, *Von der Stabilisierung zur Krise* (Zürich, Polygraphischer Verlag, 1958).

*WERNER MASER, *Die Frühgeschichte der NSDAP* (Frankfurt/M., Athenäum, 1965).

—— *Hitlers 'Mein Kampf'* (Munich, Bechtle, 1966).

*ERICH MATTHIAS, *Zwischen Räten und Geheimräten: Die Deutsche Revolutionsregierung, 1918–19* (Düsseldorf, Droste, 1969).

*—— and R. MORSEY, *Das Ende der Parteien* (Düsseldorf, Droste, 1960).

FRIEDRICH MEINECKE, *Die Deutsche Katastrophe: Betrachtungen und Erinnerungen*, 4th edn. (Wiesbaden, Brockhaus, 1949).

*ALFRED MILATZ, *Wähler und Wahlen in der Weimarer Republik* (Bonn Bundeszentrale für politische Bildung, Raiffeisendruckerei, 1965).

ALLEN MITCHELL, *Revolution in Bavaria, 1918–1919. The Eisner Regime and the Soviet Republic* (Princeton U.P., 1965).

H. MÖLLER, *Parlamentarismus in Preussen, 1919–1932* (Düsseldorf, Droste, 1985).

*HANS MOMMSEN, *The Rise and Fall of Weimar Democracy* (Chapel Hill/ London, North Carolina U.P., 1996). [Original German edition, Frankfurt/M., Propyläen, 1989.]

*——, D. PETZINA and B. WEISBROD (eds.), *Industrielles System und politische Entwicklung in der Weimarer Republik* (Düsseldorf, Droste, 1974).

DAVID W. MORGAN, *The Socialist Left and the German Revolution: A History of the German Independent Social Democratic Party, 1917–1922* (Ithaca, Cornell U.P., 1975).

*R. MORSEY, *Die Deutsche Zentrumspartei 1917–1923* (Düsseldorf, Droste, 1966).

GEORGE L. MOSSE, *The Crisis of German Ideology. Intellectual Origins of the Third Reich* (Weidenfeld & Nicolson, 1966).

*DETLEV MÜHLBERGER, *Hitler's Followers. Studies in the Sociology of the Nazi Movement* (Routledge, 1991).

A. J. NICHOLLS, *Freedom with Responsibility, the Social Market Economy in Germany 1918–1963* (Oxford U.P., 1994).

*ANTHONY NICHOLLS and ERICH MATTHIAS (eds.), *German Democracy and the Triumph of Hitler* (St Antony's College, Oxford, Publications and Allen & Unwin, 1971).

JEREMY NOAKES, *The Nazi Party in Lower Saxony, 1921–1933* (Oxford U.P., 1971).

ERNST NOLTE, *Three Faces of Fascism* (Weidenfeld & Nicolson, 1965).

P. VON OERTZEN, *Die Betriebsräte in der Novemberrevolution* (Düsseldorf, Droste, 1965).

DIETRICH O. ORLOW, *The History of the Nazi Party, Vol. I, 1919–1933* (Newton Abbot, David & Charles, 1973).

J. PETZOLD, *Die Dolchstosslegende. Eine Geschichtsfälschung im Dienst des deutschen Imperialismus und Militarismus*, 3rd edn. (E. Berlin, Akademie Verlag, 1963).

*DETLEV J. K. PEUKERT, *The Weimar Republic. The Crisis of Classical Modernity* (Allen Lane, 1991).

GAINES POST Jr., *The Civil–Military Fabric of Weimar Foreign Policy* (Princeton U.P., 1973).

*EUGEN PRAGER, *Geschichte der USPD. Entstehung und Entwicklung der Unabhängigen Sozialdemokratischen Partei Deutschlands*, 2nd edn. (Berlin, Freiheit Verlag, 1921).

GEOFFREY PRIDHAM, *Hitler's Rise to Power: The Nazi Movement in Bavaria, 1923–33* (Hart-Davis, 1973).

*P. G. J. PULZER, *The Rise of Political Anti-Semitism in Germany and Austria* (New York, John Wiley, 1964).

WOLFRAM PYTA, *Gegen Hitler und für die Republik. Die Auseinandersetzung der deutschen Sozialdemokratie mit der NSDAP in der Weimarer Republik* (Düsseldorf, Droste, 1989).

FRITZ K. RINGER, *The Decline of the German Mandarins: The German Academic Community, 1890–1933* (Cambridge, Mass., Harvard U.P., 1969).

——(ed.), *The German Inflation of 1923* (Oxford U.P., 1969).

E. M. ROBERTSON, *Hitler's Pre-War Policy and Military Plans 1933–39* (Longman, 1963).

*KARL ROHE, *Das Reichsbanner Schwartz-Rot-Gold* (Düsseldorf, Droste, 1966).

——(ed.) *Elections, Parties and Political Traditions, Social Foundations of German Parties and Party Systems, 1867–1987* (New York/Oxford, Berg, 1990).

*E. A. ROLOFF, *Bürgertum und Nationalsozialismus 1930–1933. Braunschweigs Weg ins Dritte Reich* (Hanover, Verlag für Literatur und Zeitgeschehen, 1961).

ARTHUR ROSENBERG, *The Birth of the German Republic* (Oxford U.P., 1931).

——*A History of the German Republic* (Methuen, 1936).

E. ROSENHAFT, *Beating the Fascists? The German Communists and Political Violence, 1929–1933* (Cambridge U.P., 1983).

H R. RUDIN, *Armistice 1918* (New Haven, Yale U.P., 1944).

*WOLFGANG RUNGE, *Politik und Beamtentum im Parteienstaat. Die Demokratisierung der politischen Beamten in Preussen zwischen 1918 und 1933* (Stuttgart, Klett, 1965).

KARSTEN RUPPERT, *Im Dienst am Staat von Weimar. Das Zentrum als regierende Partei in der Weimarer Demokratie, 1923–1930* (Düsseldorf, Droste, 1992).

A. J. RYDER, *The German Revolution of 1918. A Study of German Socialism in War and Revolt* (Cambridge U.P., 1967).

MICHAEL SALEWSKI, *Entwaffnung und Militärkontrolle in Deutschland 1919–1927* (Munich, Oldenbourg, 1966).

F. SCHADE, *Kurt Eisner und die bayerische Sozialdemokratie* (Hanover, Verlag für Literatur und Zeitgeschehen, 1961).

KLAUS SCHÖNHOVEN, *Die Bayerische Volkspartei, 1924–1932* (Düsseldorf, Droste, 1972).

O. E. SCHÜDDEKOPF, *Linke Leute von Rechts* (Stuttgart, Kohlhammer, 1960).

*GERALD SCHULTZ, *Zwischen Demokratie und Diktatur, Verfassungspolitik und Reichsreform in der Weimarer Republik*, vol. 1 (Berlin, de Gruyter, 1963; revised edn., 1987), vol. 2, *Deutschland am Vorabend der grosser Krise* (Berlin, de Gruyter, 1987).

——*Aufstieg des Nationalsozialismus: Krise und Revolution in Deutschland* (Frankfurt/M., Propyläen, 1975).

KARL SCHWEND, *Bayern zwischen Monarchie und Diktatur* (Munich, Pflaum, 1954).

K. SONTHEIMER, *Anti-demokratisches Denken in der Weimarer Republik Die politischen Ideen des deutschen Nationalismus* (Munich, Nymphenburger Verlag, 1962).

P. D. STACHURA (ed.), *Unemployment and the Great Depression in Weimar Germany* (Basingstoke, Macmillan, 1986).

G. STOLTENBERG, *Politische Strömungen im schleswigholsteinischen Landvolk 1918–1933* (Düsseldorf, Droste, 1933).

R. STUCKEN, *Die deutsche Geld-und Kreditpolitik 1914–1963*, 3rd edn. (Tübingen, J. C. B. Mohr, 1964).

MICHAEL STÜRMER, *Koalition und Opposition in der Weimarer Republik, 1924–1928* (Düsseldorf, Droste, 1967).

JÜRGEN TAMPKE, *The Ruhr and Revolution. The Revolutionary Movement in the Rhenisch-Westphalian Industrial Region 1912–1919* (Croom Helm, 1979).

A. J. P. TAYLOR, *The Origins of the Second World War* (Penguin, 1964).

F. TOBIAS, *Der Reichstagsbrand. Legende und Wirklichkeit* (Rastatt, Grote, 1962).

W. TORMIN, *Zwischen Rätediktatur und Soziale Demokratie* (Düsseldorf, Droste, 1954).

*HENRY A. TURNER, *Gustav Stresemann and the Politics of the Weimar Republic* (Princeton U.P., 1963).

*——*German Big Business and the Rise of Hitler* (New York/Oxford, Oxford U.P., 1985).

*——*Hitler's Thirty Days to Power, January 1933* (Reading, Mass., Addison-Wesley, 1996).

ALBRECHT TYRELL, *Vom Trommler zum Führer: Die Wandel von Hitlers Selbstverständnis zwischen 1919 und 1924 und die Entwicklung der NSDAP* (Munich, Fink, 1975).

J. VARAIN, *Freie Gewerkschaften, Sozialdemokratie und Staat. Die Politik der Generalkommission unter der Führung von Carl Legien (1890–1920)* (Düsseldorf, Droste, 1956).

*THILO VOGELSANG, *Reichswehr, Staat und NSDAP* (Stuttgart, DVA, 1962).

R. G. L. WAITE, *Vanguard of Nazism. The Free Corps Movement in Postwar Germany 1918–1923* (Harvard U.P., 1942).

ERIC A. WALDMAN, *The Spartakist Uprising of 1919 and the Crisis of the German Socialist Movement* (Milwaukee, Marquette U.P., 1958).

HERMANN WEBER, *Die Wandlung des Deutschen Kommunismus*, 2 vols. (Frankfurt/M., Europäische Verlagsanstalt, 1969).

E. WEILL-RAYNAL, *Les Reparations Allemandes et la France*, 3 vols. (Paris, Nouvelles Editions Latines, 1947).

*BERND WEISBROD, *Schwerindustrie in der Weimarer Republik. Interessenpolitik zwischen Stabilisierung und Krise* (Wuppertal, Peter Hammer Verlag, 1978).

ROBERT F. WHEELER, *USPD und Internationale. Sozialistisches Internationalismus in der Zeit der Revolution* (Frankfurt/M., Ullstein, 1975).

J. W. WHEELER-BENNETT, *The Wreck of Reparations* (Allen & Unwin, 1933).

——*Brest-Litovsk. The Forgotten Peace, March 1918* (Macmillan, 1936).

——*Nemesis of Power. The German Army in Politics 1918–1945*, 2nd edn. (Macmillan, 1936).

F. WIESEMANN, *Die Vorgeschichte der nationalsozialistischen Machtübernahme in Bayern, 1932/1933* (Berlin, Duncker & Humblot, 1975).

DORTE WINKLER, *Frauenarbeit im 'Dritten Reich'* (Hamburg, Hoffmann & Kamper, 1977).

*HEINRICH AUGUST WINKLER, *Mittelstand, Demokratie und Nationalsozialismus* (Köln, Kiepenheuer Witsch, 1972).

—— *Von der Revolution zur Stabilisierung, Arbeiter und Arbeiterbewegung in der Weimarer Republik 1918 bis 1924* (Berlin/Bonn, Dietz, 1984).

—— *Der Schein der Normalität, Arbeiter und Arbeiterbewegung in der Weimarer Republik 1924 bis 1930* (Berlin/Bonn, Dietz, 1985).

—— *Der Weg in die Katastrophe, Arbeiter und Arbeiterbewegung in der Weimarer Republik 1930 bis 1933* (Berlin/Bonn, Dietz, 1987).

*—— *Weimar, 1918–1933. Die Geschichte der ersten deutschen Demokratie* (Munich, C. H. Beck, 1993).

P-C. WITT (ed.), *Wealth and Taxation in Central Europe: The History and Sociology of Public Finances* (Leamington Spa, Berg, 1987).

J. R. C. WRIGHT, *'Above Parties': The Political Attitudes of the German Protestant Church Leadership, 1918–1933* (Oxford U.P., 1974).

Z. A. B. ZEMAN, *Nazi Propaganda* (Oxford U.P., 1964).

LUDWIG ZIMMERMANN, *Deutsche Aussenpolitik in der Ara der Weimarer Republik* (Göttingen, Musterschmidt, 1958).

4 Articles

(I have confined this list to articles cited in footnotes. They are given here in order of appearance in the text.)

ANDREAS RÖDDER, 'Reflexionen über das Ende der Weimarer Republik. Die Präsidialkabinette 1930–1932/3. Krisenmanagement oder Restaurationsstrategie?', *Vierteljahrshefte für Zeitgeschichte*, Vol. 47, Heft 1, January 1999.

WILHELM DEIST, 'Seekriegsleitung und Flottenrebellion 1918', *Vierteljahrshefte für Zeitgeschichte*, October 1966.

REINHARD RÜRUP, 'Problems of the German Revolution, 1918–19', *Journal of Contemporary History*, vol. 3, no. 4, October 1968, pp. 101–35.

LORD BRAND, 'How a Banker Watched History Happen', *Observer*, 8 January 1961.

FRITZ DICKMANN, 'Die Kriegschuldfrage auf der Friedonskonferenz von Paris 1919', *Historische Zeitschrift*, August 1963.

IMANUEL GEISS, 'The Outbreak of the First World War and German War Aims', *Journal of Contemporary History*, vol. I, no. 3, 1966.

K. D. ERDMANN, 'Deutschland, Rapallo und der Westen', *Vierteljahrshefte für Zeitgeschichte*, April 1963.

R. C. WILLIAMS, 'Russians in Germany: 1900–1914', *Journal of Contemporary History*, vol. I, no. 4, 1966.

ERNST DEUERLEIN, 'Hitlers Eintritt in die Politik und in die Reichswehr', *Vierteljahrshefte für Zeitgeschichte*, April 1959.

R. H. PHELPS, 'Hitler als Parteiredner im Jahre 1920', *Vierteljahrshefte für Zeitgeschichte*, 1963, pp. 274–330.

DIETRICH O. ORLOW, 'The Organizational History and Structure of the NSDAP, 1919–1923', *Journal of Modern History*, June 1965.

HANS W. GATZKE, 'The Stresemann Papers', *Journal of Modern History*, 1954, pp. 49 ff.

M. STÜRMER, 'Probleme der parlamentarischen Mehrheitsbildung in der Stabilisierungsphase der Weimarer Republik', *Politische Vierteljahrsschrift*, Heft I, 1967.

ATTILA CHANADY, 'The Disintegration of the German National People's Party, 1924–1930', *Journal of Modern History*, March 1967.

H. HAMMER, 'Die deutschen Ausgaben von Hitlers "Mein Kampf"', *Vierteljahrshefte für Zeitgeschichte*, April 1956.

J. NOAKES, 'Conflict and Development in the NSDAP 1924–1927', *Journal of Contemporary History*, October 1966.

HEINRICH AUGUST WINKLER, 'From Social Protectionism to National Socialism', *Journal of Modern History*, vol. 48, no. 1, March 1976, pp. 7–13.

ANDREAS RÖDDER, 'Dichtung und Wahrheit. Der Quellenwert von Heinrich Brünings Memoiren und seine Kanzlerschaft', *Historische Zeitschrift*, Band 265, Heft 1, August 1997.

HEINRICH BRÜNING, 'Ein Brief', *Deutsche Rundschau*, July 1947.

K. O. VON ARETIN, 'Prälat Kaas, Franz von Papen und das Reichskonkordat von 1933', *Vierteljahreshefte für Zeitgeschichte*, July 1966.

U. BÜTTNER, 'Politische Alternativen zum Brüningschen Deflationskurs. Ein Beitrag zur Diskussion über "Okonomischen Zwangslagen" in der Endphase von Weimar', *Vierteljahreshefte für Zeitgeschichte*, vol. 37, 1989.

JOACHIM VOTH, 'Wages, Investment and the Fate of the Weimar Republic. A Long-term Perspective', *German History*, vol. 11, no. 3, October 1993.

Index